# Praise for
## *The New Anti-Semitism*

"Written in white heat, *The New Anti-Semitism* exposes the lies and myths, the envy, corruption, and raw hatred that fuels the epidemic of anti-Semitism flaring up around the world."

—Ruth Gruber, author, *Inside of Time: My Journey
from Alaska to Israel* and *Exodus 1947:
The Ship That Launched a Nation*

"I couldn't put it down. The personal stories make this bleak narrative human, engaging, and urgent. I hope this book is widely disseminated and read by people of good will and by people who can be persuaded to become people of good will."

—Carol Ochs, author, *Our Lives As Torah:
Finding God in Our Own Stories*

"This is wonderful! I was so hungry for it. It's a really great work, and I hope it wakes up the Lefties and the misguided feminists (whom Chesler describes with such horrifying accuracy). I love the term 'alrightniks,' as well as Chesler's observations about how to identify an anti-Semite and that pacifists seem so angry."

—Judith Antonelli, author, *In the Image of God:
A Feminist Commentary on the Torah*

**Previous Titles by Phyllis Chesler**

Women and Madness

Women, Money, and Power

About Men

With Child: A Diary of Motherhood

Mothers on Trial: The Battle for Children and Custody

Sacred Bond: The Legacy of Baby M

Patriarchy: Notes of an Expert Witness

Feminist Foremothers in Women's Studies, Psychology, and Mental Health

Letters to a Young Feminist

Woman's Inhumanity to Woman

Women of the Wall: Claiming Sacred Ground at Judaism's Holy Site

# The New Anti-Semitism

## The Current Crisis and What We Must Do About It

Phyllis Chesler

JOSSEY-BASS
A Wiley Imprint
www.josseybass.com

Published by Jossey-Bass
A Wiley Imprint
989 Market Street, San Francisco, CA 94103-1741   www.josseybass.com

Jossey-Bass books and products are available through most bookstores.
To contact Jossey-Bass directly call our Customer Care Department within the U.S.
at 800-956-7739 or outside the U.S. at 317-572-3986, or fax to 317-572-4002.

Jossey-Bass also publishes its books in a variety of electronic formats. Some content
that appears in print may not be available in electronic books.

Library of Congress Cataloging-in-Publication Data
Chesler, Phyllis.
  The new anti-semitism : the current crisis and what we must do about it / Phyllis
Chesler.—1st ed.
      p. cm.
"A Wiley imprint."
Includes bibliographical references and index.
ISBN 0-7879-6851-X (alk. paper)
ISBN 0-7879-7803-5 (pbk.)
1. Antisemitism—History—20th century. 2. Zionism—Public opinion.
3. Jews—Public opinion. 4. Israel—Public opinion, Arab. 5. Public
opinion—Arab countries. 6. Arabs—Attitudes. 7. Arab-Israeli
conflict. 8. September 11 Terrorist Attacks, 2001.  I. Title.
  DS145.C5 2003
  305.892'4'0090511—dc21                    2003006448

Printed in the United States of America
FIRST EDITION
HB Printing    10 9 8 7 6 5 4 3 2 1
PB Printing    10 9 8 7 6 5 4 3 2

# Contents

# Acknowledgments

This book took several years to write—only I had to do it in six months. I worked on it full-time, both day and night, between September 15, 2002, and March 14, 2003. A fever burned in me, the task gave me no rest. Everything had to happen at once: reading, supervising the research, writing—and the daily, sometimes hourly, monitoring of breaking news. Under such circumstances, one's team makes all the difference between failure and success.

I thank my office assistant, Jenny Lander, who provided steady, devoted, and skillful administrative and research backup. My "pure" research team consisted of three people: Ariel David Chesler (who is also my beloved son), whose intelligence and passion for the subject, coupled with his legal, research, and writing skills, were invaluable; Douglas Gillison, who is divinely obsessed about the Intifada in Europe, especially in France, and whose Internet research skills are superb; and Sonia Nusenbaum (who is also my dear friend), who faithfully trolled the Internet for me both day and night. Her choice of information was always on-target. I also gratefully acknowledge Yaneev Cohen, who kept my computers up and running.

Susan L. Bender was my first reader. She has also blessed me with her financial, emotional, intellectual, and Jewish-heart support. Rivka Haut, my *chevrutah* (Torah study partner) and dear friend, read some chapters in their earliest form and generously advised me on some Torah-related questions. I received a grant from my friend Merle Hoffman, who believed in the importance of this work.

I gratefully acknowledge all my interviewees, some of whom must remain anonymous. I am especially grateful to David Rosen, who shared his considerable expertise about Israel with me. I also acknowledge the ideas and support of the following people: Judith Antonelli; Rabbi Sami Barth; Rachel Chalfi; Anselma Dell'Olio; Judith Ezekiel; Amy Goldstein, national director, Israel, Zionist and International Affairs of Hadassah; Deborah Greniman; Barbara Joans; Norma Joseph; Yehudit Moch; Frances Raday; Marilyn Safir; and Barbara Spack, national vice president of Hadassah.

I acknowledge the important data gathering and analysis upon which I have relied that are contained in published reports or mounted on Web sites by Amnesty International, The Anti-Defamation League, the Board of Deputies of British Jews, Hadassah, HonestReporting.com, Human Rights Watch, The International Fellowship of Christians and Jews, The International Policy Institute for Counter-Terrorism, Herzliya, the Israel Ministry of Foreign Affairs, the Jewish Community Relations Council, The Lawyers Committee for Human Rights, The Mitchell Report, The Middle East Media Research Institute, The Stephen Roth Institute for the Study of Contemporary Anti-Semitism and Racism at Tel Aviv University, The Simon Wiesenthal Center, The Union of Jewish Students of France, and the United Nations.

What can't I say about my editor, Alan Rinzler, who not only returned my every phone call and e-mail almost instantly but who also championed the book at Jossey-Bass/Wiley, read chapters quickly and sympathetically, and improved the manuscript immeasurably? May he live long and prosper. I am also grateful to Seth Schwartz, who untangled computer disasters most cheerfully. I would also like to thank Joanne Clapp Fullagar, Erin Jow, Karen Warner, Paula Goldstein, and Alice Morrow Rowan for their enormous efficiency and sensitivity.

And what can't I say about my agent, Joëlle Delbourgo, who also returned all calls and e-mails almost instantly, and who found Alan for me, and whose clear and bottom-line intelligence has guided and protected me? Joëlle's ability to cut through Gordian knots is heroic and her advice has consistently been right. May we grow old and wealthy together.

The following people kept my immune system in good working order as I worked round the clock: my gifted, long-time acupuncturist, Helene Kostre—the mistress of herbs and tinctures; and my hearty, cheerful chiropractor, Harvey Rossell, who expertly adjusted my work-wounded hand, wrist, arm, neck, and back and always took me out of pain. Finally, I thank my massage therapists, Meredith Kaufman and Mindy Wernick, for being fabulously adept at what they do.

I owe a special debt of thanks to Joanna Wilczyska, my opera-loving cartographer-housekeeper, for continuing to keep my home in excellent working order and for helping me host wonderful Sabbath dinners.

Phyllis Chesler
New York, New York

# Chapter One

# 9/11 and the New Anti-Semitism

On September 11, 2001, at about 11 A.M., I walked over to my computer and typed the sentence, "Now, we are all Israelis."

Always, it begins with the Jews. Osama Bin Laden called the assault on America "blessed attacks" against the "infidel . . . the new Christian-Jewish crusade." He explained that the twin towers had fallen because of American support for Israel.[1]

Both war—and a new kind of anti-Semitism—had been declared. I had no choice but to write this book.

• • •

I was not a direct victim on 9/11. I did not personally know anyone who was killed that day in the World Trade Center or in the Pentagon. I was at home in Brooklyn, transfixed before the TV set, watching it live as it continued to happen, and I did not move from my spot. I knew that when I got up, nothing would ever be the same again. I would no longer feel safe in my native city or country or in the world. I would no longer be able to assume that life as I'd known it—with all its illusions—would continue. How could it?

At 8:45 A.M. and at 9:03 A.M. two planes (American Airlines flight 11 and United Airlines flight 175) hijacked by Islamic terrorists crashed into the World Trade Center. At 9:17 A.M. the Federal Aviation Administration shut down all New York City airports and, for the first time in history, all American airports. At 9:30 A.M. President Bush announced that the country had been attacked by terrorists. At 9:43 A.M. a third hijacked plane (American Airlines flight 77) crashed into the Pentagon. At 9:45 A.M. the White House was evacuated. At 10:05 A.M. the south tower collapsed. At 10:10 A.M. a section of the Pentagon collapsed and a fourth hijacked plane (American Airlines flight 93) crashed into a field in Pennsylvania. At 10:13 A.M. the United Nations was evacuated. At 10:28 A.M. the north tower collapsed. At 10:54 A.M. Israel evacuated all Israeli diplomatic missions to the United States. At 12:04 P.M. the Los Angeles airport was evacuated and closed. And at 1:27 P.M. the city of Washington declared a state of emergency.

The twin towers had burst into flames and were tumbling down; firefighters and police officers rushed in. People with horrified eyes and covered with white soot burst out of the building; a tornado of debris whooshed after them as they kept on running. Incredibly tiny people were holding hands as they jumped to their deaths from high floors, and still the towers continued to burn and melt and fall. In my mind, they are falling still, out of heaven, into hell. Falling into memory for all eternity.

At 4:25 P.M. the American Stock Exchange, the New York Stock Exchange, and the Nasdaq announced that they would remain closed on September 12th. By late afternoon the wind began to carry bits and pieces of charred paper, smoky scraps of metal, and bits of unidentifiable debris into my neighborhood in Park Slope, less than two miles from Ground Zero, and the air smelled of scorched souls, acrid and agonizing. It was a sickening combination of industrial fuels, hate, and human cries; it burned my throat and my eyes and my mind. I will never forget it. Nor will I forget the small impromptu shrine that instantly and instinctively arose nearby: flowers, candles, an American flag, a small umbrella to shield this makeshift memorial from the elements—I paid my respects there almost every day for more than a year.

The firehouse on Union Street is located two blocks from where I live. They lost twelve firefighters out of twenty-five on that day. For months afterward, the firehouse was ablaze with lit candles and flowers. Wordlessly, tearfully, people brought baked goods and left small donations; bagpipes pierced the Brooklyn air with sonorous grief in funeral after funeral for these suddenly missing firefighters.

They will never come back, not one of them, and we will never see their like again. I made it a point to read each of the obituaries published in the *New York Times* very slowly. I thought about each person, tried to "visit" with them posthumously, grasp who they were, their hopes and achievements. I felt sorry for those who left children behind—and I felt sorry for those who had no children. I did not focus on women over men, or on whites over blacks, or on Jews over non-Jews, or on Americans over non-Americans. I focused on them all, equally. Now they all belong to me and I am part of their legacy.

I survive them, we all do. In their place and for their sakes we must find the courage to stand up to evil as best we can. There are many ways to do so. We owe it to them to speak softly, act wisely, and listen respectfully to those with whom we disagree. From now on we will be pleading their case—and the case of all civilians everywhere who are now hostage to terror.

9/11 has continued for a long time. It is still happening. It is not yet over.

I find it extraordinary that I am writing a book about a new plague of anti-Semitism, one that is so intimately connected to the events of 9/11. Who would ever have thought that such a work would be necessary in the twenty-first century?

But I must speak out. Something awful is happening to the world's Jews. If the daily violence and demented propaganda against them is not effectively countered, I fear that the Jews may again be sacrificed to a world gone mad and in search of a sacred scapegoat.

## Politically Correct Anti-Semitism

This is a book about the new anti-Semitism—a virulent epidemic of violence, hatred, and lies that are being touted as politically correct. Islamic reactionaries and western intellectuals and progressives who may disagree on every other subject have agreed that Israel and America are the cause of all evil. Israel has fast become the Jew of the world—scorned, scapegoated, demonized, and attacked.

Many of my friends tell me that I'm crazy to speak of anti-Semitism and anti-Zionism in the same breath.

"How dare you call me anti-Semitic just because I'm critical of Israel or have come to the conclusion that Zionism is a tragic mistake," they say.

And in some cases, they're right. I too have criticized certain Israeli policies—and done more. For the last fourteen years I have been part of a group who are suing the state of Israel and the Ministry of Religion on behalf of Jewish women's religious and civil rights in Jerusalem. We are known as the Women of the Wall, and we seek to pray out loud as Jews, with a Torah and in prayer shawls, in the women's section at the Western Wall, which is the site holiest to Jews the world over. I also agree that some anti-Zionists are not necessarily anti-Semitic. But frankly, I think most are.

When approached by a student who attacked Zionism, Martin Luther King Jr. responded, "When people criticize Zionists, they mean Jews. You're talking anti-Semitism."[2] I agree. And more than that: there's something unbalanced, erotic, and disturbed about the level of anger that anti-Zionists bring to bear on the subject of the Jews and the Jewish state. In the following pages I hope to show you how much the new, presumably antiracist anti-Zionist has in common with the old-fashioned racist anti-Semite. Because hidden behind that smoke screen of anti-Israeli fervor is, as we shall see, a familiar hatred of the Jew, the "other," the Christ killer, the Elder of Zion: the powerful, secret, international conspirator, the pariah and scapegoat of the Earth.

• • •

Fifty-five years ago, Israel was created to solve the problem of the old anti-Semitism. Now Israel is the Jew of the world; its citizens are being ghettoized and isolated just as Jews once were in Europe and under Islam. The Jews of Israel are facing the gravest danger, but Jews elsewhere—especially in Europe, but also in South America, Africa, and Asia—are also increasingly at risk.

Today, the new anti-Semitism speaks a hundred languages. The mob's infernal, heart-stopping chants, flag burnings, bombings, and executions are shown on television over and over again. The demonization of the Jews and of Israel has created an atmosphere in which the unthinkable and the horrific are becoming possible. There is a thrilling permissibility in the air—the kind of electrically charged and altered reality that acid-trippers or epileptics may experience just prior to a seizure: purple haze, unreality, disassociation from normalcy, responsibility.

Jews and Zionists are being blamed for 9/11 in Chinese as well as in Arabic. Nobel Prize winners, European and American academics, antiglobalization activists, and Jews on the Left have all condemned Israel for daring to defend itself while remaining menacingly silent about the suicide bombings of Israeli civilians. Doctored footage of fake Israeli massacres has now entered the imagination of billions of people; like pornography, these ideas can never be forgotten.

'Tis a season of blood that's upon us. I knew it from the moment the two Israeli reservists were lynched in Ramallah in the fall of 2000. The Palestinian crowds cheered when the smiling murderers proudly displayed their hands smeared with Jewish blood. I saw them dancing in the blood of my people, *partying,* like ghouls. No one on the airwaves drew back in horror; they showed these scenes but did not condemn them. International human rights activists and intellectuals remained silent, as did the United Nations. I wept because I understood that Jewish history was, once more, repeating itself. How foolish I'd been to think that we had finally escaped it.

But will six million more have to die before the bloodletting stops?

• • •

These days, *Israel* is far too dangerous a word to pronounce in a western intellectual or social setting. Say it—and you risk uncivil argument.

For example, it's ten months after 9/11, and I am having dinner with a friend and colleague of many years. We are talking up the usual storm, laughing a lot, enjoying each other's company, when one of us uses the word: *Israel*. My friend, a sophisticated thinker, stops talking. Suddenly the air becomes thin. She takes a deep breath. Her tone is no longer light; it has become dark, coarse, mocking.

"Israel?! It deserves exactly what it's getting. And more. And don't think America doesn't deserve what it's getting, too."

We are sitting a mile away from Ground Zero in New York City.

"Have you no compassion for the innocent?" I say, shocked by her cold, driven vehemence.

"Innocent? No one is innocent. We are all guilty. Don't tell me that you would dare to defend the Zionist apartheid state or the multinationals."

Her dear face has been utterly transformed into the face of a one-woman lynch mob. I do not want to fight; I can't bear the ridicule and intimidation. I know that I must say something; I am tired of having to do so. I do not want this friendship to shatter over the Jewish Question, that perpetual elephant in the living room of the world.

My friend is a Jew and a feminist, and she prides herself on being an independent thinker.

"According to you," I say, "only Americans and Israelis deserve to die for the sins of their leaders? I don't hear you wishing a hellish death upon Chinese or Iraqi civilians because you disagree with their government's policies." But my heart is not into making points. My heart is beating too fast. I am afraid of her anger.

• • •

I have been talking to a number of Arabs and Muslims from around the world. They are all educated and worldly people. One man, let me call him Mohammed, came for dinner last week. He is fluent in many languages, tells charming stories, and knows "everyone" in the Islamic world. He enjoys unmasking the hypocrisy of tyrants and mullahs. He shocked even me as he described the foibles of major Islamic figures who, he says, are cocaine and opium addicts, alcoholics, liars, thieves, incredibly stupid, vain, insane, and so on; they shall remain nameless because I have no way of knowing whether this information is true.

Mohammed joyfully zeroed in on hypocrisy. For example, according to my friend, "The Saudi princes *use* religion; they themselves are not particularly religious. For example, they drink. [Muslims are not supposed to drink alcohol.] Once at a conference, my host and I went to five black market liquor stores. They were all sold out. Why? Because a world Islamic conference was taking place in town!"

This man—so charming, so well-informed—earnestly pressed upon me three Internet articles that "proved that the Zionists really do run America." The fact that he himself understands that America is the world's supreme superpower does not stop him from believing that the Zionists—who run a country about the size of New Jersey—also control both America and the world. Nothing I said could change his mind. Eventually, he politely, wisely, changed the subject.

If I cannot persuade him that the Zionists really do not run America, how can I hope to persuade other educated Muslims?

Another friend, an elegant woman from an Islamic non-Arab country who has lived in exile in Paris for a long time, unsettled me with a long and eloquent diatribe against America. She reminded me of Europe's colonial past, of the untold grief it caused, of the arrogant carving up of the Ottoman Empire by Britain and France, and of America's long and ugly history of funding corrupt and sadistic tyrants in every Islamic country. She is, by and large, correct. (Strangely, she is not angry at the French, whom I have been told "went native" in a way that the British did not.)

She tells me, "Please understand, what is going on is that the frustration of the people has finally boiled over. It has come time to pay the price for America's having backed the Shah of Iran, a man who was not even royal, just the son of an army colonel, bought and paid for by the Americans. The Shah stole $36 billion from his people when he fled Iran—and who protected him and his money? The Americans. The American oil companies—that's who runs the American government! They wanted to create a pipeline running through Afghanistan and they wanted to stop the Soviets. That's why they approached and funded hardcore religious zealots in Pakistan, who turned around and created the Taliban out of the illiterate and impoverished Afghan refugees. The Taliban were originally supposed to ride shotgun and protect the new gas and oil pipeline that would run through Afghanistan. Well, that did not work out. So now America has put a new puppet, Hamid Karzai, in place. Everyone knows that Saddam Hussein is a bloodthirsty animal. But who put him there? The Americans. Again, the reason was oil and gas. If the Americans get rid of him, they'll only put another puppet in his place. *That's* why 9/11 happened."

She pauses briefly, then says, "And that's why America has got to stop backing Israel. When and if it does, that will signal to the Islamic world that America is interested in brokering some justice in the world."

I am somewhat speechless but quickly say, "Assuming that America abandons Israel to its enemies, assuming that another sacrificial bloodbath of Jews takes place, how will that change the historical record or improve matters in the rest of the Islamic world?"

She answers me by coolly saying that "15 percent of the U. S. Senate is Jewish. The American Jewish Israel Lobby is very powerful. They will never allow America to broker a just peace in the Middle East." Actually, the 108th Congress (which includes both the Senate and the House) has 535 members, of whom 37, or 7 percent, are Jews. But no matter.

Actually, most Arabs and Muslims sound angrier and far more hateful than this. In a 2001 sermon televised by the Palestinian

Authority, Sheikh Ibrahim Madhi said that the Almighty had described Jews as "apes and pigs, [and as] calf-worshipers and idol-worshipers." He also said, "We blow them up in Hadera. We blow them up in Tel Aviv and Netanya. And in this way Allah establishes us as rulers over these gangs of vagabonds."[3]

## Poetic Justice?

9/11 was a direct hit on democracy, modernity, religious pluralism, and women's rights. When Islamofascist terrorists are attacking my country, my culture, and my people, I choose to oppose them. While war is hell, self-defense is a duty. Also, just wars must be fought, not ducked. I agree with what former Czech President Vaclav Havel has said:

> Evil must be confronted in its womb and, if there is no other way to do it, then it has to be dealt with by the use of force. If the immensely sophisticated and expensive modern weaponry must be used, let it be used in a way that does not harm civilian populations.[4]

Today, Genghis Khan has megabombs and Attila the Hun has biological and nuclear weaponry. There is a vast terrorist army out there whose ace in the hole is their willingness to die, as long as they can take us and our way of life with them. What we are now up against is like an extremely bad movie, the kind in which the enemy does not stop coming at you, the kind in which the enemy you have just killed keeps coming back to life.

Americans must understand that a new kind of war has been declared upon our civilization and that we must patiently, carefully, morally, militarily, and strategically find effective ways of stopping those who wish to destroy Western civilization and individual freedom.

Some say, however, that 9/11 is all "blowback"—cosmic, inevitable retribution for the crimes of empire. America has sown death everywhere; it is poetic justice that we now reap it. Those invisible others whom we condemned to die, whose deaths remained invisible to us, have now come back from the dead to do to us what was done to them, to take us back with them.

Yes, the American government has committed terrible acts— what government hasn't? But we are the most democratic and most generous country in the world, a country in which the impoverished really can rise in what is also a rigidly class-bound society. Does the American government represent the needs of the many over the interests of the moneyed few? No, it does not—but the United States does so more than most other countries. Has our government funded tyranny and fomented countless wars abroad? Yes, and I have protested this for many years. But I also know that America is a land of opportunity for millions of immigrants from every continent who are in flight from persecution. Do I dare defend America from its critics who simplistically charge it with racism, capitalism, imperialism? Yes, with pleasure, I so dare.

As imperfect as American democracy might be, what we have achieved here would constitute a revolution in any Islamic, Muslim, or Arab country. This view is a quiet, not an apocalyptic, one. Perhaps that is why so many progressive Americans refuse to entertain it. It is true that America may have risen on the backs of others, but it is also true that Islamic countries have refused to enter the modern era. Both things are true.

• • •

Israel, like America, is a country of immigrants and a democracy. Like America, Israel has high ideals that it cannot always achieve. Because both America and Israel symbolize and promise so much— equality, democracy, justice, modernity, and the right to pursue individual happiness—people are disappointed and embittered when the promise does not include *them*.

I also know that Israel does not have a perfect government—no country does. But Israel is not a colonial, apartheid state. The Jews came to Israel in the late nineteenth and early twentieth centuries, not as conquering Europeans backed by a royal treasury but as the wretched of the Earth in search of respite from ceaseless persecution. They were impoverished, young, and idealistic. They were not mercenaries or capitalists. They had no mother country behind them, only hatred hard at their heels. They were not in search of natural resources to plunder (Israel was arid, rocky, swampy), nor did they intend to create a permanent subordinate class of workers based on racial difference. Jews and Arabs are both Semites. Jews come in all colors: black, brown, olive, yellow, white.

When Zionist idealists first returned to Israel-Palestine, what ensued was not merely a clash between white-skinned Europeans and dark-skinned Arabs. The clash that ensued—and that continues still—was also between modernity and a hidebound traditionalism that had not changed for twelve or thirteen centuries; between active doers and passive survivors; between secularists and religionists as well as between followers of different extremist religions; between those who wanted to bring modern medicine, agriculture, industry, government, and jurisprudence to the region and those who rejected such possibilities.

I am no longer willing to say that colonialism and global capitalism are solely responsible for all human suffering, that America and the West are *essentially* evil, beyond redemption and must therefore be destroyed in order to purify the world. Things are more complex than that.

European colonialism imported so-called foreign concepts such as nationalism and individual rights, which ultimately led to the overthrow of the colonialists; in addition, colonialism also sponsored practices such as education (for girls as well as the children of peasants), hygiene, health care, governmental infrastructures, and technology. So too does global capitalism, which both exploits and educates, impoverishes and enriches. The reduction of America and the West to apocalyptic rubble will not improve the material or cultural future of the rest of the world.

If Australian and European tourists stopped coming to Bali to vacation, Bali and Indonesia would not become richer; by definition, terrorism breeds poverty. However, the Islamofascist terrorists who bombed the Western nightclub in Bali in October 2002 do not care if their own people live in poverty. What they care about is killing "the infidel" and his way of life—and in so doing, terrorizing Muslim populations even further.

## Beyond Paranoia

This would be comic if it were not so tragic.

For forty years I have led and participated in national and international campaigns for civil, religious, and human rights. I have worked in the American civil rights and antiwar movements, and nationally and internationally as a feminist leader. I've written eleven books before this one, with passion, commitment, joy, and hope. My work has been translated into many European languages and into Japanese, Chinese, Korean, and Hebrew.

But I admit I resisted writing a book like this one for a long time. I did not want to become a "professional" Jew, that is, someone who earns a living by telling other Jews or the Israeli government what to do. I did not want to specialize in Judaism or to psychologically live in a ghetto. But my heart is broken by the cunning and purposeful silence of progressives and academics on the subject of anti-Semitism and terrorism.

I write "silence" to be kind. What I'm really talking about is the betrayal of the Jews, not just by the violence of the fascist right, but also by western intellectuals, some of whom are also Jews themselves. Perhaps like me they do not want to give up the larger world in order to retain their religious, racial, and cultural identities as Jews. After all, who willingly wants to wear the yellow star?

The current level of tension among Jews disunited is as high as I have ever seen it. American Jewish students are fighting for the soul of the Jewish people on campuses all across America. Some are pro-Palestinian, some are pro-Israeli. Antiwar, antiglobalization, and feminist activists, both Jews and non-Jews, are marching with banners that read, "End the Zionist Occupation" (not "End the occupation of women's bodies") and "Queers for Palestine" (where out homosexuals are tortured and killed).

One Jew I know views Israel's failure to integrate its Arab citizens as a failure of Jewish ethics and as a grave human rights violation. Another remains focused on the Holocaust and on more than fifty-five years of vicious, escalating post-Holocaust and Nazi-like Arab anti-Semitic propaganda against Jews and Israelis. A third Jewish friend views West Bank settlers as noble idealists and human shields, and the settlements as precisely what have allowed Israel to repel thousands of terrorist attacks in the last three years. A fourth believes that the settlers have jeopardized the very survival of the Jewish state.

It is important to note three things. First, these arguments at high decibel levels are taking place not only in Israel but all over the world, far from where the suicide bombers are exploding themselves and civilians in the streets and squares of Tel Aviv, Haifa, Netanya, and Jerusalem. Second, as the Jews are fighting with each other, Muslim terrorists and their allies are burning down synagogues; attacking Jews on the streets; burning Israeli and American flags; blowing up American embassies and ships; kidnapping, torturing, and executing American Jews; and doctoring footage on Al-Jazeera so that the Arab world sees only Israelis killing Palestinian women and children, over and over again. Third, much of the Western media and many of the Western intellectuals are loudly defending Palestinian rights and loudly condemning the Jewish state.

Events are spinning out of control. It's as if the political equivalent of the AIDS virus has been unleashed in the world, as if a new plague of copycat serial killers is upon us. Islamic jihadists in Asia, Africa, Israel, the Middle East, Europe, and Russia are copying each other's methods of attack and propaganda as if these terrorists were all One, as if they were all God.

Daily, the coordinated attacks against Jews and Israelis are escalating. They are synchronized and choreographed, Arafat-style, bin Laden style, so that separate attacks occur almost simultaneously. I think of this as the Islamic jihadist version of art (they are artists of death), as a maniacal fireworks display. Those for whom progress is anathema, who resonate only to stasis, uniformity, hierarchy, conformity, are now armed with the latest western weaponry—with which they hope to Talibanize the entire world.

• • •

I have lived and loved both in the Islamic and in the Jewish-Israeli world. My son's father is an Israeli who now lives in America, and I have remained active in Israeli feminist politics, first as a peace activist, then more recently as a religious rights activist. But I also remain close to my first husband, a Muslim from Afghanistan, who also lives here, and to his second wife and grown children. Both husbands are soft-spoken and charming; each has deep black eyes and an olive complexion. I think of them as the sons of Yishmael and of Yitzhak. I also understand that, unlike their Biblical proto-types, these half-brothers are now worlds apart.

I first learned how different the Judeo-Christian West and the Islamic East really are long ago, in the early 1960s, when I was a bride living in Afghanistan in an era of pre-Taliban gender apartheid. Afghanistan had never been colonized, so there were no Westerners to blame. It was there that I learned how not to roman-ticize wily, colorful, third-world tyrants.

Scholars often do not gain access to insider information for years. When they finally do gain access, they also tend to disagree with one another about what the documents mean. Today one scholar tells us that Jews flourished under Islam. A second scholar strongly disagrees and insists that Islam persecuted Jews and Chris-tians continually. A third scholar tells us that the truth is more complicated than that and may lie somewhere between "savage per-secution" and "robust flourishing." A fourth scholar says that what is happening today bears little resemblance to what happened five or ten centuries ago.

I am not a scholar in this area. I know only that I loved the "soft and easy" of Islamic and Arab countries and people, their sophisticated ceremoniality and familial intimacy, their trade-route jingle-jangle. My sense is that Islam was once more live and let live than it is today. After all, Muslims once presided over cosmopolitan cities, great crossroads of civilization, silk routes, caravans, and scientific academies. David Warren is a nonexpert expert. He is a Protestant Canadian who grew up in Lahore, Pakistan. He posted the most interesting lecture, "Wrestling with Islam," on the Internet. In this lecture he reminds us that the strength of Islam was that it

> stayed in the background. The religion wasn't oppressive because it did not have an independent church-like vanguard. . . . [During] the Golden Muslim Age in Al-Andalus the Arab Court in Spain was not necessarily religious, at least compared to the courts in contemporary Europe. The glorious city of Cordova was where Europe went in the Middle Ages to learn Greek, and some table manners; to see fabulous gardens and noble homes; paved roads and street lighting; indoor plumbing and outdoor irrigation that made the desert bloom; ladies in splendid finery; international banks—they came and felt like country bumpkins.
>
> Likewise, Baghdad, in the time before the Mongol invasion, was the center of the civilized world, the New York of the 12th century. Intellectuals would migrate there . . . looking for a job, or a chance to study. . . . [T]hey came because they preferred the more open atmosphere in the Islamic realm, the big city feel.[5]

I too have romantic memories of life in the Islamic East and of a way of life that may no longer exist. I have known utterly charming, truly enchanting Muslims. Yes, prick them and they will bleed. Long ago, in Afghanistan, I personally experienced enormous kindness, humor, and good-naturedness among Muslims—more among the women and children than among the men, but still, even among the men. The ritualized importance of guests and the stately pace of each meal were balm to my spirit. I had longed for a slower pace, a grand, biblical intimacy, and I had found it.

In Kabul, behind closed doors, I also observed many kinds of resistance: poking fun at the mullahs, the civil service, the monarchy;

protecting female relatives from their husbands' cruelties, including rape, battery, and the taking of second and third wives. I do not believe that militant Islam—which is the most serious practitioner of gender apartheid in the world—is capable of destroying such individual acts of sanity and goodness.

I sometimes experience the strangest but most profound nostalgia for Afghanistan. What can I be thinking? Forty-two years ago, when I was there, my mother-in-law tried to convert me to Islam almost every day—this, even as she proudly insisted that some of her best friends, the Sharbonis, had been Jews. My new relatives were utterly willing to accept me—but only if I became more Afghan, less American, something that I would never do.

My so-called Western feminism was certainly forged in that beautiful and treacherous country, where I observed and experienced the abysmal oppression of women, children, and servants. Forever after I was able to see gender apartheid anywhere, even in America. Although I appreciated my relative freedom as an American woman back on American soil, I no longer believed that American women were free—only privileged.

But I am not likely to forget certain heart-stopping, eerily familiar sights, sounds, tastes, and smells that, at the time, moved me so: flocks of sheep; camel caravans; fierce, tender, turbaned men armed with rifles; stars so thick and close—so clustered you'd think you could touch them (Afghanistan is more than five thousand feet above the sea); ancient bazaars; awesome mountains (I could see the foothills of the Himalayas from my bedroom window); minarets; the muezzin's hoarse call; cooking outdoors on an open fire; delicious, too-sweet candies flavored with roses (!); exquisite, salted pistachios; communal sandalis (which warmed one's feet on freezing nights); turquoise-colored ceramic hookahs (also known as hubble-bubbles), in which one smoked tobacco or hashish.

Nevertheless, my life as an American, a Jew, and a wife was cheap, and I nearly died there. All great adventures take their toll. Many Western adventurers whose hearts are in the East invariably come crawling back home with malaria, minus a limb, minus their sanity, with their tongues cut out, either literally or metaphorically. Today, romance aside, jihadic Islam is no longer soft and lovely. It is quite the opposite: aggressively programmatic, intolerant, savagely misogynistic, and militaristic in quite a new way.

The refusal of corrupt Arab and Muslim leaders to allow open societies, their long history of pocketing the wealth for themselves and of torturing and executing dissidents, and the history of honor killings, ethnic rivalries, and slavery in the Islamic world are also to blame for Arab and Muslim suffering. Such barbarous customs preceded both Zionism and the "Evil American Empire," which consequently cannot logically be blamed for such barbarisms. Unbearable suffering coupled with the dangerous consolation and stimulation of a more fanatic Islam has also changed the East.

• • •

I regret nothing. I am not recanting my ideals as a civil rights worker, as a member of the antiwar movement, or as a feminist; nor have I gone over to the dark side. And yet, and yet, I must now calmly but clearly part company with many of my former friends and comrades.

This is not the first time that an internationally minded Jew has found herself in this position. I now find it necessary and sane to think tribally as well as internationally, to think as an American and as a Jew who is concerned not only with justice for all but also with the survival of America and of the Jewish people.

There is no shame in this, only honor.

Thus, on my left stand the internationalists (some of whom are Jews). I may remain among them as long as I am strongly anti-Zionist and anti–religious Judaism. For my part, I must also remain silent as the internationalists embrace all ethnicities and demonize only one: mine. On my right are the ultranationalists and theocrats (some of whom are Jews). They will forgive my history as a firebrand feminist as long as I don't mention it, especially if I allow them to think I have renounced it.

To be a Jew is to live dangerously, on the margins, with an open, "circumcised" heart. Being Jewish means that one is meant to cross over existing boundaries; to move between countries, between this world and the next one; to trespass all natural and national borders; to be everywhere but to belong nowhere, an eternal translator between realms: God's messenger.

## Post-Traumatic Stress

Where were you the days that Malcolm X, John F. Kennedy, Martin Luther King Jr., and Robert Kennedy were shot? Most of us remember exactly where we were at those precise moments in history. Few forget.

When our children and grandchildren look up to see a plane in the sky, or when they turn on their TV sets, will they feel an utterly mysterious sense of alarm and foreboding? Will they phobically avoid tall buildings? Or will they never again go out without a cell phone? Immediately after 9/11, everyone on the streets of New York had cell phones clapped to their ears, as if they needed to be permanently and umbilically connected to one intimate other and to be disconnected from a reality too terrible to bear alone.

According to psychotherapists, some patients, both Jewish and non-Jewish, who are not directly connected to the Holocaust or to another genocidal persecution, still seem traumatized by it as a secondary and intergenerational phenomenon. For example, they may be reluctant to take showers or to close the shower door completely, or they may tend to hoard food or eat alone—habits that are mysterious to them but familiar to their European and Asian parents and grandparents.

So, if post 9/11 we are now all Israelis—who are the Israelis? What surreal level of trauma and post-trauma are they experiencing? For three years they have been bearing the burden for all of us in the West. In addition, many Israelis have lived through the European Holocaust, or their parents and grandparents have. Others have lived through Stalin's Gulag, or their parents and grandparents have. Many have fled torture, jail, and persecution in Arab lands, or their parents and grandparents have. They, their parents, and their grandparents have also lived through nine major Israeli wars of self-defense in the last fifty-five years.

Psychologically and physically, where can they be? *Israelis have experienced the equivalent of 9/11 almost every week for the last three years.* Given their population, Israeli losses to date are ten times those of America's on 9/11. Israelis have also been made to understand by Islamic jihadists, European mobs, and European and North American intellectuals that Israelis and Jews are not welcome and will not be safe in Africa or Europe or in the Middle East. And as if this were not enough, the Finns have also decided not to sell the Israelis a special kind of gas mask.

Every Israeli personally knows someone who has been killed or wounded in a recent terrorist attack. Every Israeli has lost either a spouse, a child, a parent, a grandparent, an aunt, an uncle, a cousin, a neighbor, a teacher, or a schoolmate.

One native-born Israeli woman said she feels that the last few years have been "like the Holocaust in slow motion. We have no time to recover from one blow, and then comes another one, stronger. It's better to have a war. Better for them, too. What we have now is worse."[6]

An Australian-Israeli told me that he is racked by guilt for having brought his family to Israel a quarter of a century ago. "For what? To die? To serve in the army for their entire life? To be hated by their Arab neighbors?"

Many progressive and left Israelis are demoralized, exhausted, and frightened. They have spent years denouncing the ultra-orthodox and the settlements on the West Bank and in Gaza and have assumed that, since they have done their part, the Palestinians and the Arab world would in turn do theirs and negotiate a peaceful, two-state solution and would for the first time accept a Jewish presence in the Middle East. They now understand that this was never meant to be. Their illusions are gone; so is all their hope for peace.

*Haaretz* journalist Ari Shavit, writing in the *New Yorker*, says, "I wonder whether this concept we had of a cosmopolitan, non-religious Jerusalem was plausible at all. . . . Perhaps it was self-deception."[7] In an interview in the *Forward*, Yoram Kaniuk, a pioneer of the Israeli peace movement and a personal friend, says, "Since the failure of the Camp David talks, when the truth came out, I've had to face the fact that the Arabs simply don't accept Israel being here. . . . Our (peace) partner is the suicide bomber."[8]

An American-born Israeli friend tells me that her view is now an

apocalyptic one. The subject fills me with unspeakable pain. Everywhere I go is the site of a suicide bombing. The country is full of memorials. It is one vast cemetery. Who knows how long there will be an Israel? The secular moderates on both sides never managed to confront their own extremists. The Israeli government talks peace, the settlers grab land, the Palestinians are choking. Sharon and Arafat are in a dance of death. The right-wing settlers and the Palestinians have both demonized and dehumanized each other. It's "Rashomon" over there. Each side sees everything differently.

How right she is.

So, the bill that the European colonialist powers should have paid long ago has come due, and Israel and America are expected to pay it. When I remind a Muslim friend that Arafat chose terrorism as his preferred method of political negotiation, that he is a corrupt and ineffective leader, she scoffs, "Do you think that *your* leaders are not as corrupt and murderous? Arafat's terrorism pales in comparison to the damage caused by *your* CIA in the last fifty years."

I am an American citizen and I am fortunate to be living here. I want to remind her that I have opposed a good deal of American foreign and domestic policy, but I say nothing. I have cast my lot with this country and with no other. So be it.

But, I say, "Let's assume you are right, that America has a lot to answer for. But why visit upon the small nation of Israel the crimes of another, much larger nation?"

She does not answer me.

## The Clear and Present Danger

It begins with the Jews, but if we do not stop them it will, soon enough—it already has—spread to Christians, Hindus, and Buddhists, and to Americans of all religions and races. Appeasement is no longer an option.

If we do not stop them, Islamic jihadists will surely remove the precious jewels from our houses of worship and our museums, melt down the gold and the silver, and blow up our most beautiful churches and synagogues, or they will build mosques right over them. Muslims have been doing exactly this in the Islamic world for more than a thousand years, and they continue to do so today. The moderates among them have not stopped them. Jihadists will destroy our most beautiful paintings and sculptures, especially those of non-Islamic religious figures and those of naked women—just as they blew up the beautiful Buddha of Bamiyan in Afghanistan. How can we doubt this after Islamic fundamentalists killed 250 people—living beings, more precious than gold—in Nigeria because a letter writer defended the Miss World Contest by saying that even The Prophet would have married such lovely contestants? I am no fan of beauty contests, but in my wildest feminist dreams I would not kill anyone in order to abolish one.

Conversion to Islam will not necessarily save those who wish to live at any price, nor will atheists be spared. Jihadists will enslave or kill Christians and Jews. (Trust me: they will include atheist and secular women, too, because whatever a woman says about her point of view has no real meaning to men such as these.)

I do not wish to alarm you but I am fairly and accurately describing how most Islamic extremists have treated "the infidel" for centuries (even when life was still soft and easy). Unlike the Catholic Church, which has evolved and begun to rethink and regret some of its earlier positions, fundamentalist Islam has not yet evolved. With some exceptions, it is exactly the same today as it was when Muhammad was alive. Sameness is what is valued; difference is feared and hated.

Do I sound overly anxious? Paranoid? Do I exaggerate the danger, stereotype our adversaries? Friends: the Intifada in Israel-Palestine; the Intifada in the Islamic world, in Europe, and on some North American campuses; 9/11; and the nonstop attacks on Israeli civilians have all outpaced science fiction; no adventure-horror movie can keep up with them.

For example, in America on Thanksgiving Day, 2002, which was also the eve of Hannukah, the Jewish festival of light and miracles, Israel suffered three separate attacks, two outside of Israel. Al Qaeda terrorists in Kenya, who claimed to represent the government of universal Palestine in exile, bombed an Israeli-owned hotel in Mombasa, Kenya, where many Israeli tourists had come to escape the terrorist bombings at home. "It was like being back home . . . it could have been a street in Jerusalem," said one Israeli survivor.[9] Fifteen people were killed, dozens were seriously wounded. Minutes earlier terrorists had fired a shoulder-launched missile at a crowded Israeli plane as it left Kenya, narrowly missing it.

A few hours later, shooters invaded an Israeli polling station in Beit She'han, in northern Israel, where people were waiting to vote. They shot six Israelis dead at point-blank range and wounded more than forty others. The Palestinian Al Aqsa Martyrs Brigade claimed responsibility for this—even as the Palestinian Authority condemned it. One of the shooters was seen laughing and smiling as he shot the Israelis down. Of course the Palestinian population of Jenin held the requisite party in the streets. They danced for joy and gave out candies.

Shooting whom you perceive as your enemy is serious business. What are we to make of terrorists who laugh as they kill? What are they high on? Are they psychopaths, ghouls, no longer human?

Do intellectuals still believe that such laughing shooters have been driven out of their mind by the Israeli mistreatment of the Palestinians and that they will lay down their weapons and resume a position of sanity once they have a separate Palestinian state? Really?

This book cannot keep up with breaking news. How could it? We are at war, there are too many terrible things happening every day. Like you, I am also overwhelmed by the sheer number of events and the even greater number of interpretations of the events.

Although we are not privy to inside information, still, most people have been oversaturated with information and disinformation and are fatigued by it, both morally and physically. We are unable to process it all. In the matter of the Israelis and the Palestinians, each side claims that the media are biased against them. Each side accuses its opponents of causing the trouble. Not an hour goes by without an attempted terrorist attack on civilians in Israel. Not a Friday goes by when hatred of Jews, Israelis, America, and the West is not preached in Arabic and in almost every mosque on Earth. The sermons are chilling; we will get to them later.

What I hope this book will do is provide you with the necessary historic and psychological context that will allow you to understand what is happening and what it means. We must begin at the beginning, namely, with the psychological and theological underpinnings of classical "old time" anti-Semitism. This will make it possible for you to understand what is new about both anti-Semitism and terrorism today.

# Chapter Two

# The Old Anti-Semitism

To understand and combat the new anti-Semitism, we must first understand the origins of the old anti-Semitism. Anti-Semitism has been an omnipresent factor in the life of every Jew for thousands of years. Jews are often accused of finding anti-Semitism everywhere. But the fact is, every Jew I know has had some personal experience with anti-Semitism on levels that range from the trivial to the homicidal. So for most Jews, it's not always pathological to acknowledge that in fact people may hate you, and worse, might sometimes try to hurt or kill you.

To understand the old anti-Semitism, we must also ask, What is Judaism? Is it a religion—even if the majority of Jews are not religious? Is it a race—even though Jews come in all colors, including black, brown, olive, white, and yellow? Is it a culture—even though Jews have many different cultures (American, European, Arabic, African, Asian) because they have lived on every continent? The Jews have been discriminated against for their religion, their race, their culture—and for their personal beliefs.

Psychologists and psychoanalysts, beginning with Freud, have tried to understand the origin and nature of unconscious, irrational emotions and prejudices such as anti-Semitism. They suggest that otherwise disunited groups require an outside enemy in order to stop intragroup fighting and to experience group cohesion. The outside enemy is also the one onto whom now-cohesive group members project all their own undesirable or forbidden traits. For a number of reasons, Jews have served to unite groups that would otherwise be permanently divided and at war.

Exiled from their homeland, Israel, Jews seem to be everywhere but to belong nowhere, which is unsettling and suspicious to non-Jews. What's more, Jews hold themselves apart—how infuriating and arrogant. Conversely, when Jews do assimilate, they are seen as too loud and pushy, as taking over. Jews are perfect victims because, until recently, they were powerless among the nations and therefore vulnerable.

Some psychoanalysts also say that anti-Semites tend to be insecure people who refuse to look within and who cannot accept responsibility for their own unacceptable impulses. *They* are not homosexual; the Jews are. *They* never rape their wives or daughters, resent their parents, steal, or commit murder; the Jews do. *They* are not irrationally anti-Semitic; the Jews have provoked their righteous rage and deserve their punishment.

## Scapegoating

So why are the Jews hated, feared, resented, and persecuted? How can a people so few in number, so scattered, so willing either to assimilate or to keep to themselves without proselytizing, continue to arouse the world's hatred? Many theorists have explained the persecution of the Jews as a complex psychotheological phenomenon.

One of the most prominent and credible theories is that the Jew is the scapegoat of the world. A scapegoat was an animal whom God instructed the Jewish high priest to sacrifice publicly to atone for the sins of the Jews (and only the Jews) and for the high priest's own sins. In the Torah, the offering was literally two goats, never a human being. One goat was a burnt offering, the second was thrown from a cliff.[1]

The concept of scapegoating may also be understood in more secular and psychological terms. For example, when a man is angry at his boss, or at authority in general, but can't afford to express this anger directly lest he lose his job or his life, he might redirect his rage and frustration at his child or wife, who cannot hurt him and, as a vulnerable dependent, is a safe and ever-dependable target.

Verbally abusing or beating his wife will not change his work conditions or the humiliation he may feel at work, but it may make him feel powerful over *someone*. Perhaps he has also internalized his boss's withering ways and when he visits such abuse on a wife or child, he may feel that here at least he is the boss.

What if the problem one faces goes far beyond one's own working conditions and includes collective disasters such as plagues, earthquakes, sterility, and famine? Whom can an afflicted society then blame?

For more than three centuries, the European Catholic Church killed an estimated nine to eleven million women whom it accused of witchcraft, that is, of causing male impotence, miscarriages, abortions, crop failures, plagues, and other deeds that cannot be attributed to a loving, Christian God but only to Satan—and to his most intimate mortal companion, Woman. Thus, women were scapegoated for the sins of men, and as an excuse to confiscate their property. Perhaps scapegoating also makes people feel less helpless in the grip of suffering. I suppose one might say that the women were offered up as "burnt offerings," human sacrifices, by a barbarously pagan Inquisition.[2]

The women accused of witchcraft belonged to the same ethnic and national groups that denounced them and that then laid claim to their land and possessions. The Inquisition of the Roman Catholic Church institutionalized a way to profit from the human tendency to blame and punish someone else for human suffering and for one's own misdeeds—and to offer the victims up to the gods as an atonement. I write *gods* because I agree with Freud that the Inquisition (as well as certain other Catholic rites) partook of pagan practices. In Spain and Portugal, the Inquisition was carried out not against women but against Jews. (They needed someone, and either group would do.) Women and Jews shared a vulnerability. Their persecutors knew they could get away with confiscating their earthly goods, and with torturing and killing them.

From a psychological point of view, if a man or many men—if entire nations—are suffering from poverty, disease, violence, and other conditions over which most individuals are helpless, perhaps the intimate family scapegoats—women, children, servants, and slaves, who may also be suffering—cannot be targeted. Perhaps the more reliable scapegoat is not part of oneself, but a stranger, an outsider, not one's own wife or child. Nothing unites people who are otherwise and at all times divided as well as having a common enemy to scapegoat. In fact, intimate family scapegoats may truly rejoice in having a common enemy because it lets them off the hook.

Perhaps someone of a different race or religion might better serve as the scapegoat, the one who must suffer and atone for the people's sins. Perhaps perpetual evil may be perpetually embodied by one group in particular, a group that seems to exist everywhere but does not really fit in or belong; a group that resists fitting in, rejects belonging, prefers its own ways, its own kind; an indigenous, nomadic group—secretive, strange, "different," but worldly wise and well-traveled. Smart. Monied. Filled with ideas. Who better than the Jews?

## Christ Killers

Let us return to the Bible; I am always happy to do so. God first ordered the Jewish and Muslim patriarch, Abraham, to kill his beloved son Isaac and, at the last moment, sent an angel to teach Abraham (and the rest of humanity) that God does not want men to sacrifice their children to God.

In what way can this teaching be reconciled with the Christian view that God, the Father, allowed his son, Christ, to be killed in order to redeem a sinful humanity? Perhaps this is another God entirely, or another interpretation of God's views. But there is no way that Jews can accept the sacrifice of God's own son or that such a sacrifice, by definition, can redeem humanity.

Perhaps many Christians had a psychological problem with this as well and therefore decided to blame the Jews, not God and not the ancient Romans, for Christ's murder and sacrifice. For this, as we know, is what they did: branded Jews as the killers of God's Son, the "Christ Killers," and condemned Jews to universal discrimination, persecution, exile, death, and damnation.

But this is also puzzling, for without Christ's sacrifice there would be no redemption. Thus, Christians may have at some level felt guilty that they were partaking in the body and blood of Christ, participating in or profiting from the murder of their savior.

This might be an unacceptable and painful thought. If so, Christians may have wanted everyone to join them in this primal crime; then no one could judge or blame them, because everyone would be doing it. But the Jews would not do so. Freud, in *Moses and Monotheism*, puts it this way: "[The Jews] will not admit that they killed God, whereas we [the Christians] do and are cleansed from the guilt of it."[3] Blaming the Jews thus became even more important, psychologically.

Please understand: I am not quarreling with the rights of Catholics or Christians to worship Christ as the Messiah in any way they so choose. I am horrified, saddened, outraged—a mite prickly—about the Church's centuries-long mistreatment of the Jews, its acts of both omission and commission.

I am not saying that because the Church persecuted Jews—or did too little to rescue Jews endangered by the princes of the Church—that all Christians are therefore evil. (I do agree, however, with Harvard political scientist Daniel Jonah Goldhagen that it is time for the living Catholic Church to acknowledge its role in the persecution of the Jews that culminated in the Holocaust and to make serious restitution.)[4] I am not saying that each and every Christian persecuted Jews as God-killers. Many did, some did not; some saved Jews, but most chose not to endanger themselves to prevent pogroms or Jewish extermination.

I do not mean to reduce evil to that which can be understood and therefore prevented. Like love, evil is irrational and incomprehensible. Good people can try and stop evil; they can also refuse to become evil. They can "be there" for those who have been wounded and maimed by evildoers. But they cannot prevent or abolish evil. Good people wait a long time before facing evil down, or they never do so at all. My point is that Christian theology posed certain psychological problems for Christians that were solved in a way that led to twenty centuries of anti-Jewish persecution.

## The Role of the Catholic Church

As a Jew, Catholicism frightens me. There's a long and traumatic history between the Church and the Jews. As a feminist, Catholicism often enrages me. As a person of faith, however, it tempts and gentles me, and I respect it.

Thus, I do not mean to sound overly harsh about Catholicism. Forgive me if I do. In many ways it is a good religion for women. For example, the worship of Mary—a female role model and deity—is psychologically uplifting, consoling. (I understand that Mary is also a hard act for an ordinary mortal woman to follow and that many women have been forced into loveless marriages and unwanted pregnancies in her image.)

Another attractive aspect of Catholicism is that, unlike Judaism, it allows women to be nuns. In the past, convent life was the only thing that guaranteed poor girls and women literacy, a roof over their heads, and a God-centered communal life. Nuns do not have to submit to personal marriage and biological motherhood. Although they are women, they are understood to have souls and the capacity for a serious spiritual life. Nuns may live apart from the world—and with one another. Unlike most Jewish women, in the past nuns could devote their lives to prayer and study, as well as to good deeds.

I must also say that Christ's sacrifice is a complex and fascinating concept. It is not merely the sacrifice of God's son to redeem a sinful humanity. It is also a redeeming perspective on life as it is experienced by many; like God's son, God's (other, mortal) children also know agonizing, unjust pain. This commonality has a great and comforting appeal.

Nevertheless, for nearly two millennia it was the absolute doctrine of the all-powerful worldwide Catholic Church that the Jews had killed Christ, that the Jews were Christ Killers. Thus, from this brief discussion you may understand that the first Big Lie about the Jews is that they killed Christ the Lord. But a Big Lie told over and over again eventually becomes indistinguishable from the truth.

Let us ask, Who *did* kill Christ—that most gentle, woman-friendly, and radical of rabbis? Jews did not do it, although many disagreed with Christ's views. Ancient Romans were the Christ killers, the very pagans who, over time, became the first among Catholics. Who was notoriously blamed? The Jews—for having allowed it—as if oppressed and colonized Jews could oppose the might of imperial Rome and get away with it.

All right, it's true: the Jews did not defend Christ (he seemed heretical to some), nor did they choose to fight and die to stop the Roman crucifixion—but neither did the (formerly) Jewish Mary, Joseph, the Magdalene, Peter, Mark, or Martha. Perhaps, just as in the matter of the Palestinian refugee camps in Lebanon, Sabra and Shatila, the Jews "allowed" it to happen; they allowed the Romans to crucify Christ, they allowed the Christian Phalangists to massacre Palestinian civilians in the refugee camps, and perhaps, it may be argued, Jews or individual Israelis ought to bear some moral responsibility for this.

Christians scapegoated Jews because Jews refused to admit their (original) guilt, refused to atone for the murder of God, refused, in short, to view the murder of God as a sacrament, and thus refused to convert and be redeemed. All those who refused to recognize Christ as God's Messiah merited calumny and death, but especially the Jews. How dare they remain loyal to their own God and continue to walk God's green Earth unredeemed?

## Attack on the God Killers

This view of Jews as God killers and God defilers flavored, permeated, the milk of European nationalism that Arabs and Muslims swallowed whole at the end of the nineteenth century and all during the twentieth century.

For nearly two thousand years, most Jews led fearful and cir-
cumscribed lives in both Muslim and Christian lands, where all but
a handful were condemned to poverty, denied citizenship, employment, religious and personal freedom, any dignity, and all hope.
Jews were pressured to convert and assimilate. Many did. Those
who refused to disappear were forced to live in ghettos and impoverished by tax burdens, but they were also routinely harassed,
beaten, raped, mutilated, and lynched in pogroms, forced into exile
again and again, arrested, conscripted into anti-Semitic armies, and
murdered.

The Arab pre-Islamic persecution of the Jews began as early
as the third century BCE when the Egyptians expelled the Jews as
lepers. According to Jerome Chanes in *A Dark Side of History: Anti-
Semitism Through The Ages*, pagan-era anti-Semitic writings

> have a familiar ring. The Jews are obstinate, rebellious—but also
> cowardly. There was widespread resentment of the Jews as aliens.
> Even in Rome we find the great orator Cicero resorting to an early
> form of cynical anti-Semitism when, in arguing a lawsuit against
> Jewish plaintiffs, he whispered to the court, referring to the Jews in
> the courtroom, "You see how they stick together, how influential
> they are in assemblies."[5]

In 66 CE, fifty thousand Alexandrian Jews were massacred. At
that point there was no theological basis for this persecution. This
changed, however, as Christianity triumphed and spread. According to Chanes, "At the close of the third century, the Jew was no
more than a special type of unbeliever; by the end of the fourth,
the Jew was a semi-satanic figure, cursed by God, marked off by the
[Christian] State."[6]

From then on the Jews were segregated, harassed, impoverished,
and repeatedly exiled, jailed, tortured, and murdered—all in the
name of Christ. Synagogues, Torah scrolls, and living Jews were
burned. Great centers of Jewish learning were destroyed. Jews

were falsely accused of crimes they did not commit; they were killed and their property was confiscated. In the eleventh century, when the Christian Crusaders entered Jerusalem, they massacred every single Jewish inhabitant of Jerusalem. The list of such pre-Nazi persecution in Christian lands is a very long one. I will not go into it here. Alas, there is an equally long list of comparable anti-Jewish atrocities in Islamic lands.

## The Dreyfus Affair

In response to this kind of anti-Semitism, Jews either clung to their religion, assimilated, converted, or became Zionists. Let me say that in all the years of Jewish exile from Israel, religious Jews (many of whom were reluctant Zionists) never stopped yearning to return to Zion, never stopped praying to return. Jews face east when they pray, and they pray to God about Jerusalem, God's holy city.

Assimilated, secular Jews in Europe tended to be fiercely loyal to their new "religion." If they were allowed to rise in finance, statecraft, science, or the military, their loyalty had to be above reproach. And it was.

Alfred Dreyfus was such a man. Proud, proper, he was committed to being more French than the French. His dreadful downfall as a presumably disloyal Jew also played a part in the creation of the Jewish state.

The following summary of L'Affaire Dreyfus is a bare-bones, thumbnail sketch. Even so, it may still be hard to follow, given its (unknown to most of us) French and German cast of characters and its Byzantine twists and turns. One thing is clear: When a Jew has been falsely accused and falsely convicted in France, his accusers will continue to resist exonerating him because to do so will only expose them. Those who murder Jews and ruin Jewish reputations are usually outraged when they are accused of having done so. They are anti-Semites who view this as their sovereign right. Like other racists, they do not expect to be held accountable for their racism; they will not only continue to cover up their crimes, they will also routinely threaten to murder anyone who may dare to expose the truth. They suffer no guilt.

The Dreyfus family were assimilated Jews, a line of bankers originally from Alsace who settled in Paris after the Franco-Prussian War (1870–1871). Alfred Dreyfus (1859–1935) was born in Mulhouse. He studied at the Ecole Polytechnique and began his military career as an engineer. By 1892 he was a captain on the general staff—and its only Jew.

In 1894 the French Intelligence Services accused Dreyfus of having given a secret military document to the German military attaché in Paris. Dreyfus was secretly tried. Neither he nor his lawyer were ever shown the forged documents that were used to convict him. The presiding judges unanimously handed down a guilty verdict and sentenced Dreyfus to life imprisonment (or "perpetual deportation" in the infamous Bagne, a prison camp in French Guyana designed expressly to shorten the lives of its detainees) on Devil's Island.

On January 5, 1895, Dreyfus was publicly stripped of his rank before a raucous mob of anti-Semites who shouted "Death to Dreyfus," and "Death to the Jews." Austrian journalist Theodor Herzl covered Dreyfus's trial.

Meanwhile, German officials publicly declared that they had had absolutely no contact with Dreyfus. Dreyfus's younger brother Mathieu turned to the writer Bernard Lazare to challenge the verdict. Lazare authored a pamphlet titled "The Truth About the Dreyfus Affair," which he distributed among the French Senate and to other public figures.

Following this, the new head of French intelligence, Lieutenant Colonel Georges Picquart, was given a letter that the German military attaché, Lieutenant Colonel Maximilian von Schwartz-koppen, had written to Major Ferdinand Walsin Esterhazy. The letter clearly exposed Esterhazy as the true German agent. Picquart then concluded that the secret military document that Dreyfus had allegedly written and given to the Germans had in fact been written by Esterhazy, and that Major Hubery Joseph Henry, a high-ranking member of the Intelligence Services and a conspicuous Dreyfus accuser, had forged additional documents to support Dreyfus's court-martial.

When Picquart officially revealed this, he was relieved of his duties and transferred to Africa. Before leaving, however, Picquart transmitted these documents to friends, who then showed them to left-wing Senator Auguste Scheurer-Kestner, who announced Dreyfus's innocence in the Senate. He accused Esterhazy. Nevertheless, conservative prime minister Félix Jules Méline refused to accept the evidence or the truth.

Meanwhile, Esterhazy was tried and acquitted. Picquart, the truth teller, got sixty days. Dreyfus, the innocent, remained on Devil's Island.

Then, on January 13, 1898, Georges Clemenceau's newspaper *l'Aurore* published an open letter to President Félix Faure written by novelist Emile Zola titled "J'Accuse," which accused the Dreyfus accusers themselves. It sold 200,000 copies in France.

A month later, Zola, the champion of truth, was found guilty of libel. Some officers of the general staff threatened to resign if Dreyfus were acquitted. Anti-Semitic riots broke out in different parts of the country. The Dreyfus controversy became so divisive that it split apart families and political parties. Some felt that exonerating a Jew, even if he was innocent, was not worth it if it brought the thoroughly disreputable French army into disrepute.

Protest by Picquart and others forced the new minister of war, General Louis Eugène Cavaignac, to reopen the Dreyfus case. Major Henry's forgeries were then exposed and he was arrested; he was allowed to commit a soldier's honorable suicide in his cell. Following this, a divided government resolved to vacate the sentence and to request a new trial. The decision caused complete pandemonium and forced Minister of the Interior René Waldeck-Rousseau to form a cabinet dedicated to restoring law and order. At the second trial, in 1899 at Rennes, Dreyfus *was convicted for the second time* (but not unanimously) as a traitor. He was sentenced to a ten-year term that, in light of "extenuating circumstances," was then reduced by five years for time served.

Although the "Dreyfusards" wanted complete vindication, Waldeck-Rousseau prevailed upon the Dreyfus family to drop the appeal. President Emile Loubet then pardoned Dreyfus. In 1904, a new left-wing government reexamined the case and invalidated the charges against Dreyfus without further trial.[7]

Ah, my friends, and on October 19, 2002, nearly one hundred years later, vandals painted a Star of David and wrote "Dirty Jew" on a prominent modern bronze statue of Captain Alfred Dreyfus in Paris. Witnesses said a yellow star of David, like the one Jews were forced to wear by the Nazis during World War II, had been painted over the plaque at the foot of the statue, which also had "Dirty Jew" scrawled on it.

## Theodor Herzl

And now, to our hero. Theodor Herzl was born in Budapest in 1860. He moved to Vienna when he was eighteen, studied law, and was admitted to the bar. Herzl's contemporary Sigmund Freud, the founder of psychoanalysis, could not obtain a university appointment in Vienna because he was a Jew, and Herzl could not succeed in the civil or diplomatic service for the same reason. Thus, instead, the assimilated Herzl became a successful journalist and playwright. The leading newspaper of Vienna, the *Neue Freie Presse*, sent Herzl to Paris as their correspondent. Herzl covered the Dreyfus Case, about which he wrote:

> The Dreyfus case embodies more than a judicial error; it embodies the desire of the vast majority of French to condemn a Jew and to condemn all Jews in this one Jew. Death to the Jews! howled the mob, as the decorations were being ripped from the captain's coat. A hundred years after the Declaration of the Rights of Man, the French people do not want to extend the rights of man to Jews.[8]

Herzl understood that Jews—even assimilated Jews like himself and Dreyfus—would never be accepted among the nations. Perhaps, like the biblical Moses, Herzl could see this because he himself had not suffered the worst as a Jew. Herzl had not personally endured a pogrom; he was a highly educated and multitalented middle-class European. Thus, Herzl was able to envision Zionism radically as the national liberation movement of the Jewish people and as their only hope of self-determination and freedom from persecution.

In 1896, Herzl published *The Jewish State: An Attempt at a Modern Solution of the Jewish Problem* as a political document to reawaken hope and to empower Jews to save themselves.[9] Many assimilated Jews attacked his ideas. The leading Jewish philanthropists—including Moses Montefiore and Edmond de Rothschild—refused to support him. The initially receptive German kaiser and Turkish sultan both ultimately backed down. The British colonial secretary, Joseph Chamberlain, offered him Uganda. Herzl finally understood that the Jewish *masses*, not their leaders, had to be organized to make his dream come true. In 1897, the first Zionist Congress was held in Basel, Switzerland. Afterward, Herzl wrote, "In Basel I created the Jewish State. Were I to say this aloud I would be greeted by universal laughter. But perhaps five years hence, in any case, certainly fifty years hence, everyone will perceive it."[10]

Herzl was off by only one year.

## Hitler's Unintended Results

Almost sixty years have passed since the entire world allowed Hitler to murder six million Jews.

It is true that five million non-Jewish Europeans died in the Holocaust, and that twenty to forty million Russians died at Stalin's hands, both from planned famine and in the Gulag. Arguing the case of the Jews does not mean that I have forgotten the high body count of the twentieth century. I do not think that these deaths matter less. Gil Elliot, in his *Twentieth Century Book of the Dead*, estimates that 110 million human beings died at the hands of other human beings in World War I and II; in the internal revolutions in Russia, China, Spain, France, Korea, Nigeria, India, and Pakistan; and in the Middle East.[11]

Yes, in terms of the European Holocaust the entire world allowed this to happen. Hitler did not do this alone. America refused to accept Europe's Jews as immigrants, and so did most other countries. Also, America did not enter World War II to save the Jews, and it was never America's military or political priority. Britain, America's closest ally, followed in the arrogant and bloody footsteps of ancient Rome, the Christian crusaders, and the Turkish Ottoman Empire and continued to blithely draw and quarter the Arab-Islamic Middle East in favor of the Arabs and against the Jews. Britain would not allow Jewish immigration into Palestine during World War II because Jewish immigrants—exotic outsiders in Europe—were seen as infidel Western outsiders in the only homeland the Jews had ever known. Britain did not want to offend its Arab subjects. No matter that Jews had both historic and continuous roots in Israel that preceded all other historic and tribal claims on this land.

Sometimes I think that God must have carefully chosen precisely such an arid and rocky patch of earth as the Jewish Promised Land not only to teach the Jews that they were dependent on God, who would water the land in response to their good deeds (mitzvot), but also so that other nations would not envy us for our oil, precious metals and stones, natural irrigation, and lush vegetation, which despite enormous Zionist industriousness did not and still do not *naturally* exist in Israel. Perhaps God understood that the Jews were going to be envied enough as God's chosen without adding enviable real estate into the mix. Remember how gluttonous many Holocaust-era Europeans were with Jewish crystal, artwork, carpets, hair, apartments, gold teeth, and artificial limbs. Imagine if Israel itself had natural resources.

According to Dennis Prager and Joseph Telushkin in *Why the Jews? The Reasons for Anti-Semitism:*

> Jew-hatred and its latest incarnation, Israel-hatred, are the price Jews pay for their role in history. They pay it often unwillingly and they live the role, for the most part unwittingly. But as the great French Catholic theologian Jacques Maritain noted: "Israel is to be found at the very heart of the world's structure, stimulating it, exasperating it, moving it. Like an alien body, like an activating ferment injected into the mass, it gives the world no peace, it bars slumber, it teaches the world to be discontented and restless as long as the world has not God, it stimulates the movement of history. It is the vocation of Israel which the world hates."[12]

French existentialist and Marxist philosopher and playwright Jean-Paul Sartre understood that a remnant of French Jewry, whom the French had turned over to Hitler, had actually survived and wished to return to their native country. Sartre was aware of their isolation and pariah status. He understood that anti-Semites viewed the Jew as an "alien" and as the feared and envied symbol of "modernity." To them, Jews were communists, capitalists, atheists. Sartre wished to prepare French intellectuals for the return of France's and Europe's Jews.

In 1948, Sartre published *Anti-Semite and Jew.*[13] Essentially, Sartre wished to reassure the French (and the world) that Judaism in and of itself was an empty tradition, without value, one that posed no threat to the things that mattered. Sartre envisioned that Jews would be assimilated into a future revolutionary classless society.

In 1948 of course, Theodor Herzl's prediction came true, and the State of Israel was officially launched in the world in part of what was once the Jewish biblical homeland. This geographic area was also inhabited at the time by Arabs, who had also lived there for generations. The Arabs refused to accept the Palestinian state that the British and the United Nations offered them. Instead, the

Palestinians and five Arab nations attacked the new and tiny nation of Israel. For a brief time the Israelis were considered heroic Davids against the Goliath who attacked them at birth, but the fickle tide of public opinion has radically shifted and the Jews are now the ogres of the Middle East, hated and vilified by nearly every other country on Earth.

Herzl and Sartre were both right, but they were also both wrong. Neither the existence of a Jewish state nor Jewish assimilation into other nation states has led to the abolition of anti-Semitism in the world. Instead, a global and modern society has emerged that, paradoxically, is more fractured than ever by tribalism and ethnic rivalries.

## The Last Acceptable Prejudice

In a politically correct, multicultural world, anti-Semitism is the last acceptable prejudice. Today, Jews in Israel, Africa, Europe, and South America have been taunted, beaten, terrorized, blown up, shot, wounded, disabled for life, and murdered; their synagogues have been torched, their cemeteries vandalized. Many intellectuals have justified or minimized these criminal acts.

In the past it was clear that right-wing fascists, nationalists, and racial supremacists had led the mobs in torching the Jews. Left-wing intellectuals only worked with Jews who had fled the narrow confines of the ghetto and of a religious Jewish life; otherwise, they viewed Jews with suspicion, as being rigid, intolerant, narrow, unenlightened, and hopeless on the question of individual and women's rights—which often was all too true.

Although most Jews lived in abject poverty, left-wing intellectuals viewed them as monied capitalists because some Jews were indeed wealthy. International working-class-oriented intellectuals did not respect Zionists, whose very existence suggested that intellectuals were no better than others when it came to the Jews. Some Russian Jews had learned this the hard way and had thrown their lot in with the Zionists, not the Bolsheviks.

The Jews have been accused not only of killing God, but also of running the world's newspapers, controlling all governments, and oddly enough, of plotting communist revolutions.

Christian anti-Judaism and anti-Semitism may be the boilerplate, the template for all subsequent racisms. This fight against the Jews is almost as old as the Jews.

• • •

In the past, in Europe, Jews were ritually and continually slaughtered and did not, could not, fight back, partly because they were forbidden to arm themselves. To cover their considerable nakedness, some Jews either embraced or were seen as embracing a form of pacifism that is not always recommended in the Torah. This does not mean that the Torah is a Nazi-like document that preaches war, hatred, and racial superiority, for that is far from the truth. Any number of secular liberals, leftists, and feminists have said this, but *I* say they are wrong. The five books of Moses, the Prophets, the Writings, the Mishna, and the G'mara, which together compose the Talmud, are amazing, complicated texts filled with ethical laws, fabulous tales, horrifying deeds, and interpretations both divine and absurd.

Anti-Semites love to judge the Jews harshly for refusing to behave like dead Jews or good Christians, and while the Torah definitely has some hair-raising scenes in it, so does the world and so does every other sacred book. Although the Prince of Peace might have been nonviolent, his followers were decidedly less so. The doctrine of surrendering to one's fate nonviolently and of forgiving one's enemies may indeed be Christ-like, but this oriental fatalism and courage were not easily transplanted to Europe, and thus many of Christ's followers subsequently launched the most aggressive military crusades against other Christians and against Arabs, Muslims, and Jews. Incidentally, most Catholics did not view the Church, the Crusades, or the Inquisition as anti-Christian because they practiced war, not peace.

Today, modern anti-Semitism also partakes of a new uncon-scious psychological dynamic. Today, anti-Semites are enraged when their designated Christ-sacrifice fights back, refuses to turn the other cheek, and arms himself not only spiritually but with sky-commanding Phantom Jets and atomic weaponry. Enter the hatred of Israel as a new form of anti-Semitism.

Let me be clear: I am not suggesting that Jews are Christ-like, only that anti-Semites often expect this to be so. This is a horren-dous expectation. May I suggest that, psychologically, this precise expectation is often at the root of disappointment with the Jewish people when we turn out not to be ready to die for the sins of oth-ers, and when we turn out to be no better than other people either. The very world that so readily demonizes Jews also unconsciously expects Jews to be better than everyone else, to be that "light unto the nations," and when we are not, the heartbreak and rage are very great, which leads to the demonization and to the collective pun-ishment of the Jews.

Sometimes some Jews *are* better than barbarians; in many ways the state of Israel towers above its neighbors both morally, politi-cally, and in terms of religious freedoms—but some say, sadly, only barely. David Ben-Gurion, that most admirable of secularists and Israel's first prime minister, would be horrified by some of the fundamentalist excesses practiced by both his religious and anti-religious children and grandchildren. Sometimes Israelis behave in the same way that people of other nations do, and for this we are not forgiven. All the incredibly positive things that Israel also does are instantly forgotten because we are not supposed to make any mistakes, not to mention really terrible ones.

## Chapter Three

# Modern Anti-Semitism Before 9/11

The period immediately after World War II was one of unprecedented worldwide sympathy for the Jews. As the facts of the Holocaust became known and the tiny state of Israel struggled for its life, global and particularly American public opinion seemed to shift dramatically in favor of the Jews as long-suffering innocent victims and in support of the Jewish State as the heroic underdog nation suffering attack on all sides by forces that had overwhelming numerical superiority.

But the truth about this "quiet period" in the history of modern anti-Semitism is more complex. Anti-Semitism never disappears entirely. There are always so-called quiet periods that are not really quiet. The world does not always note ongoing violence against the Jews, although it does tend to note negatively all instances in which Jews defend themselves against such violence.

So yes, from 1948 to 1968 there was a brief honeymoon period between the world and the Jews, but even then, during these "best of times" for the Jews, the persecution continued as always and, in fact, gradually began to grow and accelerate as it became evident to the Arab nations and to the rest of the world that the Jews and their nascent state of Israel were not going to go away quietly.

A careful examination of the facts reveals, therefore, that anti-Semitism was alive and well in the Middle East before, during, and after the Holocaust. To understand the historical origins of our current crisis and to set the record straight on significant events in the Middle East, let's review some relevant historical information beginning early in the twentieth century.

# A Brief History of Arab Attacks Against Israel, 1908–1970s

In 1948, Britain offered the Jews a very small state composed of mainly nonarable desert. Britain also offered the Arabs mainly fertile land for their state. At the time the Palestinian Arabs rejected Britain's offer. Had they accepted it, they would now be celebrating fifty-five years of statehood. Perhaps the two-state solution could have come into being nonviolently. The Israelis accepted a far-less-than-ideal amount of nonarable land. The Arab and Islamic nation wanted the Jews out of the Middle East more than they wanted the Palestinians to have their own nation-state, and therefore rejected all offers of sovereign land.

During the late 1930s and throughout the Holocaust, colonial Britain viciously and with malice aforethought stopped all Jewish immigration into Palestine. Britain thus single-handedly doomed many Jews of Europe. (To be fair, at the time no one was entirely clear about the extent of the Nazi Holocaust against the Jews.) Britain continued this policy after the war. At the time, Arabs were Nazi sympathizers and supporters and viewed themselves as at war with colonial Britain. In addition, in 1947 to 1948, Britain tried to stop all shipment of arms to the Jews, while fully arming the Arabs for the war against the Jews. The Arabs lost that war, but they have continued to fight the same war over and over again ever since.

What follows is by no means a complete or comprehensive list; rather, it is merely a sample that indicates the spectrum of incidents in Jewish-Palestinian history over the past century.

## 1908–1915

Galilee pioneers established the first kibbutzim (collective settlements). Arabs invaded the Jewish settlements, so David Ben-Gurion and his colleagues decided to build a self-defense force called *Hashomer,* or "the Watchmen." Ben-Gurion's *Memoirs* cites this as the beginning of Jewish-Arab friction in Palestine.

> One can say without exaggeration that the kibbutzim constitute a social experiment from which peoples everywhere can take inspiration and ideas. And they are the one true example in

today's world of a democratic form of socialism, combining the most advanced economic practices with a respect for individuality and the inalienable rights of every human being, that has never been attained elsewhere.

My group stayed working in Sejera and the surrounding area for two years. Though most of us were new to manual labour, the labour itself caused little hardship. What hurt us more was worry and lack of sleep. We were an isolated community surrounded by nomadic Bedouins. Their intent was not to hurt us or to drive us away, but plain theft. They bothered the Arab settlements as much as they did us.

The villages used to hire Circassian guards to keep watch over life and property. We in Sejera, true to the idea of being dependent on no one but ourselves, resolved to organize our own defense. To do otherwise seemed an abdication of our autonomy, the potential sacrifice of freedom.

Jews did not readily take to bearing arms. As a people we have an ingrained abhorrence to violence. In the centuries of exile we were often martyred. Yet we submitted in abnegation, rarely fighting back. Our weapons were intellectual, based upon reason and persuasion. But for Jews to take rifles and defend that which they had sown seemed at first as going too far.

But one day, three of our group who were hiking back from a short trip to the coast were ambushed by Arab nomads. A few wild shots were exchanged, both sides probably intending merely to scare the other. But an Arab bullet hit one of the Jewish boys and the incident turned into a pitched battle that ended with one Arab lying on the ground seriously injured. Our boys made it back to Sejera without further trouble and we were able to treat the wounded one who wasn't hurt seriously. But we knew that if the Arab bandit died, we could expect a vendetta of revenge that would unite nomads and villagers against us in accordance with the age-old law of an eye for an eye.

Well, the wounded man did die. We knew it when our sheep disappeared, stolen. Then, armed horsemen began roving menacingly round our settlement and our fields. All we could do was triple the guard and wait in anguish for an attack to come.

The first victim of this sorry situation was a newcomer, Israel Korngold. He had just joined the group and was taking one of his first turns at guard duty. He left the Sejera inn, our head-quarters, at two in the afternoon armed with his rifle. Shots rang out. We grabbed our weapons and ran to help him. It was too late. He was lying dead on the road and his rifle was missing. That same day the Arabs killed a Jewish carpenter named Shimon Melamed. It was then I realized the wider implications of this small clash. Sooner or later, Jews and Arabs would fight over this land. . . . [A]ll the intelligence in the world would come to naught, I knew, faced with the rigid traditions and blood code of the East.[1]

In 1915, approximately 83,000 Jews and 590,000 Muslim and Christian Arabs lived in Palestine.[2]

### 1920s

In 1920–1921, "Arab terrorism was rampant during a wave of anti-Jewish riots . . . characterized by the brutal murder in Jaffa of the prominent Jewish author Y. Brenner. . . . [There were similar 'distur-bances' in 1929 that included the massacre of the entire Jewish community in Hebron] and during the Arab Revolt of 1936–1939."[3]

Joseph Trumpeldor, Zionism's greatest military hero, was shot down by Arabs in the Galilee.

The Arabs kill Jews in acts of scattered violence, the Jews cre-ated a defense force called the *Haganah.*[4]

The Mufti of Jerusalem, Hadj Amin el-Husseini, used the slogan "Death to the Jews." He wanted to expel all non-Arab elements and instigated a massacre of Jews in Jerusalem by telling everyone that the Jews were planning to rebuild the ruined Temple on the site of the Mosque of Omar. Husseini directly provoked the Arab-Jewish friction.

On August 23, 1929, Arabs invaded the Jewish areas of Jerusa-lem and attacked the entire population. Riots then ensued in Hebron, Jaffa, and Safed. In total, at least 140 Jews were killed and thou-sands were injured. The riot in Hebron targeted defenseless people in a Yeshiva community—rabbis, yeshiva students, and their wives and children were all slaughtered.[5]

## 1930s

The Arab revolt lasted from 1936 to 1939. It began when riots broke out in Jaffa, in April 1936. Sixteen Jews were killed, and many more were wounded. The Arab Higher Committee, headed by the Husseini, led the campaign of terrorism against both Jewish and British targets. Husseini proclaimed a strike and boycott of Jewish enterprises and products. The committee made the following demands on the British Mandate:

1. Stop Jewish immigration.
2. Stop transfers of land to Jewish owners.
3. Establish a "general representative government."

After the strike, Jewish property was burned, Jewish pedestrians were killed, and Jewish settlements were attacked. Also, British police and army were attacked by terrorists.

By August 1936, the British launched an attack against the terrorists. The Arab strike ended in October 1936, and peace existed temporarily, for almost a year. In September 1937, the violence resumed after the report by Britain's Peel Commission.

The violence continued through early 1939. Eighty Jews were murdered by terrorist acts during the labor strike, and a total of 415 Jewish deaths were recorded during the 1936–1939 period of Arab rioting.[6]

On April 15, 1936, cars on the road between Tulkarm and Nablus were held up by Arab highwaymen. After the armed robbers removed valuables from the cars, three Jews were forced to sit together in a truck and were shot.[7]

On April 19, 1936, a Jew was stabbed to death near Town Square and another was beaten to death in Manshieh Quarter. Near Morum's Corner, two private cars were violently attacked by a mob.

On April 20, 1936, there were further riots between Jaffa and Tel Aviv. In Catton, Manshieh, and Saknat Abu Kebir quarters, two Arabs and two Jews were killed and twenty-six Jews and thirty-two Arabs were injured.

From April 19 through 22, 1936, five Arabs died, sixteen Jews died, thirty-one Arabs were severely injured, twenty-six Jews were severely injured, forty-one Arabs were slightly injured, and forty-nine Jews were slightly injured.

By the end of April 1936, Jewish buses were frequently stoned and fired upon. The Jewish settlements in the Northern District were constantly victims of arson, and damage was done to the trees and crops.

In May and June 1936, in Jerusalem and the Northern and Southern Districts, there were attacks on public and private Jewish property, and sabotage on railways and telegraph and telephone communications.

On May 16, 1936, three Jews were murdered and two wounded leaving a Jerusalem cinema.

## 1940s

In 1939 the British White Paper announced that an independent Arab state would be created within the next ten years; Jewish immigration was limited to 75,000 over the next five years, after which it would cease altogether. Jews were forbidden to purchase land in 95 percent of the territory. The British refused to allow Jews to enter Palestine for the duration of World War II.

On June 6, 1946, President Truman urged the British government to allow 100,000 Jewish immigrants to enter Israel. Ernest Bevin, Britain's foreign minister, replied that the United States wanted the Jews in Palestine "because they did not want too many of them in New York."[8]

From August 1945 to May 1948, Jewish resistance organizations smuggled Jews into Palestine. Sixty-five illegal immigrant ships carrying 69,878 people arrived from Europe. In August 1946, the British captured and detained fifty thousand immigrants in camps in Cyprus. Twenty-eight thousand were still imprisoned after Israel declared independence.[9]

On February 16, 1948, the first organized Arab attack was made on the Jewish village Tirat Tzvi by thousands of Syrians and Iraqis. The kibbutz repulsed the attack.[10]

The water supply was cut off in the Western sector of the city, the area where the Jewish people lived. And in mid-March the Arabs were threatening the single two-lane highway that Jerusalem depended on to bring food from the Jewish settlements.

The crisis came in 30 March when the Mufti's men attacked a large convoy trying to get up to the city. It was a slaughter and dozens of our trucks were also destroyed. We realized that the road to Jerusalem was definitely cut.

The British failed to intervene to protect our people or clear the road. In fact, on one occasion in March, they stopped a Jewish truck convoy, disarmed its members and subsequently distributed their weapons to the Arabs.[11]

The winding road up to Jerusalem became the site of bloody massacres as food convoys were attacked at Sha'ar HaGai. To this day the rusted ruins of the destroyed trucks remind Israelis of the sacrifices made to keep Jerusalem from starving.[12]

On March 11, 1948, the Jewish Agency headquarters was blown up by Arabs.

On April 13, 1948, the Arabs slaughtered doctors and nurses on their way to Hadassah Medical Center.

By 1949, the British had allotted 87,500 acres of the 187,500 acres of cultivable land to Arabs and only 4,250 acres to Jews.[13]

### 1950s

After the War of Independence, Arab terrorism expanded in scope. In 1952, when "fedayeen" terrorist border incursions reached their height, there were about three thousand incidents of cross-border violence, extending from the malicious destruction of property to the brutal murder of civilians.

In 1951–1955, 503 Israelis were killed in attacks originating from Syria and Lebanon. This anti-Israel violence encompassed both frontier settlements and population centers and was perpetrated, for the most part, against innocent civilians, most of them new immigrants.[14]

### 1952

On January 1, 1952, seven armed attackers killed a nineteen-year-old girl in her home in Beit Yisrael, Jerusalem.[15]

### 1953

April 14, 1953, marks the first time that terrorists tried to attack Israel by sea. It was an unsuccessful attempt; one of the boats was intercepted and the other escaped.

On June 8, 1953, Jordan and Israel signed an agreement by which Jordan would prevent terrorists from crossing into Israel from Jordanian territory. A day later, on June 9, a group of terrorists attacked a house in Hadera, near Lod, a farming community. One of the residents was killed. The terrorists threw hand grenades and sprayed gunfire in all directions.

On June 11, 1953, a couple from Kfar Hess were shot to death by terrorists in their own home.

On September 2, 1953, terrorists from Jordan threw hand grenades in all directions in the neighborhood of Katamon, in the heart of Jerusalem. Miraculously, no one was hurt.

## 1954
On March 17, 1954, terrorists about twenty kilometers from the Jordanian border ambushed a bus traveling from Eilat to Tel Aviv. When the bus reached Maale Akrabim, in the northern Negev, the terrorists killed the driver and wounded most of the passengers. They shot each passenger one by one, killing eleven. The survivors said that the murderers spat on the bodies and abused them.

## 1956
On April 11, 1956, three children and a youth worker were killed and five more were wounded at a synagogue. Terrorists opened fire at a synagogue full of children in the farming community of Shafrir.

## 1958
On April 22, 1958, two fishermen near Aqaba were killed by the gunshot of Jordanian soldiers.

On May 26, 1958, Jordanian attacks on Mt. Scopus, in Jerusalem, killed four Israeli police officers.

On December 3, 1958, at Kibbutz Gonen, a shepherd was killed, and in the artillery attack that followed, thirty-one civilians were wounded.

## 1960s

## 1965
January 1, 1965, marked the first attack carried out by the Fatah faction of the Palestine Liberation Organization (PLO). Palestinian terrorists attempted to bomb the National Water Carrier.

On May 31, 1965, two civilians were killed and four wounded. Jordanian Legionnaires fired gun shots on the neighborhood of Musrara in Jerusalem.

On July 5, 1965, explosives were planted by the Fatah faction at Mitzpe Massua and on the railroad tracks to Jerusalem.

On September 29, 1965, an Arab terrorist tried to attack Moshav Amatzia and was killed.

## 1966

On May 16, 1966, two Israelis were killed north of the Sea of Galilee and south of Almagor when their jeep hit a terrorist land mine. Tracks led into Syria.

On July 14, 1966, terrorists attacked a house in Kfar Yuval in northern Israel.

### Post 1967 War
## 1968

On September 4, 1968, one civilian was killed and seventy-one were wounded by three bombs exploding in central Tel Aviv.

On November 22, 1968, Al-Fatah terrorists bombed Mahaneh Yehuda market. Fifty-two civilians were injured and twelve were killed.

## 1969

On February 21, 1969, two people were killed and twenty injured when Palestinian terrorists exploded a bomb in a crowded supermarket in Jerusalem.

### 1970s

In 1974, Yasser Arafat was the first non-state leader to be invited to speak before the United Nations. On November 22, the United Nations granted observer status to the PLO; only the United States and Israel opposed it. On November 10, 1975, the UN General Assembly passed its resolution equating Zionism with racism. It also established the Committee on the Exercise of the Inalienable Rights of the Palestinian People. Alan M. Dershowitz writes:

> The U.N. General Assembly even went so far as to encourage Palestinian terrorism directed against Israeli and Jewish

civilians. In 1979, it approved an exception to the international convention against the taking of hostages. The
amendment, which expressly intended to permit hostage
taking by Palestinians, went as follows: "The present Convention shall not apply to an act of hostage-taking committed in the course of armed conflicts, . . . in which people are
fighting against colonial occupation and alien occupation
and against racist regimes in the exercise of their right of
self-determination."[16]

I hope this outline of events dispels the notion that there was
much of a "quiet period" in Jewish and Israeli history. Moreover, as
we shall see, in addition to all the events mentioned here, from
1968 on, the Palestinians, under the command of Arafat, began a
nonstop campaign of airplane hijackings and synagogue bombings
all across Europe.

In 1972 the Palestinians murdered eleven Israeli athletes at the
Olympic games in Munich, and in 1976 they hijacked a planeload
of Israelis to Uganda. Israeli Defense Forces rescued the hostages in
a stunning commando operation.

In the 1980s, Palestinian terrorist Abu Nidal was the bin Laden
of his time. According to *Le Monde*, in the presumably more
"peaceful" 1980s, Nidal led an attack on a group of Jewish children
in Antwerp in 1980 and on a synagogue in Vienna in 1981; he also
attempted to assassinate the Israeli ambassador to London in 1982.
In 1980, Nidal was implicated in the anti-Jewish attack against the
synagogue at *rue Copernic* in Paris (four died), and, in 1982, at *rue
des Rosiers* in Paris (six died).[17] One of his last big operations was the
1985 bloody attacks at the ticket counters of the Israeli airline El Al
in the airports in Vienna (three died) and in Rome (fifteen died and
one hundred were wounded).

At the time, people said that none of this was anti-Semitism; it
was "only" a political statement about Israeli military policy, that is,
a disagreement about whether Israel did or did not have the right to
exist and to defend itself when it was attacked.

## The Beginning of Modern Pogroms

I remember visiting the bombed synagogues of Paris, Vienna, and Rome in the early 1980s and other times thereafter as well. Policemen were guarding the Jewish houses of worship, and I was glad of it, but sobered, troubled, by what it meant: that the Jews of Europe were still not safe; that killing six million of us (a fact still hotly disputed by European and American Holocaust deniers) had not been enough of a blood offering; that those who want to destroy Israel would not stop at Israelis but would strike out at the world's Jews as well; and that there weren't enough bobbies, police, *carabinieri,* and *polizei* to protect the Jews from right-wing, left-wing, and radical Islamic foes.

By the late 1970s I had begun working for the United Nations. I coordinated a conference in Oslo that took place right before the 1980 United Nations World Conference on Women in Copenhagen. I saw with my own eyes how the entire agenda, both officially and unofficially, was hijacked by the PLO. The official United Nations conference voted 94 to 4 for a 186-point "plan of action" that included a paragraph that listed Zionism as one of the world's main evils, along with colonialism and apartheid. Cuba submitted this amendment when the conference formally opened.

This was my first postmodern "pogrom," and I put this in quotes because it was not like the pogroms of old, in which synagogues were torched, Jewish women raped, babies thrown up on bayonets, Jewish men tortured and murdered. It was something else: a pogrom of nonstop words and ideas, an exercise in total intimidation, perhaps similar to those perfected in Russia and China that are supposed to result in ego breakdown, "confession," a show trial, and death. There is no absolution. The method was now being finetuned for use in an international setting filled with ardent, active, naive women.

Official delegates blamed their own intransigent regional problems on Zionism and apartheid. Bands of thirty to fifty Russiantrained Arab women, headed by PLO representatives, roved the hallways. They had been trained to interrupt each and every panel and to take them over with propaganda against America and Israel. Their behavior was that of attackers on the march— bullies. They did not pretend to be feminists or to be concerned with women. They did not have to be—no one held them to this standard.

The bullies made no eye contact with anyone as they yelled, "Jews must die! Israel must die! Israel kills babies and tortures women. Israel must go!" Many of the unofficial panels were also rigged so that moderators called on only pro-PLO speakers from the audience. In one panel, they interrupted a speaker for five full min- utes with the following chant: "Cuba si, yanqui no, PLO, PLO!" I heard women say, "The only good Jew is a dead Jew" and "Zionism is a disease that must be attacked at the cellular level."

I observed how such hooligans managed to utterly silence an Arab Jew, Simha Choresh, when she tried to talk about her Jewish husband's torture and execution in Iraq and about her consequent flight, but they really outdid themselves when a Pakistani woman tried to talk about the Afghan refugee tragedy that followed the Russian invasion of Afghanistan.

Mina Ben Zvi, who had commanded the Israeli women's armed forces in the 1948 war of independence, wept in my arms. She could not believe that both Israelis and Jews could still be so irrationally hated. Many Jewish women were completely unprepared for the battle-level animosity, its uniformity, omnipresence, and ruthless- ness. I had personally sent for civil rights member of Knesset Shula Aloni, the founder of Israel's Civil Rights Party (Meretz), to debate Leila Khaled, who in 1969 became the first Palestinian woman to hijack a plane (TWA), which she had flown to Damascus.

"I will only talk to her out of the barrel of a gun," Khaled said.

Aloni was unfazed, as was Tamar Eshel, then head of Na'amat, the movement of working women and volunteers. But most other Jewish women experienced Copenhagen as a psychological pogrom. For months afterward, many could not and would not talk about it. They would start talking, then start crying, or start talking and abruptly stop. They said they were unable to convey in words what Copenhagen had been like.

Thus, anti-Jewish and anti-Zionist goon squads were already well trained and on the march long before Israel invaded Lebanon in 1982. Such programmed hate was upon us long before Sharon ascended the Temple Mount in 2000. And it rained down upon us from both the left and the right, and from all four corners of the globe.

In 1980, in Copenhagen and in Oslo, I met otherwise pleasant and progressive Scandinavians who automatically supported the PLO and automatically hated Israel—reason be damned. As socialists, they had already been well programmed to espouse the most profound disgust and hatred for all things American, Jewish, and Zionist—and in the most aggressive manner.

Their considerable anger with religion did not lead them to march against the Vatican, but it did lead them to march symbolically against the Zionists. Their anger at imperialism did not lead the Danes or their counterparts all over Europe to demand that France, England, Holland, Spain, and Germany pay serious reparations to all those whom they had formerly colonized; but it did lead them and their European counterparts to scapegoat both America and Israel, as America's "imperialist" outpost in the Middle East. The one thing I have always noted about European and American socialist-pacifists is how very angry they are.

• • •

Thus, ideological and other kinds of terrorism against Jews, Israel, and the United States were well launched and under way during the so-called quiet period. The international conference in Copenhagen was only one of hundreds, perhaps even thousands that took place, and that are still taking place—conferences that are maniacally obsessed with demonizing and isolating Israel. During this period, the Russians and the Europeans commandeered the propaganda war against Israel. The Palestinian and Muslim terrorists took to the streets, so to speak.

In 1980–1981, post-Copenhagen, I did three things: I persuaded the Israeli government to allow me to organize a truly radical feminist conference and to hold it in Jerusalem; I wrote about the Copenhagen Conference for *Lilith* magazine, but under a pseudonym so as not to jeopardize the safety of feminists from Arab and Islamic countries whom I was inviting to this conference-that-never-was in Jerusalem; and I initiated and moderated a panel on feminism and anti-Semitism for the annual National Women's Studies Association meeting in Storrs, Connecticut. I did these things because I didn't want to tell people that American feminists were anti-Semitic and anti-Zionist only behind closed doors. I wanted to present the facts publicly "to my people," so to speak, and to give them a chance to include anti-Semitism in their thinking about racism and in their antiracism statements.

I was also concerned about the rumors that had begun to circulate among *Ms.* magazine staffers and, through them, among international feminists, namely, that Jewish women, myself included, were "paranoid" about what had happened in Copenhagen and were perhaps no longer the "right" kind of feminists. The feminist party line—even back then, in the 1970s and 1980s—was strictly pro-PLO and anti-Zionist. Feminists, both those who had presumably broken with the Left and those who had not, viewed Israel as the symbol of patriarchy, capitalism, and religious misogyny.

I therefore made it a point to "come out" as a Zionist at the Storrs panel. I talked about Zionism as the national liberation movement of the Jewish people. I described how feminist reports of anti-Semitism in our ranks were often seen as exaggerated, groundless. I said, "If we understand why women need separate shelters for battered women, coffeehouses, music festivals, land trusts, Women's Studies programs, can't we also understand why Jews might need a Jewish state?"

I asked my assembled feminist sisters, "Who'd hide me and all the other Jewish feminists and our families in their attics when the Nazis come for us again?" "I will, I will," promised an earnestly distraught Susan Griffin. She was the only one who responded. Everyone else remained absolutely silent. Afterward, it became clear that some powerful (white) feminists, both Christian and Jewish, were disgusted, dismayed, and disappointed by the presentation; and some women of color were angry because, once again, the (white-skinned) Jews seemed to be competing for the limited antiracism flavor-of-the-month slot.

Friends: some major feminists wrote me off after Storrs. These were the same feminists whom I had chased, often fruitlessly, all through the 1970s for their signatures on petitions for Israel vis-à-vis the United Nations. Please understand: nothing dramatic happened. Things happened subtly, and over a long period of time. Some academic feminists simply stopped inviting me to certain private and public events; others stopped asking my advice. In the past I had usually been included in meetings with visiting feminist dignitaries from abroad; from Copenhagen on—definitely post-Storrs—I rarely was. I would learn that someone had been to New York only after she'd returned to Africa or Asia or Europe because she'd then write and say she'd expected to see me at so-and-so's party or at the meeting, and when I wasn't there she'd assumed I had been out of town.

From 1980–1981 and onward, I had many passionate conversations with individual Christian feminists, both white and of color, who emotionally seemed to believe that twentieth-century Jews and Zionists were more responsible than anyone else on Earth for the death of "the" Goddess three thousand years ago and for the slave trade four centuries ago; that Zionism is responsible for racism in America today, and for all forms of American and Western imperialism; that all Jews are rich, powerful, reactionary, and racist; and so on.

Post-Storrs, I turned over our panel tapes to Letty Cottin Pogrebin, who used some of the information in her important article on anti-Semitism among feminists, which was published in Ms. magazine in 1982 and became the basis for her book Deborah, Golda and Me.[18] The article caused quite a stir. A number of Ms. feminists asked me privately whether I thought Letty was exaggerating, grandstanding, merely applying for a position in the Jewish establishment, and so on. I told them she was telling the truth.

## Continuing Attacks on Jews, 1980s–1990s

Thus, before the new anti-Semitism emerged, Jews were continually attacked outside of Israel on every continent. For example, in September 1986, Palestinian-born terrorist Nidal was accused of being involved in an attack on a synagogue in Istanbul (twenty-four died), and in 1988, on a Greek cruise ship, the *City of Poros* (nine died). In 1987, the group took its first hostages when it captured eight "Israeli spies" of French and Belgian nationality onboard a pleasure boat, the *Silco*. The hostages would later be freed, but Al-Fatah would later be cited in the kidnappings of Westerners in Lebanon.[19]

Europe was not the only theater of the war against the Jews in these times. For example, in the 1990s, long before the emergence of the new anti-Semitism, Argentina—that country of the "disappeared"—also made life hell for its Jews. In March 1992, at least 28 people were killed and more than 220 injured in the bombing of the Israeli embassy in Buenos Aires. While this incident remains unsolved, experts believe that Iran funded the attack.[20]

In 1994, in Buenos Aires, eighty-six people were killed and many more injured in an explosion that destroyed a seven-story building that housed the Argentine Jewish Mutual Association and the Delegation of Argentine Jewish Associations. According to a report by the Stephen Roth Institute for the Study of Contemporary Anti-Semitism and Racism at the University of Tel Aviv, "It is believed that although the bombing was carried out by Muslim militants, they were aided by the local police, who provided them with the necessary intelligence, vehicles, explosives and immigration documentation."[21]

Let us recall that Eva and Juan Peron's Argentina refused to allow European Jews to immigrate there during World War II but became a haven, thereafter, for escaped Nazi war criminals. Adolph

Eichmann, Josef Mengele, Klaus Barbie, and 297 others of their kind sought and received secret, priority asylum in Argentina. Evidence exists which documents that the Catholic Church collaborated in this Nazi-Argentina secret network. To this day, Argentina continues to resist opening certain archives on this subject.[22]

On March 9, 2003, Argentinian judge Juan Jose Galeano indicted four Iranian officials in the infamous 1994 bombing of the Jewish Center in Buenos Aires. The Iranian officials cited were Ali Fallahian, a former Minister of security and intelligence; Mohsen Rabbani, formerly the Iranian cultural attaché in Buenos Aires; Ali Balesh Abadi, a diplomatic courier; and Ali Akbar Parvaresh, a former education minister and a former deputy speaker of the Iranian parliament.[23]

Let us not forget the long history of lawsuits on behalf of Holocaust survivors and their heirs. Enormous sums of money, property, jewelry, artwork, real estate, and factories were all stolen from the Jews of Europe. Many contemporary Europeans either deny that the Holocaust ever happened or demand impossibly high levels of documentation. Some Europeans—especially the so-called neutral Swiss—deny they have stolen anything and resent it when they are proved wrong. Brigitte Sion, a Swiss Jew, writes the following:

> Beginning in 1996, investigations had revealed the extent of Holocaust victims' dormant accounts in Swiss banks, money which the Swiss government had made no attempt to return to the families of its rightful owners. These reports triggered a wave of graffiti and insults, boycott campaigns and physical aggression against Jews in Switzerland. Politicians and bank officials made shocking statements: then-President Jean-Pascal Delamuraz said that Switzerland was the victim of "blackmail" and "extortion," while one of the leaders of the nationalist Swiss People's Party, Christopher Blocher, accused the Jews of being "only interested in money."[24]

In 1997 in Austria, three Jewish cemetery desecrations were recorded and two bomb threats were received by Jewish institutions in Vienna. Also in 1997, a group of Italian Jews visited Austria in August. They left their hotel and they left Austria after the inn-keeper shouted anti-Semitic insults and physically assaulted two of them.[25] In 1998 in Holland, the home of a Jewish mayor was daubed with swastikas and a synagogue was defaced with swastikas and the words *Forbidden to Jews* and *Juden raus*.[26] That same year, in two sep-arate incidents, swastikas were painted on the monument erected in memory of local Jews murdered in the Holocaust.

For a long time, anti-Semitic slogans have characterized the be-havior of soccer fans in the Netherlands. In 1998, the Center for Information on Football Vandalism reported that at matches in-volving Ajax (a team incorrectly perceived as Jewish), cries of "Jews to the gas" and "They forgot to gas all of you Jews in the Second World War" were routine. Despite the suspension and nonadmis-sion of the most serious player-offenders, the stadium itself seethed with hatred, and the Ajax team was taunted by anti-Semitic chant-ing. Objects were also thrown at them. At one match, the police arrested thirteen people for shouting racist slogans.

In 1997 in Italy, Molotov cocktails were thrown at a building on an island in the Tiber River housing the Temple of the Young synagogue and a Jewish hospital. No casualties were reported. In addition, a firebomb was hurled at Rome's central synagogue, which caused minor damage to the entrance. Italian police detained a thirty-four-year-old Egyptian who seemed drunk or mentally dis-turbed. As in previous years, there were also anti-Semitic graffiti and threats. For example, anonymous telephone threats were received at the office of the Venice congregation and at the home of its cantor. They included anti-Semitic curses and slogans such as "Hitler did not finish the job and we will continue."[27]

Please understand that I am describing only a mere handful among thousands of such anti-Semitic and anti-Jewish incidents that took place all over Europe during the so-called "quiet time."

• • •

After twenty centuries of pogroms that culminated in the Holocaust, who could ever have predicted the forceful return of anti-
Semitism to Europe? This has not happened suddenly. Over the last
thirty years, synagogues have been bombed on a regular basis, usually by Palestinian terrorists, sometimes by North African and Arab
Muslim terrorists. Were they signaling, winking, to the Europeans
that they, the Muslims, "got it"? That they understood that the
Europeans did not really like their Jews and would permit the Muslims to go after them?

### Islamic Terrorism Against the United States, 1970s–1990s

After the War of Independence, the Palestinians fully expected the
Arab world to rise up on their behalf and drive Israel into the sea. In
1967, four Arab armies declared war on Israel. Unexpectedly, Israel
won this war of self-defense. Within a year, Palestinian Arabs began
to attack airplanes and shoot Americans, and so on.

For example, on June 5, 1968, Christian Palestinian Arab Sirhan
Sirhan fatally shot Senator Robert F. Kennedy in the kitchen pantry
of the Ambassador Hotel in Pasadena, California. Sirhan initially
pleaded not guilty to one count of murder and five counts of assault
with a deadly weapon, but while the jury was absent, he shouted in
the courtroom, "I killed Robert Kennedy willfully. . . . I'm willing to
fight for [the Arab cause] . . . I'm willing to die for it."[28] He then
requested to change his plea to guilty on all counts, announcing the
intention to request execution, but the court denied this.

Defense witnesses testified that Sirhan had been psychologically
scarred by his exposure to the Israeli war of independence as a child
in Jerusalem, where he was born in 1944. The defense also testified
that Sirhan had become enraged when Senator Kennedy pledged
military support for Israel ("fifty phantom jets") if necessary.

Sirhan stated at trial that he "'read everything about the Arab-
Israeli situation he could lay his hands on,' including publications
from the Arab information center in the United States and a book on

Zionist influence on U.S. policy in the Middle East." He also testified that, on seeing an advertisement for a march in support of Israel, he was "brought back to the six days in June of the previous year," and that "a fire started burning inside of him as a result of the ad."[29]

Evidence produced at trial suggested that Sirhan was insane and inclined to outlandish mysticism, and that he had an intense loathing for the state of Israel and for Jews. He was sentenced to death, but this sentence was commuted to life in prison. All attempts at obtaining parole have been denied and he remains in a California State prison.[30]

• • •

The war against America has been under way for a long time. Here is another brief history, this time a partial list of incidents of Islamic terrorism against the United States.

On November 4, 1979, Iranian Islamic seminarians in Tehran stormed the U.S. embassy and held fifty-three Americans hostage for 444 days.

On April 18, 1983, a suicide car bomber blew up the U.S. embassy in Beirut, killing sixty-three, including seventeen Americans.

On October 23, 1983, terrorist operatives blew up the U.S. Marine barracks and French military headquarters in Beirut, killing 241 marines and 58 French paratroopers. Jeffrey Goldberg, staff reporter for the *New Yorker,* attributes this attack to Hezbollah (a.k.a. the Islamic Jihad Organization, a.k.a. the Organization of the Oppressed on Earth).[31] Prior to 9/11, it was the most deadly terrorist attack on Americans.

On June 14, 1985, Hezbollah seized a TWA jet and commandeered its flight to Beirut, demanding the release of seven hundred Arabs held in Israeli jails. One U.S. Navy diver was killed and thirty-nine Americans were held hostage until July 1.[32] Goldberg reported that the United States held one of Arafat's former bodyguards, Imad Mugniyah, responsible for most of Hezbollah's anti-American attacks, including this one.

On April 5, 1986, a bomb, putatively Libyan, exploded in a Berlin nightclub, killing 2 U.S. servicemen and wounding 230 other people. "Libya is blamed," according to the Associated Press (AP).

On December 21, 1988, Libyan terrorists blew up Pan Am flight 103 over Lockerbie, Scotland, killing 270 people, including some on the ground.

On February 26, 1993, a car bomb planted by radical Islamists exploded in the parking garage beneath the World Trade Center towers, killing six and wounding more than a thousand. The four convicted perpetrators were all linked to the blind Egyptian radical Sheik Omar Abdul Rahman, himself indicted as the leader of a larger alleged conspiracy to destroy the United Nations headquarters and the Lincoln and Holland tunnels.

On June 25, 1996, a truck packed with explosives exploded outside the Khobar Towers in Dharam, Saudi Arabia, killing nineteen U.S. servicemen and wounding hundreds. According to Goldberg, the U.S. also suspects former Arafat bodyguard Mugniyah of involvement in this case.[33]

According to the *Washington Post,* however, American investigations in 1998 pointed exclusively to Iranian agents.

On November 17, 1997, Jemaah Islamiyah operatives shot and killed more than sixty tourists visiting the temple of Queen Hatshepsut at Luxor, Egypt. There were Japanese, Swiss, German, and British among the dead.

On August 7, 1998, Al Qaeda detonated two car bombs and destroyed the U.S. embassies in Nairobi and Dar-es-Salaam simultaneously, killing 224 and wounding thousands. The AP reported that bin Laden was suspected.

On October 12, 2000, Al Qaeda attackers bombed the U.S.S. *Cole* as it refueled in the Yemeni port of Aden, killing seventeen sailors. Again "bin Laden [was] suspected."[34]

## Palestinian and Islamic Terrorism Against Jews, 1970s to 1990s

During this same period (1979–2001), Palestinian and Islamic terrorists continued to attack Jews, mainly civilians, in Israel proper as well as Westerners. I list here only a handful of such incidents. I do not want to overburden you with lists of the dead; however, it is important that you understand that anti-Semitic violence against Jews, on every continent but especially in Israel proper, has been a fairly continuous phenomenon, not one pegged to some particular outrage committed by Zionists in a particular year.

## 1970s

On May 30, 1972, the Ben-Gurion airport was attacked. Twenty-six died and seventy-six were wounded.[35] El Al planes were attacked in August 1976 in Istanbul and in May 1978 in Paris.

In December 1974, a Tel Aviv movie theater was bombed, killing two and wounding sixty-six.

In March 1975, a Tel Aviv hotel was attacked, leaving twenty-five dead and six wounded.

On July 4, 1975, a bomb in Zion Square, in Jerusalem, killed fifteen people and wounded sixty-two.

## 1980s

On April 7, 1980, Kibbutz Misgav Am was attacked, leaving three dead and sixteen wounded.

In October 1980, terrorists bombed a Paris synagogue.

In August 1981, a Vienna synagogue was attacked, leaving two dead and nineteen wounded.

On September 19, 1982, a synagogue in Brussels was attacked.[36]

In October 1982, a Rome synagogue was attacked.[37]

In November 1985, eight people were killed in the hijacking of an Egyptian plane.

On October 8, 1985, Leon Klinghoffer, a wheelchair-bound American Jewish tourist aboard the Achille Lauro, was killed by members of the PLO's Palestine Liberation Front, who hijacked the ship and threw Klinghoffer over the side.

On December 28, 1985, Palestinian Arab terrorists from the Abu Nidal group attacked the El Al terminal at the Rome airport. Five Americans were killed.

On September 6, 1986, Rajesh Kumar, of Huntington Beach, California, was killed when Palestinian terrorists hijacked a Pan Am jet at the Karachi, Pakistan, airport.

Between 1980 and 1982, European synagogues in Paris, Vienna, Brussels, and Rome were attacked.

As Palestinian terrorists were attacking Jewish houses of worship, Pope John Paul II decided to welcome Arafat to the Vatican in

1982. Following the 1986 attack on the synagogue at Istanbul, the Pope invited Arafat again.

### 1990s

On December 6, 1991, near Hebron, Mordechai Lapid and his son, Shalom Lapid, nineteen, were shot to death by terrorists. Hamas claimed responsibility for the attack.

On October 29, 1993, Chaim Mizrahi, a resident of Beit-El, was kidnapped. Three terrorists captured him from a poultry farm near Ramallah. They murdered Mizrahi and burned his body.

On February 19, 1994, Zipora Sasson, a resident of Ariel who was five months pregnant,  was killed by shots fired at her car on the trans-Samaria highway. The terrorists were members of Hamas.

On February 25, 1994, an eighty-year-old man, Sam Eisenstadt, was assaulted with an axe in the center of Kfar Saba. He died shortly after the attack.

On July 24, 1995, six people were killed on a bus in Ramat Gan by a suicide bomber.

On August 21, 1995, four people were killed by a suicide bomber on a bus in Jerusalem.

On September 5, 1995, a terrorist broke into Daniel Frei's house in Ma'aleh Michmash. He was only twenty-eight years old.

On February 15, 1996, Hamas claimed responsibility for the suicide bombing of bus 18 near the central bus station in Jerusalem. Twenty-six people were killed, seventeen civilians and nine soldiers.

On March 3, 1996, bus 19 on Jaffa Road in Jerusalem was attacked by a suicide bomber. Eighteen people were killed (sixteen civilians and three soldiers).

On March 4, 1996, in Tel Aviv, outside Dizengoff Center, a suicide bomber detonated a twenty-kilogram nail bomb. Thirteen people were killed, twelve civilians and one soldier.

On June 16, 1996, in the village of Bidiya, an off-duty policeman, First-Sergeant Meir Alush, forty, was shot and killed in a toy store.

On March 21, 1997, three people were killed (Michal Avrahami, thirty-two; Yel Gilad, thirty-two; and Anat Winter-Rosen, thirty-two) and forty-eight wounded by a suicide bomber on the terrace of a Tel Aviv café.

On July 30, 1997, 13 people died and 170 were wounded in two consecutive suicide bombings in Mahaneh Yehuda market in Jerusalem.

On September 4, 1997, three suicide bombings on Ben-Yehuda pedestrian mall in Jerusalem killed 5 people and wounded 181.

On August 20, 1998, Rabbi Shlomo Ra'anan, sixty-three, was stabbed to death in the bedroom of his caravan in Hebron.

On October 29, 1998, Sergeant Alexey Neykov, nineteen, was killed by a terrorist who drove his explosives-laden car into an Israeli army jeep carrying forty elementary students from the settlement of Kfar Darom in the Gaza Strip.

On January 13, 1999, terrorists opened fire near Hebron, at Othniel Junction. Sergeant Yehoshua Gavriel was killed.

On August 6, 1999, a body, shot in the head, was found in a burned vehicle.

On August 30, 1999, two people, Yehiel Finfeter, twenty-five, and Sharon Steinmetz, twenty-one, were murdered by terrorists in the Megiddo Forest while they were hiking.

We are getting closer to the full-fledged eruption of what constitutes the new anti-Semitism, but we are not quite there yet. First, I would like to describe what a group of international academic feminists did in the summer of 2000. (The latest, ongoing Intifada did not begin until the fall of 2000.) This was not a headline-making synagogue burning or homicidal bombing but rather an early example of the insidious anti-Semitic campaign in the academic, feminist, and politically left-wing international community.

## Academic McCarthyism

On July 27, 2000, two months before Ariel Sharon ascended the Temple Mount in Jerusalem, which subsequently unleashed and became the excuse for the long-planned Intifada of 2000, Marilyn Safir, an American-born academic who had lived in Haifa for more than thirty years, was disinvited to an autonomous academic conference on female sexuality that had been scheduled to take place in Istanbul, Turkey, during the Jewish High Holidays.

The fact that Safir was a pro-peace, pro-Palestinian Jewish feminist who had been conducting academic research with her Palestinian counterparts at Al-Quds (Jerusalem) and An-Najah (Hebron) Universities did not matter. The fact that she was an Israeli *Jew* is all that mattered. Thus, after a warm and congenial series of conversations, the conference's co-sponsors, Women for Women's Human Rights and the International Women's Health Coalition, abruptly rescinded Safir's invitation.

The Turkish conveners, Pinar Ilkkaracan and Leyla Gulcur, disinvited Safir because, they wrote, "the lack of agreements reached between Israel and Palestine at Camp David . . . [has created] an atmosphere of tension and we were told that the Arab participants would boycott the meeting in finding out that participants of Jewish-Israeli background were also coming."[38]

Safir asked them to resist such pressure and to reconsider their decision. The Turkish conveners not only refused to do so, but they also claimed not to understand what Safir meant by "giving in to outside pressure." Their aim had been the creation of a network of Middle Eastern women; they perceived *Israel* as the outsider, not the Arab women who had allegedly threatened a boycott. Ilkkaracan and Gulcur wrote that Safir's insistence that "we should take 'another' stand on this issue could also be described as 'pressure.'"[39] Adrienne Germaine, president of the Health Coalition, agreed with their decision.

What was to have been a nonpolitical, free-standing feminist conference had been taken hostage by the Islamic Jihad and the PLO.

On August 11, 2000, more than two weeks later, Safir shared news of this troubling incident with other feminist academics and activists. I wrote a letter on her behalf to selected feminists. In response, British-born Israeli law professor Frances Raday strongly condemned the disinvitation.

She wrote that "the preparedness of women who are members of human rights groups to associate themselves with a boycott on

Jewish (but not Muslim or Christian) women from Israel makes a mockery of the very concept of human rights. . . . [S]ince the conference is concerned with the rights of women against governments, it is self-defeating to exclude women on the grounds that their governments are allegedly not behaving in accordance with your standards regarding human rights."[40]

Conversely, a number of Jewish Israeli feminists excused Marilyn's disinvitation. One woman wrote, "[S]ince Israel is the dominant power in the Middle East [this disinvitation] cannot be viewed as a human rights violation. . . . [Arab women] may not feel comfortable 'sharing' with a white European woman."[41] A second woman deplored the disinvitation but also suggested that, from a practical point of view, Arab women may view the creation of Arab-only space in which to discuss "sexuality" as their *feminist* priority over and above solidarity with Jewish Israelis.

These are both plausible points of view, yet I cannot help but note how dangerously good Jews are at understanding the "other's" point of view, and at expecting Jews-only and Jews-first to betray their loyalties to their own tribes. Arab and Muslim women would be killed on the spot if they did so. Therefore, Jewish and Christian feminists often set a lower standard for Muslim and Arab feminists.

When I mentioned this disinvitation in American feminist circles, a sympathetic groan was heard in the land—not for Safir, but for the "poor" Turkish women and for "poor" Adrienne Germaine, who had clearly been pressured into an unfortunate decision and who would no doubt be raked over the coals by the Zionist colonialists from hell. When I raised the possibility that the decision was an anti-Semitic one, most feminists begged to differ. "No, they probably weren't thinking clearly, who knows what pressure they were under."[42]

Women, you see, cannot be accused of racism—unless, of course, they are *Jewish* women. Whatever other women do is entirely due to undue male pressure for which women can never be held accountable.

On August 19, 2000, Germaine called Safir. "She was extremely apologetic," Safir wrote, "for not understanding my viewpoint, for not consulting with other people, and for the nature of the response written by the conference coordinators." Safir confirmed that it was never her intention to have the conference cancelled, "but to challenge the thinking that went into the disinvitation."[43]

So the conference was cancelled due, we were also told, to the "intense international reaction."[44] However, no one had called for a boycott of Turkey, nor had the conference organizers been harassed, fired, kidnapped, tortured, or executed. A handful of academics had written letters.

My conclusion: this group of international feminists chose to cancel an entire conference rather than to allow *one* Jewish Israeli to attend it. Yes, Safir was the only Israeli Jew who had been invited.

• • •

Although I was disgusted and disheartened by this turn of events, I was not at all surprised. I had first encountered anti-Semitism among women on the feminist left in the late 1960s. During that period it was quite fashionable among the "radical chic" to despise Israel as a racist, Eurocentric state, a puppet of U.S. imperialism and oppressor of the newly underdog Palestinians. Never mind the actual racial, ethnic, and cultural diversity of the emerging Jewish state and the intransigence of the surrounding Arab nations in their stated intention to destroy Israel. No, my feminist friends and colleagues could not tolerate this little nation's struggle for identity and survival against overwhelming odds, because the Israelis were Jews, and Jews were held to a different standard. They were fair game for self-righteous attacks from progressive feminists who were, in my opinion, guilty of frank and outright anti-Semitism.

I called anti-Semitism by its rightful name immediately and have not stopped doing so ever since. But my credentials as a radical were impeccable, so when I began wearing big Jewish stars to rallies, I was neither challenged nor shunned. Perhaps my star of David was seen as a mere fashion statement; perhaps I got away with it because back then I was the "right" kind of Jew: secular, ideologically sophisticated, universalistic, antiracist. I had even been married to a Muslim. I had worked with Iranian Muslims against the Shah. I was one cool Jew.

What do I mean by anti-Semitism? I mean the raw and filthy kind, in which the prejudice is both blatant and eroticized, without any left political cover. For example, I once rescued a (Christian) feminist colleague from being psychiatrically institutionalized against her will. Afterwards, she treated me to a monologue about how "the Jews are dirtying up the beaches." Poor soul, she reminded me that when one goes mad, one's political or philosophical orientation cannot withstand the ideas embedded in our collective unconscious. A stream of anti-Semitic vitriol came flying out of her mouth.

Another (Christian) feminist confided in me. She said that in her view "the pushy Jews had taken over the feminist and lesbian movements," and she was very unhappy about this. She was proud of her friendship with one particular Jewish woman, but she also viewed the "pushy" Jewish women as "slutty, sexy" scoundrels.

A third feminist, an African American (Christian) woman of enormous beauty and dignity, continually confronted me, albeit privately. She said, "How can you call yourself a feminist and still support Israel, an apartheid state?" Nothing I ever said about Israel ever got through to her. She understood the symbolic and political importance of African Americans converting to Islam, of African nationalism; she simply did not extend the courtesy to the Jews.

A fourth feminist told me that she'd been thrown out of her feminist consciousness-raising group for being "too pushy, too smart, too verbal."

I was astounded. "Are you Jewish" I asked? "Was anyone else Jewish in your group?"

"No, I was the only one. But I never thought of it this way."

A fifth feminist blamed what she perceived as Betty Friedan's homophobia and woman hatred primarily on her "heterosexual Judaism." A sixth feminist blamed what she saw as Bella Abzug's rage and overweening but self-destructive ambition on her Judaism and probable Zionism. (I must say that Bella was as compassionate as she was angry and that her Zionism was of a limited and situational sort.)

Encountering such anti-Semitism within progressive political circles sent me straight to Israel for the first time. In 1972, when I was in Tel Aviv, I remember coming upon a review of my recently published first book, *Women and Madness,* in *Time* magazine. Freud was caricatured as a big-nosed, ugly, pygmy-midget, clearly "in lust" with the tall, blonde Viking princess on his couch. The pure racism just leapt off the page at me. I was shocked. I hated the anti-Semitic illustration even more than the reviewer's anti-feminist bias.

Between 1973 and 1975, I tried but, with the exception of Aviva Cantor and Cheryl Moch, failed to interest other Jewish feminists in meeting on a continuous basis to discuss the problem of anti-Semitism. At the time, one rising feminist light said, "Phyllis, it may be *a* problem, but it's not *my* problem." Another said that she didn't identify as a Jew anyway—and hoped I'd give it up too. (Within a decade, both women would have important things to say on this very subject.)

## The Turning Point

I hope that by now we are all well aware of the continuing anti-Semitic war against the Jews and the Jewish state. It has been relentless, but also regionalized and technologically low-level. Today, in our times, a new kind of anti-Semitism is happening, one that is more threatening and dangerous to Jews than anything that has occurred since World War II.

The war against the Jews is now also the war against America and the West, and against our shared cultural values. On September 11, 2001, Al Qaeda operatives hijacked four planes simultaneously.

Three were deliberately crashed into the two towers of the World Trade Center and into the Pentagon. The final plane crash-landed under mysterious circumstances in Pennsylvania. The death toll from all events reached 3,031. Al Qaeda claimed responsibility.[45] Since then, a dizzying series of events have followed.

## Post 9/11 Islamic Terrorists Against the West

On November 13, 2001, bombs exploded in the U.S. bank Citibank and the U.K. bank Barclays in Athens, Greece. A third bomb damaged the studio of a Greek American sculptor.[46]

On April 10, 2001, in Rome, Italy, a bomb ripped the door off a building that houses a foreign affairs think tank and the affiliated U.S.-Italian relations office.

On May 27, 2001, the Abu Sayyaf group claimed responsibility for the kidnapping of three Americans and seventeen Filipinos from Dos Palmas Island, Philippines.

On January 31, 2002, after having been kidnapped eight days earlier by Pakistani Muslim extremists, *Wall Street Journal* reporter Daniel Pearl, thirty-eight, was murdered by his captors. CBS News aired a videotape of the execution (with the moment of death omitted) that was filmed by his captors and titled "The Slaughter of the Spy Journalist, the Jew Daniel Pearl." In the recording, Pearl can be heard repeating a statement prepared for him immediately before his execution: "My father's Jewish. My mother's Jewish. I'm Jewish. . . . We Americans cannot continue to bear the consequences of our government actions such as the unconditional support given to the state of Israel."[47]

The BBC reported that Pearl was kidnapped by "the previously unknown National Movement for the Restoration of Pakistani Sovereignty, who demanded the release of al-Qaeda and Taliban fighters being held by the Americans in Cuba in return for Pearl's release."[48]

On April 11, 2002, a truck driven by an Al Qaeda operative crashed into a synagogue on the Tunisian resort island Djerba, exploding and killing sixteen people, including eleven German nationals. German interior minister Otto Schily told the BBC on April 22 that he could not be absolutely certain that Osama bin Laden's Al

Qaeda network was behind the attack, but the BBC reported that the London-based *Al-Quds Al-Arabi* printed a letter from Al Qaeda claiming responsibility, and that French authorities matched the author's name to the registration of the truck.

On May 8, 2002, Muslim extremists bombed a bus in Karachi, killing fifteen, including ten French nationals working for a submarine construction company.[49] The BBC reported on July 9 that Pakistani authorities had arrested three people in connection with the bombing, claiming that the suspects—members of the Harkat-ul-Mujahideen offshoot al-Alami—confessed to police.

On September 23, 2002, a grenade exploded in a car outside the U.S. embassy in Jakarta, killing a vehicle occupant. Police said this was a failed attempt at throwing the grenade at the embassy.

On October 6, 2002, operatives from the Aden-Abyan Islamic Army are believed to have attacked the French oil tanker *Limburg* off the coast of Yemen. The attack killed one crew member, injured twelve, and caused a large oil spill. An Arab-language newspaper *Al-Sharq al-Awsat* reported receiving a communiqué from the *Aden-Abyan* Islamic Army claiming that the real target had been a U.S. Navy frigate in the area.

On October 12, 2002, Al Qaeda operatives bombed the Sari Club, a discotheque at Kuta Beach in Bali, that killed at least 180 and wounded hundreds of others. Australian writer Thomas Keneally noted that the device used in the explosion was in fact "a cunningly constructed series of devices" intended to kill as many as possible and obviously used to great effect.[50]

On October 28, 2002, Islamic extremists shot dead Lawrence Foley, sixty, an administrator for the U.S. Agency for International Development, as he was walking to his car in Amman, Jordan. A group calling itself Shurafaa' al-Urdun claimed responsibility.

On November 9, 2002, the *New York Times* reported that a suspect in the investigation of the bombing of the Sari Club told his interrogators that the blast was in fact intended to kill Americans (there were seven Americans among the dead) and that in fact he regretted having killed the Australians.[51] According to the *New York Times,* a "senior Western diplomat" said that evidence in the investigation "point[ed] in the direction of" an Indonesian individual named Hambali, one of two local leaders of Jemaah Islamiyah (an international Muslim fundamentalist group), and a Southeast Asia operator for Al Qaeda.

On November 12, 2002, the Arab satellite news channel al-Jazeera broadcast an audio recording putatively containing the voice of Osama bin Laden in which the Saudi militant reportedly spoke of recent attacks as "a taste of things to come," mentioning "the death of German tourists in a synagogue explosion in Tunisia on April 11; the attack against the French tanker in Yemen on October 6; a bombing of French naval experts in Karachi on May 8; the killing of an American marine in Kuwait on October 8; the October 12 explosion in Bali, with its high toll of Australians and Britons; and the hostage taking in a Moscow theater on October 23."[52] The voice also claimed that the defense of the Palestinians had united the world in an anti-Islamic coalition, with the "false and spurious title of the war against terror." The *New York Times* also reported that "Mr. bin Laden's previous claims that he was helping the Palestinian cause or the Iraqi's suffering under sanctions have been widely dismissed by Arab governments and Muslim religious leaders, who say that he has done nothing but harm their cause, but the statements carry a certain popular appeal."[53]

Also on November 12, 2002, the English-language Japanese news outlet *Japan Today* reported that McDonald's had announced plans for a major retrenchment of operations in several unspecified Middle Eastern markets. "The corporation said the pullout was a result of lagging returns on investment."[54]

*Japan Today* summed up recent events in this area, noting that since the beginning of a "grass-roots boycott campaign in the Arab world" of U.S. goods and services in 2000, two of Jordan's six McDonald's franchises (one in Amman and another in a Palestinian refugee camp) had already closed. McDonald's has gone so far as to change its name in Egypt and to fight public rumors that McDonald's employees had donated a day's pay to Israel. Some franchises in Egypt even required police protection. Other products boycotted in this way included Coca-Cola, Pepsi, Kentucky Fried Chicken (KFC), Marlboro, and Heinz.

Also on November 12, 2002, Reuters reported that bomb blasts occurred at three U.S. fast-food outlets in Beirut and North Lebanon, and that these were "the latest in a string of bombings of fast-food outlets associated with the United States."[55] According to witnesses, the blasts occurred in the night at a Pizza Hut and a Winners. Another Pizza Hut was hit simultaneously in the northern town of Tripoli. The latter "destroyed the building's façade, shattered glass and left tables scattered in the car park."[56] The bombings began in May, when one person was injured in a blast at a KFC outlet, also in Tripoli. Earlier in the year, Lebanese franchise owners took out newspaper advertisements asserting that they and their employees were all Lebanese and not American.

On December 5, 2002, a bomb detonated in McDonald's restaurant in the Indonesian city of Makassar, killing two. The explosion, which occurred on the last day of Ramadan, came shortly after Iftar when the restaurant was busy, according to Reuters.

On December 30, 2002, three missionary aid workers were shot and killed by a Muslim extremist in Yemen.

• • •

The American government finally declared a serious war on such terrorism—the same kind of terrorism that has plagued Israel for so long—and invaded Afghanistan and then Iraq.

## The Defective Race

As we have just seen, for thirteen centuries Eastern and European Christians extorted money from, exiled, scapegoated, and killed Jews. By the middle ages, they expanded such barbaric practices to include white European women accused of witchcraft. White European racism turned genocidal against Native Indians and African Americans in the "New World." Spain and Portugal spared their women and persecuted their Jews instead. (Interestingly, through the diplomatic and financial intervention of a woman, Donna Gracia HaNasi, Islamic Turkey provided a haven for these very Jews.)

In the eighteenth and nineteenth centuries, enlightened European thinkers proposed a doctrine of universal human equality. All men (alas, this did not yet include women) were equal. In response, less enlightened European thinkers proposed a counterargument: that the white race was biologically different from and superior to all other races.

Nonwhite races—for which Jews were the prototypes—did not deserve universal equality. Thus Christians could, with impunity, enslave, exploit, persecute, tax, even murder Africans, Native Americans, and Caribbean Indians, and countless other nonwhite and non-Christian groups. Like Jews, they were deemed inferior and dangerous.

By the 1870s, Jews were no longer seen only as Christ killers and deniers; they were increasingly also viewed as biologically defective and racially criminal. They were *Semites*. Jews were defined as a "race" rather than as an ethnic, cultural, and religious group. Hitler's *Mein Kampf* blends mystical and pseudoscientific concepts of racism and anti-Judaism.[57]

Today, we are dealing with at least two kinds of racism. One is right-wing, neo-Nazi, and traditional; the other (and here's where it gets complicated) is left-wing, anticolonialist, anti-imperialist, and ostensibly antiracist, but also pro-Islamofascist.

Today, right-wing (white) racists tend to target culture instead of race. Thus, today certain cultures are viewed as inferior and unredeemable, such as African cultures and Islamic culture. Not surprisingly, these same cultures are also inhabited mainly by nonwhite, non-European, and non-Christian peoples. In turn, the left-wing racist targets American and European culture as doomed and damned.

Nobody accuses either white people or nonwhite people of being biologically defective. The new racism is coded as culture.

Left-wing antiracists target white Europeans and Americans as racists, colonialists, and imperialists. *All* Americans and *all* Europeans are seen as guilty of having inflicted poverty, disease, and a deep hopelessness upon the Third World. This group refuses to hold any Third World dictator responsible for the crimes he commits because his smaller evil is always due to the larger evil of Western colonialism and imperialism. Thus, suicide-terrorists are freedom fighters.

For example, the French writer Bernard-Henri Lévy is especially eloquent on this point. In his 2001 book *Reflections on War, Evil, and the End of History*, he writes of "the confrontation between the developed, historic world and the peripheral lands we have condemned to slowly edge their way out of the present day." Lévy, an Algerian-born Jew who lives in Paris, imagines that those whom we have condemned will return as ghost-terrorists. "You ignored us when we were alive; now here we are dead; you didn't want to know about our deaths as long as they happened in our own countries. . . . [W]e who were invisible when alive will become clear to you as suicides."[58]

There is some power to this poetic, metaphoric way of thinking. However, it is limited and potentially dangerous. If a man or a woman murders an innocent stranger just because the murderer has been abused in childhood or culturally oppressed is no excuse for the murder itself. Jews have been oppressed for centuries. They are not blowing themselves up in shopping malls and pizza parlors.

How can progressive ideologues forget who the Jews are? Are Jews too momentarily successful, both in Israel and in America, to pass the "sniff" test for victims? Are American and European Jews too white? Is that it? Has our white-skin privilege allowed us to prosper too quickly and too well in Europe and in the United States while other, darker races, including other immigrants, have not? (My God, is this the fault of the Jews? Will this infernal, invidious comparison of bleeding wounds ever stop?)

Do people actually believe that the Jews are the ones who brought racism and slavery to the New World? Will it make any difference if I point out (as I have in this chapter) that the Jews were the first to suffer racism at the hands of European Christians? Will it make any difference if I point out that Jews are also black, brown, and olive as well as white?

Can I persuade the anticolonialist ideologues that the Jews were the original native Indians of the Middle East? That the Jews were there in Judaea-Israel three millennia before the same strip of earth was called Palestine by the British colonialists?

## The "Niggers" of the World

I have always thought that American Jews felt uncomfortable and guilty that another group occupies what had been the traditional Jewish position in society. Yes, African Americans (not Jews) are the Jews in America, but Jews are the world's "niggers." Do I endanger us by saying so? Do I risk the ire of African Americans who are tired of hearing Jews complain about their well-documented suffering but who have been able to fund Holocaust Museums in America, Europe, and Israel while African Americans still do not have even one Museum of African slavery in America? (There is no Rape Museum anywhere in the world either—but don't get me started.)

In presenting the Jews as the people who have been persecuted for the longest time (that's partly because we have managed to survive for the longest time), am I saying that a Jew cannot be guilty of a crime because anything and everything a Jewish person does is and must be forgivable? Of course not. If a Jew steals, deals drugs, beats his wife, beats his child, or murders another human being, he must be tried for his crime, not excused for it because he is a member of an oppressed group.

Am I saying that Zionist policies in terms of most of the settlements are a disaster, both morally and in terms of Israel's public image? Yes! They may have to go—although I am increasingly persuaded that the Israeli Defense Forces (IDF) have been able to repel more than 27,000 terrorist attacks that were launched against Israel between 2000–2002 only because the IDF controls the West Bank and Gaza right down to the Mediterranean Sea and the Jordan River.

Granted, it would have been lovely if the Arab and Islamic world had absorbed their Arab-Palestinian brethren and accepted the Jewish state in their midst long ago—but this did not happen. Granted, it would have been lovely if Israel could have traded the West Bank and Gaza for real peace—but this did not happen either. The settlers came to stay—the government funded them to do so. Wealthy Arab governments could have done likewise for the impoverished Palestinians—but they failed to do so. The Palestinians could have accepted a state in the 1940s—but they refused to do so.

The contrast between impoverished Palestinians and Israeli Jewish settlers is startling. To the uninformed it does look like apartheid: shacks and a few goats on one side, modern buildings with running water and indoor plumbing on the other side. But Zionist Israel is not Nazi Germany; recent Zionist policies on the West Bank and in Gaza (however much I may beg to differ with them) are not apartheid or colonial policies.

Some pioneer Zionists believed that they would live collectively and cooperatively with the Arabs in socialist communes. If they could uproot themselves and leave Poland, Russia, and Judaism behind them, then surely the Arabs would also be able to uproot themselves from Islam and reactionary ways of life. (How misguided and well-intentioned these Zionists were!)

There is a long history of buying and selling land and houses in the Middle East. Some Zionists believed that the Arabs (who did not yet think of themselves as Palestinians) could simply be paid to leave and that they would settle nearby in what became Jordan or in what was southern Syria. Some Zionists did not "see" the Arabs in their midst. Those who did, did not see a *racially* different enemy: everyone was a Semite. The differences were cultural and political. The clash was one between European concepts of modernity and Arab and Islamic concepts of antimodernity.

Today, as Palestinians suffer a 70 percent unemployment rate and are so desperate that they are willing to die to enter Israel for employment, I must ask: Why don't wealthy Arab countries employ Palestinian Arabs? Why don't wealthy Arab countries fund the development of infrastructure and industry in Palestine? Why expect the small and struggling Jewish state to shoulder the burden of the entire Islamic world?

Shall we describe Saudi Arabia, Kuwait, and the United Arab Emirates as apartheid states because they have systematically imported unskilled Indian, Pakistani, and Filipino laborers who, in order to feed their families, are forced to live apart from them for many years—and whose lodgings are no better than those of Palestinians in the worst refugee camps?

I am saying: Let my people go. Why pay so much attention to us? Why treat us as "special"? If we claim that we're special, that's entirely our delusion. Leave us to our ideas. Do not scapegoat us for them. Why hold us up to special, higher standards and then kill us when we fail to live up to them? Consider us merely a backward Middle Eastern tribe. Forget about us for at least one hundred years. Let us struggle with our enemies, stew in our juices on our own.

• • •

The term *anti-Semitism* does not do justice to what the complex prejudice against the Jews is about. Jews have been persecuted for theological reasons, that is, they presumably killed Christ and refused to accept Christ as their Messiah. Jews have also refused to convert to Islam. They have been persecuted for cultural and racial reasons. They were too Oriental, too Semitic for Europe, and too white-European for the Middle East. In addition, Jews have been feared and hated for their various cultural and intellectual choices. For example, they have been seen as symbolizing modernism, capitalism, free love, and free thought—but they have also been seen as symbolizing backwardness, poverty, and superstition.

Anti-Arabism or anti-Semitism toward Arab Semites is not the same thing. Arabs and Muslims do not have a Jewish history of being driven into exile and punished as Christ killers, nor have they permanently lived in foreign cultures that demanded but resented both assimilation and separation. Many nineteenth- and twentieth-century European colonizers had a romance with the noble Arab abroad that they never had with the Jews at home. Some European adventurers "went native," but they did not become Jews; they became Arabs.

We must remember all this when people say that anti-Semitism against Arabs also exists. It does—but its source is a somewhat different one. The prejudice against Jews exists even when Jews have white skins and are culturally totally assimilated. In the case of Arabs, in some instances it is dark-skin-color prejudice, pure and simple, that is at work, without any theological overtones at all. In other instances it may be resentment against an impoverished and illiterate immigrant population taking up European and American jobs and social services.

Most recently, Arabs may be feared and hated because so many acts of terrorism (airplane hijackings, American Embassy bombings, 9/11) have been committed by Arabs and Muslims. Jews and Zionists are not the ones who have been hijacking planes or blowing up civilian populations around the world. Jews have not taken their local war global. Only Arabs and Muslims have.

Nevertheless, the progressive left in Europe and America have already mounted pro-Arab civil rights campaigns lest Arabs lose their civil liberties in America's war against terrorism. And I agree: the profiling, arrest, and detention of innocent Arabs and Muslims is reprehensible. But we must also balance our commitment to civil liberties with that of national security needs in time of war. Many leftists have also sided with the Palestinian terrorists and people against the Israelis. These leftists remained entirely silent for more than three years about the enormous Israeli Jewish civilian loss of life. Perhaps they do not see the Jewish right to exist as an important civil right.

No one questions the right of Arabs—however bestial their leaders may be—to continue to live in their countries. Everyone continually questions the rights of the Jews to do likewise. Zionism has become the dirtiest of words. If the Jews don't measure up—that's it, they're out. They are not worthy enough to have a country.

• • •

Nothing has been the same for any of us, in America or the rest of the world, since 9/11. The global economy; international travel; the focus of worldwide media; the war on terrorism, and consequent military actions both threatened and executed; the domestic status of our constitutional rights and civil liberties—it has all changed dramatically in ways we could never have predicted.

In addition, at the very core of this crisis, both as a cause and an effect, has been the new anti-Semitism.

Yes, welcome to the very bloody twenty-first century. Who would have imagined that there could ever be a new kind of anti-Semitism, one that is shared worldwide by both the old right and the new left, by the media and by intellectuals, and by Muslims everywhere—an anti-Semitism that is more virulent and dangerous to the identity and safety of Jews than anything since Hitler?

## Recent Arab Terrorism Against Israel

### 2000

On November 20, 2000, right alongside a bus carrying children to school in Gush Katif from Kfar Darom, a roadside bomb exploded. Miriam Amitai, thirty-five, and Gavriel Biton, thirty-four, were both killed.[59]

On December 8, 2000, a schoolteacher at Beit Hagai, Rina Didovsky, thirty-nine, was shot and killed by a car full of gunmen. Didovsky and the driver, Eliahu Ben Ami, forty-one, were killed in the van near Kiryat Arba.

### 2001

On January 23, 2001, two cousins from Tel Aviv, Motti Dayan, twenty-seven, and Etgar Zeitouny, thirty-four, were abducted from a restaurant in Tulkarm by masked Palestinian gunmen and executed.

On March 28, 2001, Eliran Rosenberg-Zayat, fifteen, of Givat Shmuel, and Naftali Lanzkorn, thirteen, of Petah Tikva, were killed in a suicide bombing at the Mifgash Hashalom gas station, several hundred meters from an IDF roadblock near the entrance to Kalkilya, east of Kfar Saba. Hamas claimed responsibility for the attack.

On May 9, 2001, two fourteen-year-old teenagers, Yossi Ish-Ran and Kobi Mandell, both of Tekoa, were found stoned to death in a cave only two hundred meters from their home, a small community south of Jerusalem.

On May 15, 2001, Palestinian terrorists fired thirty bullets, nineteen of which hit a family car enroute to a wedding on the Alon Highway. Idit Mizrahi of Rimonim, twenty years old, was fatally shot.[60]

On June 1, 2001, a suicide bomber blew himself up outside the discotheque Dolphinarium in Tel Aviv just before midnight on a Friday evening. Twenty mainly young people were killed and 120 were injured.

On August 9, 2001, in the center of Jerusalem, on the corner of King George Street and Jaffa Road, a suicide bomber entered a Sbarro pizzeria and killed 15 people and injured approximately 130. Hamas and Islamic Jihad claimed responsibility for the attack.

On September 20, 2001, Fatah claimed responsibility for a shooting near Tekoa, south of Bethlehem, which killed Sarit Amrani, twenty-six, and seriously wounded her husband, Shai. Traveling in the vehicle with their parents, the couple's three children were not injured.

On December 1, 2001, at 11:30 P.M., a Saturday night, a suicide bomber killed 11 people aged twelve to twenty-one, and wounded 188 people in Ben-Yehuda pedestrian mall in Jerusalem. Twenty minutes later a bomb exploded in a car. Hamas claimed responsibility for the double suicide bombing.[61]

## 2002

On January 17, 2002, six people were killed and thirty-five injured at a bat mitzvah in a banquet hall in Hadera. A Palestinian gunman opened fire with an M-16 assault rifle, and Fatah Al-Aqsa Brigades claimed responsibility.

On March 9, 2002, the Fatah Al Aqsa Brigades claimed responsibility for two Palestinians throwing grenades and shooting at cars and pedestrians in Netanya on a Saturday evening, close to hotels and the boardwalk. About fifty people were injured, and Avia Malka, nine months old, and Israel Yihye, twenty-seven years old, were killed. The terrorists were killed by Israeli border police.[62]

On March 27, 2002, Hamas claimed responsibility for a suicide bombing during a Passover holiday seder with 250 guests in the Park Hotel in Netanya. Twenty-two people were killed and 140 were injured, twenty of them seriously. By May 5, seven more people died of their injuries, bringing the total death count to twenty-nine.

On June 5, 2002, Egged bus 830 was traveling from Tel Aviv to Tiberias when a car packed with explosives struck the bus, bursting into flames. Seventeen people were killed and thirty-eight injured. The Islamic Jihad claimed responsibility.

On July 31, 2002, Hamas claimed responsibility for the bomb that went off at the Frank Sinatra Cafeteria on Hebrew University's Mt. Scopus campus during lunchtime. Eight people died, eighty-six were injured, fourteen seriously. Five of the eight who died were Americans.[63]

On September 19, 2002, on one of Tel Aviv's busiest streets, opposite the Great Synagogue, six people were killed and sixty injured by a bomb exploding on a bus. The Islamic Jihad and Hamas claimed responsibility for the attack.

On Sunday, November 10, 2002, Palestinian gunmen attacked Kibbutz Metzer late at night. The gunmen kicked down Revital Ohayon's house door and killed Ohayon, thirty-four, and her two children, Matan, five, and Noam, four, in their bedroom.

On November 21, 2002, Hamas claimed responsibility for a Palestinian suicide bombing during rush hour that killed eleven people and injured forty-seven on a bus filled with passengers, including school children, in the Kiryat Menahem neighborhood in Jerusalem.

On November 28, 2002, six people were killed and more than forty wounded by two terrorists who threw grenades at the Likud polling station in Beit She'an. Al Aqsa Martyrs Brigades claimed responsibility for the attack.

On December 20, 2002, Islamic Jihad claimed responsibility for the killing of an Israeli rabbi. He was shot in his car while driving with his wife and six children on the Kissufim corridor road in the Gaza Strip.

On December 27, 2002, Islamic Jihad claimed responsibility for the killing of four students and the injuring of ten. The terrorists broke into a dining hall at a yeshiva in Otneil, south of Hebron, and attacked students working in the yeshiva kitchen.

## 2003

On January 2, 2003, the Fatah Al-Aqsa Martyrs Brigades claimed responsibility for the killing of an Israeli from Menahemiya. His body was found in a burned-out car in the northern Jordan Valley.

On January 5, 2003, the Fatah Al-Aqsa Martyrs Brigades, the Islamic Jihad, and Hamas all claimed responsibility for killing twenty-two people and wounding about 120 in a double suicide bombing near the old central bus station in Tel Aviv.

On January 12, 2003, terrorists from the Palestinian Islamic Jihad infiltrated the Moshav Gadish community and shot and killed Eli Biton, a forty-eight-year-old resident.[64]

On January 17, 2003, terrorists entered Netanel Ozeri's home on a Friday night, shot and killed him, and injured his four-year-old daughter.

On January 24, 2003, Palestinian terrorists opened fire and killed three IDF soldiers near Hebron.

On January 25, 2003, a donkey rigged with explosives blew up next to a bus near the West Bank village of El Khader.[65]

On January 29, 2003, a father and his eight-year-old son were shot in a car by a Palestinian gunman near the settlement of Beit El and south of the Ofra settlement.

On March 5, 2003, a suicide bomber detonated a bus in the northern city of Haifa. The blast killed at least sixteen people and wounded more than fifty. This bombing of a bus in Haifa was done by a twenty-year-old member of Hamas, Mahmoud Kawasme, who, in his farewell note, praised the 9/11 attacks.

On March 7, 2003, armed terrorists disguised as Jewish worshippers entered the Kiryat Arba home of Rabbi Eli Horowitz, 52, and his wife, Dina, 50, when they were celebrating the Sabbath. The rabbi and his wife were killed and five others were wounded. Hamas claimed responsibility for the attack.

On March 10, 2003, Palestinian gunfire near the West Bank city of Hebron, close to the settlement of Kirya Arba, killed one Israeli and wounded three.

How could this happen and what does it mean?
Let us proceed . . .

*Chapter Four*

# What's New About the New Anti-Semitism?

First, let us be clear: the absence of anti-Semitism is what's unusual, not its presence. As we have seen, for more than two thousand years, classical anti-Semitism denied individual Jews the right to live safely or with dignity as equal citizens anywhere in the world.

Today, this historical strain of anti-Semitism continues, but in the last fifty years it has also metamorphosed into the most virulent anti-Zionism, which in turn has increasingly held Jewish people everywhere, not only in Israel, accountable for the military policies of the Israeli government.

## The Double Standard

The world—including many people in the Jewish world—still seems to have one standard for Jews and for the Jewish state (and it's a high standard) and another, much lower standard for everyone else. Most barbarism goes completely unnoticed; no one is ever held accountable, the crimes are denied and covered up, the whistle-blowers killed or imprisoned. In contrast, Israel's most minor imperfection is continually criticized; serious mistakes are demonized. This has led to a whole new rationale for stigmatizing Israel, and Jews all over the world who support it, as proponents of the most heinous political crimes.

As a result, we have what I call the *new* anti-Semitism. And what's new about the new anti-Semitism is that for the first time it is being perpetrated in the name of antiracism and anticolonialism. Because the charges of apartheid Zionism are being leveled by those who champion the uprising of the oppressed, what they say, by definition, presumably cannot be racist. Therefore, when such champions of freedom chant "death to the Jews" or "divest in apartheid colonialist Israel," by definition these are not racist remarks. The new anti-Semites are not anti-Semites because they *say* they're not. Even George Orwell would be astounded.

What's new about the new anti-Semitism is that acts of violence against Jews and anti-Semitic words and deeds are being uttered and performed by politically correct people in the name of anticolonialism, anti-imperialism, antiracism, and pacifism. Old-fashioned anti-Semitism was justified in the name of ethnic, Aryan, white purity, superiority, and nationalism. Many Nazi-era Germans and Americans viewed Jews as inferior racially and biologically. The new anti-Semite cannot, by definition, be an anti-Semitic racist because she speaks out on behalf of oppressed people.

What's new about the new anti-Semitism is that the new anti-Semite may also be Jewish, and female.

What's new about the new anti-Semitism is the speed and frequency at which anti-Semitic thoughts and deeds are being displayed and repeated over and over again, twenty-four/seven, around the world. Nazi-era anti-Semitism attacked Jews mainly on one continent. Now Jews are being verbally and visually attacked everywhere. Superior technology and communications allow people to spread lies as well as truth, to save lives as well as to commit murder more efficiently.

What's new about the new anti-Semitism is that the Israeli government, which has been under siege from the moment of its birth, has now been given to understand that Jews who are not Israeli citizens may be taken hostage by Islamic and Palestinian terrorists because of Israeli policy.

In the last three years, the most soul-shaking incidents of anti-Semitism have increased enormously in Israel, in the Western world, in both Europe and North America, in the Islamic world, on campuses, at demonstrations, and at international conferences: ugly words, sneers, threats, beatings, riots, broken bones, broken windows, torched synagogues, vandalized synagogues—the works. It's as if Hitler's Brown Shirts have returned from the dead, in greater numbers, and are doing their dirty Kristallnacht work everyday, everywhere.

The Jews are experiencing four simultaneous Intifadas: one in the Islamic world, a second in Europe, a third on North American campuses, and a fourth directed at America and the West by Al Qaeda.

Jews are facing the full force of two thousand years of racism (anti-Judaism, anti-Semitism) recycled. Lies, propaganda, myths, and half-truths are being advanced through modern technology and presented as if they were factual. Right-wing politicians in Europe, left-wing politicians in North America, print and broadcast media pundits of all stripes, feminists, filmmakers, journalists, students, esteemed professors—all proclaim Big Lies to be the truth. As advertising companies well know, most people eventually come to believe whatever they continually hear and see. We are the species that hums the jingles from commercials.

Indeed, this is also what is new about the new anti-Semitism: that it is worldwide, and that it is carried around the world instantly via mass communications. And as this epidemic of violent deeds and propaganda rages, the world media and prominent left-wing Western intellectuals and activists either deny that this plague is happening or they merely note it in passing, without context or mercy; or they simply blame Israel for causing the anti-Jewish violence. By definition, Israel is a rogue state because it is a *Jewish* state that insists on defending itself.

This global technology is also what's new about terrorism. Al Qaeda is able to operate a *virtual* terrorist network. According to counterterrorism expert Jonathan Stevenson, writing in the *Wall Street Journal*, al Qaeda has demonstrated an "ominous adaptability." He credits "technology [and] the multinational allure of jihadism." Today, central command posts and training camps may no longer be needed. Local sleeper cells may assemble bombs in safe houses and use notebook computers, the Internet, and global travel to strike anywhere in the world. If anyone is caught or killed, others are ready to take their place in the name of Islamic jihad. Thus, according to Stevenson, the "process is self-perpetuating."[1]

The "new" anti-Judaism and anti-Christianity is a worldwide phenomenon. An overwhelming amount of propaganda is being created in the Islamic world. For example, Saudi Arabian textbooks teach young children "intolerance and contempt for the West, Christians, and Jews." Eighth-grade Saudi students are taught that a "malicious Crusader-Jewish alliance is striving to eliminate Islam from all continents." Saudi children are "implored not to befriend Christians and Jews."[2] It is no surprise that fifteen of the nineteen terrorists who attacked America on 9/11 were from Saudi Arabia. In addition, Saudi textbooks and curricula are exported to other Islamic countries.

And in the scheme of things, Saudi Arabia is an American ally.

## Visual Propaganda

What's new about the new anti-Semitism is the way visual propaganda is being purposely created and used to indoctrinate and hypnotize people on a scale that was neither imaginable nor possible fifty years ago. Films are being expertly doctored and played over and over again in order to brainwash the viewers.

What's new about the new anti-Semitism is the horrific hardcore visual propaganda perpetrated against Israel and the Jews, including illustrations, graphics, photographs, videos, and films. Nazi-era cartoons in which Jews were depicted literally as devils and rats are back, and mainly in Arabic. The new Arab-Muslim anti-Semite also says that the Holocaust did not go far enough, and that they aim to finish the job. The most blatant Nazi-like propaganda is being energetically circulated all over the Middle East. Grotesque cartoons of Jews as lice, rats, devils, gluttons, monsters, bloodthirsty Nazi-type soldiers, leering and promiscuous big-nosed men, and Christ crucifiers are making the rounds. Arabs and Muslims do not feel at all guilty about this propaganda. They enjoy it and they believe it. This is not latent; it is quite blatant.

I have just viewed a collection that appeared in the Palestinian Authority's official newspaper. I will not reproduce it in this book. Suffice it to say that from 1997 to 2001, Jews have been characterized as monsters, bugs, lice, octopi, death skulls, and devils with pitchforks and tails. When shown as human, Jews and Israeli leaders are also depicted as leering, crafty brutes who are literally dismembering and piercing Arab men and female symbols of peace.[3]

What's new about the new anti-Semitism is how the old propaganda is being visually recycled as historical truth via satellite to one hundred million viewers a day. For example, in 2002, the Protocols of the Elders of Zion—a long defunct Czarist-era fraud—was turned into a television series. It aired in forty installments every day in Egypt during Ramadan. The popularity of the Protocols is partly the legacy of European colonialism that taught the Muslim world to think nationalistically and to blame the Jews for all their ills.

In February 2003, the Iranian supreme leader Ayatollah Ali Khamenei charged that "the explosion of drugs and prostitution" in Iran were "a conspiracy by Israel and the United States to dominate the world." In Khamenei's view, Israel and the United States want to "destroy Islamic culture by propagating immorality."[4]

On October 11, 2002, Israeli Government Press Office director Daniel Seaman alleged that foreign journalists had coordinated their coverage of the Israeli-Palestinian conflict with Fatah leader Marwan Barghouti and had paid Palestinian photographers to forge damning and false anti-Israeli photographs. Seaman charged some foreign media with paying impoverished Palestinians to pose for pro-Palestinian/anti-Israeli photos.

Seaman said, "Barghouti used to call them. . . . They always received early warning about [Palestinian] gunfire on [Jewish Israeli] Gilo. They then shot for TV only the Israeli response fire on Beit Jala. These foreign producers advised Barghouti how to get the Palestinian message across better." When the Israel Defense Forces demolished an *empty* house, foreign photographers would pay a starving Palestinian family "300 dollars for a picture of a crying

child sitting on the rubble. They've degraded photography to prostitution."[5]

Recently, Peter Maass described the kind of journalism practiced by Yosri Fouda, the most popular al-Jazeera commentator, as
"a journalism of access." Fouda was blindfolded and taken to the
leaders of Al Qaeda; to obtain such cloak-and-dagger interviews,
Fouda must remain in the "good graces of the giver of access." By
tossing "scoops" to Fouda, bin Laden "helps ensure that one of the
most influential voices in the Arab media stays on the fence."[6]

In 1991, journalist Peter Arnett reported on the Gulf War for
CNN. At the time, he showed images that "proved" that American
forces bombed a baby-milk factory. However, this may or may not
have happened, since Arnett may have chosen to sacrifice critical
objectivity in order to obtain and maintain journalistic access. On
February 27, 2003, in the pages of the *Wall Street Journal*, Arnett
himself explained that if you don't follow Iraqi Press Corps guidelines you will find yourself banished from the war. Indeed, other
American journalists had been thrown out for refusing to follow
Iraqi guidelines. Arnett remained and perhaps gave us the only Iraqi
version of that war.

What conclusion may we draw? That at least one highly visible
*American* journalist was as forced as his Arab Muslim counterparts
to compromise the truth—a "trade-off that is not worth the price in
a democracy."[7]

It is important but unsettling to realize that photos, films, and
numbers *can* lie. If we can't believe our own eyes, if our very senses
cannot be trusted, how can we understand reality? I don't have an
easy answer. However, my goal is to persuade you that because doctored realities and canned "spins" are upon us, we must exercise extraordinary vigilance and independence of mind.

In the past, the news of real lynchings and pogroms traveled
more slowly. Today, technology ensures live, universal coverage.
The entire world can at the same moment see and react to the same
doctored images and propaganda as if it were a neutral, objective account. Inflammatory images are not presented or analyzed in con-

text. They rely upon our already ingrained biases for their interpretation.

The mass media—their images, intimacy, and round-the-clock comfortingly parental presence—not only pacify and render viewers passive, they also hypnotize and brainwash vast populations, many of whom are not literate or educated, have short attention spans, and lack context and perspective—in short, they are relieved to have their minds made up for them, to have one less thing to worry about.

Al-Manar, the Lebanese based Shi'ite television station with at least ten million viewers, broadcasts hate-Israel-all-the-time videos twenty-four/seven. These videos are synchronized to a musical beat and aimed at viewers of different ages, beginning with those who are under five years old.[8]

Such propaganda is apparently working—witness an interview on May 7, 2002, on Egyptian television, with a three-year-old girl named Basmallah. When asked if she likes the Jews, Basmallah said no, because God in the Qu'ran says "they are apes and pigs." Basmallah also knows that "a Jewish lady tried to poison Mohammed."[9] None of this is at all true, of course.

On April 24, 2002, a Jordanian program interviewed two fathers, including the father of Said Al-Khotari, the suicide bomber who blew up the Dolphinarium in Tel Aviv. The first father explained how he is "preparing" his son to become a martyr. When the boy asks, "'If I carry out an operation and blow myself up, will Allah give me a car, a rifle to shoot with, toys?' I answer him, 'You will get everything you ask for.'" Al-Khotari's father has been on television before, saying, "We are willing to sacrifice our four children." Proudly he reports that upon hearing this his smallest (fifth) child said, "Why can't I?"[10]

Similarly, the men who executed *Wall Street Journal* reporter Daniel Pearl captured both his execution and the executors' joy on a video and replayed it over and over again. After forcing Pearl to admit that he was an American Jew who came from a family of Zionists, his captors beheaded him on camera and held his head aloft as a warning to other Jews, as part of their death pornography. (I am reminded of what the Taliban in Afghanistan did to women; in one grisly instance they cut a woman in half, from head to toe, and mounted both halves of her on a door, offendingly naked, for all to see, as her corpse slowly rotted.) Such Arab-Muslims are barbaric and primitive; they do not hide their joy when they kill, and when their enemies are killed. They literally dance in Jewish and Christian blood; they hand out candy.

Granted, I may think it immoral and obscene to drop a bomb on civilians from a great, safe height, but I do not think that most Americans or many Jews delight in the death of their enemies in quite the same way. Some of us even mourn such "necessary" deaths incurred as part of a just war or in self-defense. Religious Jews are taught to feel compassion for the deaths of their enemies, even for Pharaoh's soldiers as they drowned in the Red Sea in hot pursuit of the escaped Jewish slaves.

I have great affection for and am quite sentimental about all things Arabian, Middle Eastern, Islamic, and Jewish. Therefore, I am not necessarily offended when a Middle Easterner stretches the truth by more than a yard merely to please or impress me. On the contrary. I allow the speaker's extreme enthusiasm and emotionality to sweep me along, but only for the moment. Such a speaker's ability to exaggerate, talk for hours, make up things, is also the way of dreams and of the oral tradition. Of course, things can turn quite deadly if your storytelling host means to lull you into a false sense of security before he robs, kidnaps, or kills you.

Granted, Islamic culture was once at the forefront of scientific knowledge, but that was a long time ago. After I returned from Kabul, I understood that Western concepts of objectivity and independent truth-seeking occupied a lesser place in a tribal, impoverished, illiterate, and religious Islamic world that prided itself on its *non*-evolution. When I was younger, I was outraged and frightened by this difference. In time, I learned that I had a weakness for "Eastern" emotionality and hyperexaggeration and that I therefore had to protect myself by double-checking the information that came my way.

You have to have lived in the Islamic East to believe what I am about to tell you. Actually, let me quote the Afghan-American writer, Tamim Ansary, on the phenomenon. In *West of Kabul, East of New York*, Ansary describes a visit to the Islamic world in 1980, long before the Taliban and Al Qaeda really started brainwashing people. Ostensibly in search of his Islamic roots and some good stories, Ansary records conversations with Muslim men. In Tangiers, Morocco, Ansary asked a group of men

> about Muammar Quaddafi, the Libyan strongman who was making a particular ass of himself on the world stage just then. "Is he a good Muslim?"
>
> "No. Quaddafi is a Jew."
>
> "A *Jew*? Really?"
>
> "Oh yes," came the sage reply, "placed in power many years ago by the Israelis to blacken the reputation of Islam! How else can you explain his actions?"[11]

Another conversation between Ansary and a group of fanatics (who do not pray in mosques because, they insist, mosques purposely mislead people), yielded the following information: that Islamic "religious scholars" have "sold themselves" to Muslim governments so that the people will be "lost," and the "gangsters (will be) safe." Perhaps there is some truth to that. But, amazed, Ansary asks

> "You don't consider the government of Morocco to be Muslim?"
>
> "Ha-ha! Muslim! They are Mafia! Just like in Iraq! Saudi Arabia! Egypt! Gangsters! Zionists!"[12]

This sincere belief in fanciful absurdities might be charming over an open campfire, but it is very dangerous in matters of war and peace, life and death, truth and falsehood.

Most Americans and Europeans have not had the opportunity to learn this lesson. Thus, when individual Palestinians or the Arab media insist that the Israelis have blown up the hospital in Jenin, purposely killed ten children in Gaza, poisoned the drinking water (and, according to Yasser Arafat's wife, Suha, poisoned this water in a way that only affected Palestinian women—or so she advised Senator Hillary Clinton), I would advise us all to look for some independent evidence. If the Palestinian Authority announces that Israel has a secret weapon that it has begun to use on Palestinians, I do not automatically assume that this is true.

I hope that I am not offending the millions of Muslims who share what I am calling a Western-standard of truth-telling and objectivity. As for those who are prone to exaggeration without guilt and who are usually the first among the highly offended: I hope you do not try to kill me!

• • •

In terms of visual propaganda, movies are the perfect weapon against America and against the Jews.

Films are like our dreams: they are real but not real; everything is true, nothing is true. If I am out of touch with reality, my reality is like a dream; nothing is real but what I feel or think. Even if I am hearing imaginary voices, they are very real to me. If all I can hear is the sound of my own voice, and if I have absolutely no tradition of objectivity, have not learned to separate myself from either Id or Superego, have been permitted no individuality with which to set myself apart from my family, tribe, religion, and community, the medium of movies will best express my intimate and private as well as public group reality. Movies can lie to tell the deeper truth. Movies can also lie to function as effective propaganda, to indoctrinate people into the father-leader's most intimate reality.

Recently, Muhammed Bakri directed a film about the nonmassacre in Jenin. Of course, Bakri himself had not been in Jenin at the time of the so-called massacre. The film was recently aired at a private screening in Jerusalem. On November 11, 2002, David Sangan, a physician who *had* been in Jenin at the time, was startled by the film and wrote about it in the Israeli newspaper *Ma'ariv*. The piece was titled "Seven Lies About Jenin."[13] People in the film talk about the bombing of the Jenin hospital, a baby-killing and the disappearance of a baby's body, the shooting of an elderly man, atrocities by Israeli tanks, and a mass gravesite.

Dr. Sangan writes that contrary to what one Dr. Abu Riali says on camera, there was no Israeli shelling or bombing of the hospital in Jenin; in fact, Israeli soldiers carefully guarded the hospital's water and oxygen supply and blew up nothing, even though the hospital served as a refuge for several wanted fugitives. Dr. Riali was the man previously interviewed by Al-Jazeera television and who spoke about "thousands of victims" in Jenin.[14] In addition, the elderly male inhabitant of Jenin shown on camera complaining about the Israeli doctors was in fact treated by them—but not in Jenin (where he was refused treatment) but in an Israeli hospital in Afula.

On camera, someone talks about a particular baby who was shot and who died because Israeli soldiers refused to allow the baby to be evacuated to a hospital. On camera the baby's body was said to have subsequently "disappeared." Dr. Sangan asks for the name of this baby because, he insists, no such incident occurred—nor did Israeli tanks run over living people many times until they were completely flattened, as the film claims.

Dr. Sangan says that all of this—which is "real" in the film—did not happen in reality. The film is fiction, but it is utterly persuasive. Dr. Sangan writes, "The film systematically and repeatedly uses manipulative pictures of tanks taken in other locations, artificially placing them next to pictures of Palestinian children. In general, this is a vulgar but extremely well done work of manipulation."

The film was given a standing ovation at the premiere in Jerusalem. Immediately after the lights came up, however, Dr. Sangan mounted the stage, took the microphone, and began listing the "lies and inaccuracies." Whispers, scornful calls, erupted. He was called "a murderer" and a "war criminal." "Intense hatred" was directed at him. He only got as far as his second point when a man aggressively took the microphone away from him. Only a few people stood up for Sangan's "right to free speech."[15]

Perhaps people have grown accustomed to graphic death as a form of entertainment. If the footage is real, not fiction, if the agony is part of a live war—who can tell the difference? Who cares? If the footage is pure fiction, that does not make it psychologically less real.

Films are perfect for demagogues. Imagine what Hitler would have done had he lived in an era of mass communications, television, cinema, the Internet. Well, Hitler lives on in this kind of media; contemporary propagandists are creating anti-Jewish and anti-Zionist propaganda in his honor.

• • •

In response to really Big Lies one can only tell the truth. No doubt human rights violations did occur in Jenin. The Palestinians are running a bomb and terrorist factory there; the Israelis are trying to stop them. But contrary to what you may have heard, the Israeli army is one of the most civilized (and mainly civilian) armies in the world. Military policy does not target enemy women for rape, nor do soldiers systematically engage in kidnapping women and children to brutalize and to sell as sex slaves. Many other standing armies do this all the time, especially in Third World countries.

Israeli soldiers do not confiscate property and valuables for personal use. Israeli soldiers have not targeted Palestinian women and children to shoot or blow up. As we shall see, the majority of Palestinians who have been killed in the last three years have been armed (male) soldiers and (male) suicide bombers. The majority of the Israeli dead have been civilians, an overwhelming number of whom have been women and small children.

The Palestinians, the international human rights community, and the world media said that the Israelis conducted a "massacre" in Jenin. Israelis were now the "Nazis," and the only "Holocaust" that mattered was the one that the Israelis were inflicting upon the Palestinians. By the time the United Nations actually documented that there had been no massacre in Jenin, the damage had been done; the truth did not have the power to untarnish Israel's reputation.

Israel was also attacked for not allowing the media into Jenin. But according to retired British army colonel Larry Hollingworth (who is the coordinator for the United Nations Relief and Works Agency for Palestine Refugees in the Near East for Jenin), the Israeli checkpoints are like "kindergarten" compared to the Serb ones. "Here we are dealing with arrogant, bored, 18 and 19 year olds—not drunken Serbs. The worse thing that happens to us is that we're delayed."[16]

When Israeli military experts insisted that Jenin was a bomb factory and that terrorists had been hiding among the civilian population, the world did not believe it. But then the United Nations hired demolition experts to clean up Jenin. Guess what? They found bomb factories galore, and what they called thousands of "live" items.

Ian Rimmell, also British, works for a Scandinavian explosives-disposal company. *Village Voice* correspondent Sylvana Foa quotes him as saying, "Guys with guns [in Jenin] would show up and demand their bombs back. I always give them back—I have a wife and family."[17]

Jenin, it turns out, actually has a reputation not unlike that of Chechnya. It is rife with outlaws who live beyond the law. According to Foa, "Jenin's own Palestinian police never dared venture into its Casbah-like maze of winding alleys."[18]

## Little Mohammed

Remember the tragic and infamous case of "little Mohammed," the Palestinian boy who was shot to death in his father's arms in September 2000? A French camera crew (France 2) filmed and broadcast the boy's death. Everyone presumed that Mohammed Al-Dura (for that is his name) had been shot by Israeli gunfire. Charles Enderlin was the journalist who headed the French team.[19]

The footage is real, the event really happened, the boy tragically but *accidentally* died. No one planned to shoot him. However, there's one thing that's wrong with this picture: the Israelis may not have been the shooters.

A number of journalists, experts, government officials, and filmmakers have suggested that it is unclear who shot the boy, and it is as likely—possibly more likely—that the boy was shot by Palestinians as that he was shot by Israelis. A German television documentary that aired in March 2002 strongly concluded that "it is not possible to determine with absolute certainty that Palestinians shot the boy, but the extensive evidence points, with high probability, to the fact that the Israelis did not do it."[20] Israeli shooters were all stationed in low places, and the boy was shot from above. The documentary charged that France 2 did not release all the video footage in its possession. In fact, Channel 2's Palestinian cameraman had initially claimed that no Palestinians had been firing when the boy was killed.

Ah, friends: as I read about this German documentary I began to look for the name of its director. I found it: Esther Shapira. Oh no, I think, she's probably Jewish and no one will believe her. I decided that I was getting paranoid. And then I found the director's own words on the subject. She said that because she was Jewish, reports were already circulating in Germany suggesting that her work had been produced in cooperation with the Mossad, Israel's secret service.

Daniel Shek, director of the Israeli Foreign Ministry's European division, consoles me—but only barely—when he says that "the documentary is very significant because it leaves doubt. Doubt is healthy." But then he also says that "Mohammed Al-Dura will remain part of the Intifada's mythology; it will not matter what kind of proof you bring to the contrary."[21] I agree with him.

French journalist Clement Weill Raynal reports that the French Press Agency continued to blame the Israelis for the boy's death long after this view had been effectively challenged.[22] Israeli

Government Press Office director Daniel Seaman insists that the entire Al-Dura incident was staged.[23]

I do not know whose bullet killed this child. Perhaps we will never know. However, I do know that Israel has been permanently damaged both by the footage and by the initial presumption of Israeli guilt. Everyone who was outraged by the footage and by the many photos of it all immediately assumed that the Jews did it *on purpose*, that it was no accident. Imaginations and memories have been permanently altered by this early interpretation. Second and third interpretations two years later do not carry the same emotional resonance. Questioning the *meaning* of the footage and photos is not as powerful as the photos themselves.

One picture is, indeed, worth a thousand words.

## Media Bias

Palestinians and pro-Palestinian anti-Zionists claim that the media are biased against them because the media are run by Jews. I actually think that quite the opposite is true. In fact, the new anti-Semite's rule of thumb is that nothing a Jew, a Jewish Israeli, or a Jewish or a Zionist organization ever says can be true. Zionists are all liars, vermin. To an anti-Semite, there is no such thing as a Jew who tells the truth. The "true" truth, the only satisfying truth that an anti-Semite wants to hear, is an anti-Jewish truth.

Language is—and should be—related to the truth. Otherwise, it disconnects us from reality. Propaganda, however, uses language to confuse and indoctrinate. It reduces political analysis to a cartoon, or to a neon light that flashes over and over again in a rigid, continuous, persistent way. It is hypnotizing and worthy of Hermann Goering at his best.

For example, French journalist Raynal (I wonder if *he's* Jewish) exposed an epidemic of anti-Jewish and anti-Israeli bias in the French media. (He must be Jewish; a Jewish organization published his work. Look: the anti-Semites have me doing this, too.) Raynal deconstructed the Agence French Presse (AFP) coverage of Prime Minister Ariel Sharon's visit to the Temple Mount on September 28, 2000. Raynal notes that by omitting certain background facts—and by then downplaying or denying them—the AFP was able to blame Sharon—and not the Palestinians—for the Second Intifada. The world press did the same thing.

Raynal reminds us of the facts: two Palestinian suicide bomb attacks occurred the day before Sharon's visit, which killed an Israeli soldier who had been escorting a civilian bus in Gaza. Sharon's September 28th visit had been announced several days beforehand and had received the approval of the Muslim authorities. Sharon was accompanied by Knesset members, including Arab Knesset members. Responding to intelligence reports, the group was escorted by one thousand police officers. Sharon never entered the mosques. Upon his expected arrival, one thousand Palestinian demonstrators threw stones, heavy rods, and metal objects at him. Sharon's police escorts responded by firing rubber bullets. Thirty Israeli policemen and four Palestinians were wounded in a period of a few minutes.

Within four hours of Sharon's preapproved visit, Yasser Arafat, in a radio broadcast, declared the visit to be a "serious step against Muslim holy places." He called upon the Arab world to "move . . . against Israeli practices against holy Jerusalem." Palestinian Legislative Council speaker Ahmad Quray, on the voice of Palestine radio, described the visit as one that "defiled" the mosques; Palestinian Culture and Information Minister Yasir Abd Rabbuh decried the "Judaization" of Jerusalem.

What was reported and commented upon both in France and in the world media was the "provocation" of Sharon's visit and the "outrage" of Sharon's soldiers killing and wounding Palestinians.

No Palestinians died that day.

More annoying facts: since the failure of the peace talks in July, Israeli intelligence had known and the Israeli media had reported that the Palestinian Authority had been planning a return to violence. In the early hours of September 29th a Palestinian policeman, Nail Suliman, killed an Israeli border guard with whom he had been carrying out a joint patrol.

These facts in this exact sequence were the beginning of the Intifada. They were buried, over and over again, not only in the French press but everywhere else as well.[24]

A full thirty hours after Sharon's visit, Palestinians threw large, sharp, heavy stones at Israeli soldiers and at Jewish worshipers praying at the Western (Wailing) Wall. The soldiers responded. At day's end there were 7 Palestinians dead and 220 wounded. That was the beginning of the Intifada as far as the world was concerned.

The original AFP reports of September 29 written by those "on the ground" did in fact mention the annoying facts cited earlier, but the information died right there; it had no informational legs. From then on, AFP blamed Sharon and the Israelis for the violence of the Intifada. *He* provoked it. According to Raynal, the first dispatch to reflect this view was not even written in the Middle East; it was written in Paris, and it relayed the views of the Palestinian Authority's representative in France, Leila Shahid.

The French and the world media essentially functioned as Yasser Arafat's private public relations firm—which did not stop the Arabs and the Palestinians from charging that the media were biased against them and run by Zionists.

Other bulletins sent from the Arab capitals followed closely in these footsteps and, Raynal notes, often took "the tone and vocabulary of governmental communiqués, of official press and of Palestinian organizations (whose words they echoed)."[25]

Raynal notes the following with suspicion: at 11:50 A.M., an AFP bulletin from Damascus was titled "Damascus Denounces the 'Massacre' at the Esplanade of Mosques in Jerusalem." An hour later, the Damascus spokesman for the Democratic Front for the Liberation of Palestine said that "the massacre committed by the Israeli forces of occupation on the esplanade of mosques, after the profanation of this esplanade by the terrorist Ariel Sharon, shows the absurdity of pursuing peace negotiations."[26]

By the second day of the Intifada, the AFP told the entire

French press corps as a matter of fact that "the violence was started by Ariel Sharon's visit to the esplanade of mosques which is home to the third most holy site in Islam."[27] On October 1, this view was repeated thirteen times by the agency, and on October 2, more than twenty times.

According to Raynal, over the following months AFP repeated this explanation at every opportunity. At the same time, they continued to fail to make any mention of the Palestinian decision to return to violence, the Palestinian shooting of two IDF soldiers in two separate instances, the Palestinian attack on Sharon, or the Palestinian attack on the worshipers at the Western Wall. The bulletins kept mentioning Al-Aqsa as "the third holiest site in Islam" but rarely mentioned that it was also the single most holy site in Judaism. Day after day, the bulk of the AFP dispatches relating to violence in the region relied solely on Palestinian sources, with those few that contained Israeli information sent largely at the end of the day, after editorial staffs had gone home.

• • •

The barrage of information, disinformation, lies, and propaganda is overwhelming. Whom can one believe or trust?

Even Orwell would weep at some of the utter linguistic distortions of reality. Today Israelis are "Nazis" and the hatred of the Jewish state is therefore really a fight against Nazism, fascism. The new star of David—pinned to each Israeli and to each Jewish breast—is a swastika. For example, Palestinian Police Chief Ghazi al Jabali claims that the Jews and the Nazis cooperated during World War II. "There is no difference between Hitler and Ben-Gurion."[28]

As I have noted in Chapter Three, the anti-Semitic propaganda in Arabic in the Islamic world is filthy, manically exaggerated, and quite defies belief. No distinction is made between Jews and Zionists, and both are accused of being subhuman exploiters and champion liars. The Holocaust against the Jews never happened—but if it did, the Jews themselves were in charge of it. And they used it to

their advantage. The official newspaper of the Palestinian Authority, *Al-Hayat Al-Jadidah*, has this to say:

> Everywhere, the Jews have been the subjects of hatred and disdain
> because they control most of the economic resources upon which
> the livelihoods of many people are dependent. . . . The winds began
> blowing in their favor when the campaign of persecution against
> them was begun by Hitler the Nazi. . . . [T]he international Jewish
> communications media under their control exploited this in the best
> possible way, and then the show started. They began to disseminate
> frightful pictures of mass executions and invented the shocking story
> of the gas ovens, where Hitler allegedly burned them. . . . [T]hey
> focused on women, children and old people and have exploited this
> to arouse sympathy for themselves when demanding financial com-
> pensation, donations and grants from all over the world.
>
> The truth is that the persecution of the Jews is a deceitful myth
> which the Jews have labeled the Holocaust and have exploited to
> get sympathy. . . . And even if it is possible that Hitler's assault
> against the Jews hurt them a little, the fact is it did them a clear ser-
> vice whose fruits they are reaping until today.[29]

I must note that the Palestinians seem to be accusing the Jews
of doing exactly what I am accusing the Palestinians of doing: creating deceptive propaganda about a nonexistent genocide for the
purpose of gaining sympathy, money, and power.

• • •

In October 2000, an Algerian man stabbed a twenty-year-old rabbinical student, Mayer David Myers, twenty times on a North London bus. In September 2002, a judge ordered the assailant, Nabil
Ouldeddine, twenty-nine, held indefinitely in a hospital for the
criminally insane. On being arrested Ouldeddine told police, "Israel
are the murderers. They kill women and children. So I stabbed
him."[30] An article by Francis Marion posted online with the

National Free Press refers to the rabbinical student as "an alleged homosexual" and to the Algerian as a "freedom fighter." The article also says:

> "Decent people the world over applaud his noble action against Zionism. As a result of the stabbing incident, Jewish women in the Stamford Hill neighborhood have stopped riding the buses. How nice it must be to at least have even a brief respite from the presence of obnoxious, hateful Jewish women when riding a bus in North London!"[31]

The Islamic counternarrative charges the Jews not only with organizing the (non) Holocaust but also with masterminding 9/11. Interestingly, the Jews are accused of distorting photos to prove that a European Holocaust really happened. In fact, the Palestinians and Arab Muslims (with the assistance of the Western media) have been specializing in this themselves. One might say that these jihadists and anti-Zionists are projecting their own misdeeds onto the Jews—and then reacting to it in a paranoid way.

## The Cover of Intellectualism

What's new about the new anti-Semitism is that the campaign to burn synagogues, to vandalize cemeteries, to harass, intimidate, beat, bomb, wound, and kill living Jews, both in Europe and in Israel, is being led, in Israeli journalist Avi Becker's phrase, "under cover of intellectualism."[32] Yet again the Jews themselves are to blame for what is being done to them. (That's old, of course, but it's coming from an entirely new cast of characters.) I will focus on this in another chapter.

According to French theorist Alain Finkielkraut, the doctrine of "original sin" has become the doctrine of "original oppression." America and its archagent and symbol Israel can never be redeemed. Neither Christ nor Marx (the secular Christ) will do so. These two empires must die for their crimes of "original oppression"—

even if such crimes have also been committed by others. The scape-goats have been chosen and they must die.[33]

What's new about the new anti-Semitism is that it has become politically and psychologically acceptable to be anti-Semitic. It has also become easier, as we have seen, to hide one's own anti-Jewish prejudice even from oneself by claiming that one is only anti-Zionist, not, God forbid, an anti-Semite.

What's new is that all those people in Europe and North America who never liked the Jews anyway but who felt they could not openly say so now feel morally justified to shout the old Big Lies from the rooftops. Moreover, the Jews have metamorphosed into the Nazis—witness the so-called Israeli Holocaust of the Palestinians. Thus, either the Holocaust never happened or it has been vastly exaggerated. Even if it did happen, the Jews have turned into their former tormenters and are no longer worthy of the pity that a dead and exterminated Jewish people might have elicited.

• • •

Today, as I've noted, Jews and Israelis are suffering from a horrifying overscrutiny that has reached the level of an obsession. People are possessed. As Alan Dershowitz has noted:

> Though Israel may often be deserving of criticism, what is missing is the comparable criticism of equal or greater violations by other countries and other groups. This constant, often legitimate criticism of Israel for every one of its deviations, when coupled with the absence of legitimate criticism of others, creates the impression currently prevalent on university campuses and in the press that Israel is among the worst human rights violators in the world. . . . [I]t is not true, but if it is repeated often enough, it takes on a reality of its own.[34]

At the same time, Palestinians are romanticized as the most grievously oppressed, and therefore the noblest group in the world. The Palestinian uprising has increasingly been seen as the uprising of all oppressed peoples against their colonial oppressors, that is, Jews, Zionists, and Americans. The overthrow of these groups, both real and symbolic, is imagined as some sort of Second Coming, even by the staunchest of secularists, and of course by the Islamofascists with whom they have made common cause.

In the past, Islamic commentators said that the Holocaust, which killed six million Jews, really did happen, but it happened in Europe and should be resolved there, both morally and politically, and not in the Middle East; Palestinian Muslims should not have to lose their homes and unchanging way of life because of Christian European anti-Semitism or, for that matter, because of the three-thousand-year Jewish attachment to the land of Israel. "Let them get over it," say the very people who held up keys to Palestinian Muslim houses lost a mere fifty years ago, too recently to have created an entire soulful culture of mourning and yearning.

Today, they (the jihadists, the Islamic media, the mullahs, the masses, the various European and Arab experts) tend to agree with the European Holocaust deniers or "negationists": The Jews have lied about the Holocaust (which never happened) in order to rob the Palestinians and the Muslim world of land and money. But they also argue that Hitler did not do a good enough job of finishing off the Jews and that they will finish his work.

Today, the Islamic jihadists also say that the Jews and the Zionists run the American government and control all Western global corporations, that Jews and Zionists (not Saudi al-Qaeda terrorists) carried out the attacks against America on 9/11. Jihadists say that the Zionists warned the Jews to stay away from work that day. No facts are brought to support any of these allegations and none are wanted. In the Islamic world, the most hysterical fantasy often passes for truth. Argue against it—and you may find a price on your head. In fact, the more outrageous the allegation against the Jews or against Christian America might be, the more it tends to be believed.

## Terrorists or Freedom Fighters?

In a recent interview in London, Leila Khaled, who once hijacked planes for the Palestinian cause, says she does not consider herself a terrorist; only Israelis and Zionists are terrorists.[35] Movsar Bareyev, the leader of the Chechen suicide hostage takers in Moscow, had his own linguistic and conceptual spin. He told journalist Mark Franchetti, "We are not terrorists. If we were, we would have demanded millions of dollars and a plane to escape."[36]

Everyone lives in their own fractured reality, the master of their self-definition. From the multicultural point of view, there is no objectivity, no truth. Everyone (except Jews and Israelis) are entitled to define their own separate reality. Khaled is a freedom fighter, not a terrorist; the Chechen rebels are not terrorists because . . . they say so.

• • •

In the last decade, the Irish, Indian, and Kashmiri "troubles" have continued to simmer, and the genocidal atrocities in Iraq against the Kurds, in Rwanda against the Tutsi, and in the former Yugoslavia have all made headlines. Nevertheless, the international community has not demonized the British, Irish, Hindus, Moslems, Hutus, or Bosnian Serbs. It has increasingly, solely, demonized Israel.

While the Christian and Islamic world focuses obsessively, unnaturally, on Israel as wrongdoer, and while it continues to blame Ariel Sharon for what Christian Phalangists did to Palestinian Muslims in Sabra and Shatila, Lebanon, in 1982, that same world fails even to note, except in passing, that in 1995, two hundred Dutch UN peacekeepers failed to protect seven thousand Muslim men in Srebrenica, who were therefore massacred by Bosnian Serbs. This happened while the city was under UN protection. In 2002, a Dutch-initiated report was published that led to the resignation of some members of the Dutch government. My point is that Muslims and Christians worldwide have not been targeting Dutch products, Dutch academics, or the Dutch as monsters, nor have they been chanting "death to the Serbians."

I do not understand why Muslim countries did not denounce the Bosnian Christian Serbs long ago for their systematic rape of Muslim women and for their slaughter of Muslim men. Can the Israelis be responsible for this, too? Or, if Jews and Israelis can't possibly be blamed, does that mean that the slaughter of the innocents does not matter? The war in the former Yugoslavia was Nazi-like, surreal, conducted by human fiends, and yet the world has not obsessed about the Serbs; they have not become the scapegoats for us all.

The information that came out of Bosnia defies belief; it confirms the worst nightmares of second wave feminists. The former Yugoslavia has been rebalkanized, cursed really, by paramilitary fascist-nationalists, virulent racists, misogynists. No matter who the aggressors were, their victims were mainly civilians. Male soldiers attacked civilians (who were often their neighbors) with ferocity and hatred. Male soldiers treated female civilians the way "kinky Johns" treat whores, the way psychotic batterers treat their wives.

Perhaps this is what men think is "manly" in the Balkans.

According to Alexandra Stiglmayer, editor of *Mass Rape: The War Against Women in Bosnia-Herzegovina*, Serbian male soldiers made their entrance cursing, often drunk; broke into houses where frightened women huddled; taunted, shoved, punched, slapped, and beat the women; put cigarettes out on their flesh; cut them with knives; called them whores; demanded that they smile; ripped their clothes off and raped them right there, where their children or mothers could see it, then herded the "terminally dishonored,"[37] half-naked, or completely naked women away to rape camps, where many other soldiers repeatedly gang-raped the starving, naked, soiled women. Bosnian women were also kidnapped off the street, blindfolded, held in cellars or gymnasiums for one to three months, and repeatedly raped. Afterward, they were often killed, although many were released, especially if they were pregnant with "Chet-nik" babies. The men gang-raped seven- and eight-year-old girls *to death*, but did not allow the grown women to comfort them as they lay dying. The rapists did not use condoms. They beat women if they thought they were using birth control. They filmed some of the rapes, and they aired some live, both on radio and television.[38]

Many—certainly half—of the rapes were committed by men whom the women knew. When the rapists were coworkers, neigh-bors, or former teachers, they were harder, not easier, on their victims—especially if the women called them by name.

The rapists were not out of control; they were implementing Serbian military ethnic cleansing policy. They were following orders. Yes, fascist-nationalist Croat and Moslem male soldiers raped women, too, with as much ferocity, although perhaps on a smaller scale.

In a ghastly replay of World War II, Serbian soldiers ordered the men-gypsies-Jews out of the house, lined them up, and shot them in the street or marched them out of town and shot them down into mass graves. Those men "lucky" enough to survive endured beat-ings, starvation, and hideous tortures in concentration camps. Serbian soldiers sometimes castrated and killed those Serbian men and boys who refused to systematically rape women. The soldiers slaughtered the able-bodied men outright, and sentenced the women to living deaths.

The Arab and Islamic world has not risen up against the Serbs. Only Western-trained international humanitarians and legal schol-ars have forced the hand of the United Nations to do so. Only America and NATO actually invaded the former Yugoslavia. Saudi Arabia did not help. The PLO sent no one.

While the war in Bosnia raged on, millions of women world-wide endured rape. Moslem women in Bosnia were not the only Moslem women to be systematically raped by soldiers. In fact, rape has consistently been used as a political weapon against Moslem women by Moslem men for the past fifteen years in Afghanistan, Algeria, Bangladesh, India, Iran, and Pakistan.

According to attorney Karima Bennoune, Algerian fundamentalist men have committed a series of "terrorist atrocities" against Algerian women from 1992 on. Bennoune describes the "kidnapping and repeated raping of young girls as sex slaves for armed fundamentalists. The girls are also forced to cook and clean for God's warriors. . . . One seventeen-year-old girl was repeatedly raped until pregnant. She was kidnapped off the street and held with other young girls, one of whom was shot in the head and killed when she tried to escape." As in Iran, "unveiled," educated, independent Algerian women have been seen as "military targets" and increasingly shot on sight. According to Bennoune, "the men of Algeria are arming, the women of Algeria are veiling themselves. As one woman said: 'Fear is stronger than our will to be free.'"[39]

According to Bennoune: "Terrorist attacks on women [in Algeria] have had the desired effect: widespread psychosis among the women; internal exile–living in hiding, both physically and psychologically, in their own country." In Bennoune's view, "the collective psychosis" is due to the "escalation of violence" by the "soldiers of the Islamic state." According to Michael Curtis, an American volunteer-physician for Doctors Without Borders: "In Bosnia's Tuzla camp, the leading cause of death is suicide, probably the only refugee camp in the world where that is the case."[40]

## The Demonization of Jews

In 1948, an estimated 500,000 to 700,000 Palestinians fled their homes. Many were forced to leave, many were afraid of Jewish rule, and many believed the promise of neighboring Arab nations that their exile would be only temporary and that soon the Arab nations would drive Israel into the sea. Some Palestinians were also killed— perhaps even massacred—by Israeli forces. Some Palestinians left and went directly to Jordan, which many say is *the* Palestinian homeland. This is the refugee plight that is very much on the world's mind.

Over the next two decades, an even larger number of Jews (850,000) who lived in Arab lands were forced to flee their countries. More Jewish Arabs fled from Arab lands such as Iraq, Yemen, Egypt, Syria, Algeria, Morocco, and India than did Palestinians from Palestine-Israel. Tiny Israel absorbed these Arab Jews. Twenty-three Arab states did not and would not absorb their Palestinian-Arab brethren. The nonabsorbed Palestinians were kept by their Arab hosts in temporary refugee camps, for which Israel has always been blamed.

The world was, and still is, unconcerned with the flight of Jewish refugees from Arab lands.

• • •

For a moment, let's compare Israel to Iraq, which is not a real country but one cobbled together by British imperialists. It is not even an exclusively Arab country. Iraqis speak eleven languages, only one of which is Arabic. But my main point (based on Amir Taheri's many points in a recent op-ed piece in the *New York Times*[41]) is this: between 1972 and 1980, Saddam Hussein expelled nearly a million Persians who had been born and raised in Iraq. He did this in order to "Arabize" Iraq. In addition, he "relocated" four thousand Kurdish villages from north to south. He also exterminated thousands of Kurds and used poison gas against them and against Iranians.

While it is true that Iraq and Iran engaged in prolonged warfare, did Saddam Hussein ever become demonized in the Islamic world in the way Israel has? Were his mass expulsions and use of biological warfare the subject of Muslim-initiated international conferences? Is *Iraq* synonymous with evil in the *Arab* world—or is only Israel?

• • •

"What about Gujarat?" asked my anguished Indian feminist colleague. (Gujarat is the site of bloody Hindu-Muslim clashes.)

"What about AIDS in Africa?" asked my South African colleague. They are out of luck. According to Gillian Gillison, "if it's not about the Jews, it's not news."[42] The world does not seem to care quite as much about atrocities if Jews cannot be accused of committing them or are not the victims. Whose fault is this? Surely one cannot blame the Jews for this.

Actually, anti-Semites can and do. "The Jews run the newspapers and own the banks" is what they say. (This is too surreal and spooky even to repeat; I repeat it anyway.) Even when I think an article or a program has presented the Jews in a biased and awful light, today's anti-Semite reads the same article, sees the same program, and denounces it as "too" pro-Jewish. The Zionists, the Jewish lobby, are behind the program; they sigh, "What else can you expect?"

Today's anti-Semite does not believe that the Jews and Zionists can ever do anything right or that the Arabs and Palestinians can ever do anything wrong. Therefore, if the facts line up in such a way as to present the Jews sympathetically—clearly the story must be a hoax. The anti-Semite trusts her prejudice, not the facts.

Statistics, not just photos, can also be doctored or "spun" in such a way as to serve one's biases, not the truth.

For example, for two years the media, the Arab rioters, European intellectuals, and the immediate world said—and kept saying—that brutal "Nazi" Israeli soldiers were shooting young Palestinian children at point-blank range, and using the most powerful military weaponry in the world against barefoot stone throwers. Israeli soldiers were accused of perpetrating a holocaust upon innocent civilians on the West Bank and in Gaza. The proof was not only in doctored and undoctored photos repeated ad nauseam, but in the numbers themselves. For example, from September 27, 2000, through October 30, 2002, sixteen hundred Palestinians but only six hundred Israelis were killed.

But these true numbers do not represent the "truth."

The International Policy Institute for Counter-Terrorism, a prestigious think tank located in Herzliya, Israel (oh dear, they must be Jews), released an objective analysis of these numbers *based entirely on Palestinian sources*. (Okay, the Jews may be smart but you still can't trust them.) The report is titled, "The al-Aqsa Intifada—An Engineered Tragedy." According to Don Radlauer, the casualty figures just cited

> distort the true picture: They lump combatants in with noncombatants, suicide bombers with innocent civilians, and report Palestinian "collaborators" murdered by their own compatriots as if they had been killed by Israel. . . . Israel is responsible for around 617 Palestinian *noncombatant* deaths, while Palestinians have killed more than 471 Israeli *noncombatants*. . . . Over 54 percent of the Palestinians killed were actively involved in fighting—and this does not include stone-throwers or "unknowns." . . . Palestinians were themselves responsible for the deaths of at least 203 of their own number.[43]

On the Israeli side, 80 percent of those killed were noncombatants, most of whom were women and girls. *Israeli female* fatalities far outnumbered *Palestinian female* fatalities by either 3 to 1 or 4 to 1. (So far I have heard no feminist complaints about this; have you?) Israeli women and girls constituted almost "40 percent of the Israeli noncombatants killed by Palestinians."[44] Of the Palestinian deaths, more than 95 percent were male. In other words, Palestinians purposefully went after women, children, and other unarmed civilians, and Israelis fought against armed male soldiers who were attacking them.

Still, Palestinians were not demonized for their cowardly approach, and Israelis *were* demonized for defending themselves in battle.

For the Jews in Israel, it has ever been such. In the past, the Arabs learned to respect Israeli Jews only when the Jews learned that if they were to live in peace with their Arab neighbors they would have to defend themselves; otherwise, they would all soon be dead. What's new is that today the entire world is attacking Israel for defending itself.

Now that we have an idea of what is new about the new anti-Semitism, I would like to focus on the Intifada in Europe and in North America, in terms of both deeds and ideas. Western intellectuals have provided incredible cover for the mob actions against Jews and Israelis.

## Chapter Five

# The Betrayal of Truth, Part One

## The European Intifada

The lies of the new anti-Semitism, the partial truths, the diabolical distortions, the raw filth, the hate, are perhaps too hard for any one person to confront and combat.

Over the years I have debated many practiced liars and agenda maniacs. I no longer do so. In my view, one cannot find and communicate the truth of a given matter by engaging in a snappy, polarized debate in which there is a "winner" and a "loser." That format is sheer entertainment, like mud wrestling or a quiz show, and is no more nourishing than white bread, no more illuminating than a video game. At best, it is a diversion.

The truth is no match for lies. Lies take no work; one simply makes them up and keeps on repeating them. As Sir Winston Churchill said, "A lie gets halfway around the world before the truth has a chance to get its pants on." The truth about a complex and difficult matter may be reached, or approximated, only after a long time in the library, at lectures, on site, talking to the people involved in an ongoing way, not just once. In doing so, one becomes something of an expert in the matter at hand and is recognized as such by other experts. An expert is not the keeper of divine and infallible truth but, rather, someone who has the necessary background to understand context, who keeps track of a thousand threads, and who can therefore venture an informed opinion about the matter.

I am sure this does not sound easy. It isn't; it is damned hard, and most people do not become experts, not even as a hobby, although some do. It is far easier to read one newspaper, to watch one or two television channels, and to conclude that what you've read or heard is "probably the truth." After all, journalists are experts, right? Ah—wrong; many are merely television actors, entertainers; and many more have been hired because their views conform to those who own the station or the paper. They are not always allowed to venture independent views. Some journalists mainly rely on their own personal experience and take pride in trusting their own instincts. This is not a crime, but it does not qualify as expertise.

Still, at some point one must put one's faith in those with whom one agrees or whose way with words one admires. In my case, I have tended to read and to trust certain public intellectuals. The current crisis has proved to me that I cannot do so, at least not lightly, and not on this particular subject. Worse, I now understand that many intellectuals are ideologues, not freethinkers.

Many brilliant, brave, eloquent journalists do exist. However, the nonideologues among them are often maddeningly "objective"— which means they do not believe in taking sides and must therefore allow Hitler and Jack the Ripper their fair say if they are interviewing their surviving victims. Some journalists are also scholars who hold doctorates, medical degrees, or law degrees; others are ideologues, expert on bending or using facts to fit their ideology. No civilian is a match for them, and few civilians can understand a debate between two journalist-ideologues; eventually a civilian walks away, puzzled, disgusted.

Most American and European intellectuals have not stood up to the orgy of racism against Jews; on the contrary, they have been leading the racist mobs—and in the name of antiracist politics. Why have so few Jewish intellectuals (outside of France) confronted or unmasked Palestinians at conferences and in demonstrations all across the Western world as the Palestinians have shed copious, practiced, on-camera tears in order to gain world sympathy by telling lies about Israelis and Jews? Why have no responsible academics confronted Palestinian and pro-Palestinian rioters on campus? Why have so many scholars deserted the path of objectivity, neutrality, sanity? For example, why did the Portuguese Nobel Prize winner José Saramago write the following in *El Pais*:

> Intoxicated mentally by the messianic dream of a Greater Israel which will finally achieve the expansionist dreams of the most radical Zionism; contaminated by the monstrous and rooted "certitude" that in this catastrophic and absurd world there exists a people chosen by God and that, consequently, all the actions of an obsessive, psychological and pathologically exclusivist racism are justified; educated and trained in the idea that any suffering that has been inflicted, or is being inflicted, or will be inflicted on everyone else, especially the Palestinians, will always be inferior to that which they themselves suffered in the Holocaust, the Jews endlessly scratch their own wound to keep it bleeding, to make it incurable, and they show it to the world as if it were a banner.[1]

Saramago is condemning Judaism as a faith but he is also condemning Judaism as a culture, a race, and a political entity. He is denying the historicity of anti-Semitism. He seems to resent the role that memory has played among the Jews, and therefore the skill that Jews have brought to bear on reminding the world of Jewish persecution. To Saramago, it is a fiendish trick, a theatrical tic, and it enrages and disgusts him. Saramago does not sound sorrowful or grave; he sounds disgusted, offended, outraged. He is an anti-Semite.

Am I the only intellectual in America to feel this way? Am I wrong? Is everyone else right? Are the Israelis so evil that they deserve to be demonized and destroyed? If I am even partly right, then how can we understand the silence of so many presumably antiracist intellectuals? How has the politically correct academy, both here and in Europe, so betrayed complexity and truth, and displayed such cowardice, conformity, cruelty, and narrow tunnel vision?

# The European Intifada

*Intifada* is a word that has been used exclusively to describe the uprising among the Palestinians against the Israelis. But I choose to use the word here also to describe the uprising and attack against Diaspora Jews in Europe and North America. In essence, Jews are being attacked outside of Israel in retaliation for Israel's continued existence and as part of a general propaganda-driven resurgence of anti-Semitism. Let's begin with the anti-Semitic deeds in Europe.

The anti-Semitic attacks in Europe have included the desecration of Jewish cemeteries; use of Molotov cocktails, firing of guns, and other attacks on synagogues; stone throwing; physical assaults on Jews in the street; anti-Semitic graffiti and drawings of swastikas; signs denying the Holocaust; distribution of anti-Semitic materials; hostile demonstrations; bomb and other threats; arson; burglary of Jewish property; and attacks on Jewish students, schools, and homes.

According to the Stephen Roth Institute for the Study of Contemporary Anti-Semitism and Racism, in 2000 and in the first few months of 2001, there were 1,378 clearly visible and reported incidents of anti-Semitism in Germany, 405 in England, 146 in France, 100 in Italy, 46 in Holland, 15 in Spain, 13 in Austria, 8 in Belgium, and 5 in Denmark. In short, according to this one source, 2,116 such incidents—about three or four incidents per day—occurred over a period of about fourteen months in Europe.[2] Such incidents continue, and in many other countries, too, for which we don't have accurate statistics.

But this is only the tip of the iceberg. According to an August 2002 report released by the Lawyers Committee for Human Rights, European governments record such incidents only sometimes, and rather vaguely. Whether this is done intentionally or accidentally, the result is a continued "disappearance" of the problem.[3] Jewish community centers and regional monitoring bodies are often forced to collect this information—which is then often discredited as parochial, biased, and noncredible—on their own.

European governments' failure to keep serviceable data on racially motivated crime is a well-known problem that has long cried out for a remedy; none has been offered, however. In 1997, the European Union created a body known as the European Monitoring Centre on Racism and Xenophobia (EUMC). In 1999, EUMC passed a resolution for improvements in record keeping; however, it later issued a statement in which it despaired because of hopeless discrepancies between official and unofficial reports.[4] Yet whatever the technical difficulties, the numbers available on the rise of anti-Jewish violence provide concrete evidence of widespread violence, harassment, and hatred. The methodologies employed by various organizations and groups may lack coordination, but all compilations rely on scrutable reports.

Nevertheless, according to the Anti-Defamation League, the Coordination Forum for Countering Antisemitism, the Jewish Telegraph Agency's daily briefing, the Union des Étudiants Juifs de France and SOS Racisme,[5] and the Stephen Roth Institute for the Study of Contemporary Anti-Semitism and Racism, anti-Semitic incidents have recently occurred in the following countries: Belgium, Belarus, Czech Republic, Denmark, Finland, France, Germany, Greece, Ireland, Italy, Latvia, Lithuania, Moldova, Poland, Romania, Russia, Slovakia, Spain, Sweden, Switzerland, Ukraine, and the United Kingdom.[6]

For our purposes, I will focus mainly on the countries that have seen the greatest number of anti-Semitic incidents.

## Germany
According to the Stephen Roth Institute, Germany has experienced the greatest number of incidents, with 1,378 in 2000 and early 2001.

Shortly before Yom Kippur [2000], a crowd of about 100 Palestinian and Lebanese demonstrators tried to storm the Old Synagogue in the German city of Essen, today a Jewish museum and Holocaust memorial center. German Foreign Minister Joschka Fischer instantly condemned the attack and declared that Germany would not permit institutions to be targets of violence.

Other incidents during October 2000 included violent attacks on synagogues in Dusseldorf and Berlin and desecration of cemeteries, as well as threats and fake letter bombs addressed to representatives of the Jewish communities. On

July 27, 2000, ten persons were injured, six of them Jews, when the Wehrhahn railway station in Dusseldorf was bombed.

Throughout the year Jewish cemeteries were once again the main targets of right-wing extremists throughout Germany. These included the cemeteries of Göttingen, Erfurt, Guben, Georgsmund, Hanover, Hillersleben, Uckermunde, Anklam, Eberswalde, Potsdam, Leipzig, Grabow, Saarbruecken, and Solms. . . . Synagogues and Holocaust memorials were also the targets of extreme right violence. The Erfurt synagogue, for example, was torched on April 20, the anniversary of Hitler's birthday. Since 1945 Jewish cemeteries and property have been damaged on more than 1,000 occasions.[7]

On September 5, 2002, the Wittstock Museum, which honors the victims of a Nazi death camp, was firebombed. Outside the museum, vandals painted a three-by-eighteen-foot anti-Semitic slogan as well as a large red swastika.[8]

According to the Stephen Roth Institute, due to a new system of German record-keeping, it is difficult to compare the anti-Semitism statistics for 2001 with those of 2000. Nevertheless, the evidence indicates a steady increase in such incidents. Thus, in 2001 there were 1,424 reported anti-Semitic crimes in Germany, including 18 violent crimes by the far right. Jewish public figures and sites received special police protection. Some states, including Berlin, saw a 100 percent rise in reported anti-Semitic "manifestations,"[9] while the number of far-right anti-Semitic acts shot up drastically.

For example, on March 13th, unidentified individuals rubbed feces on a Berlin memorial to deported Jews. The same month there was an arson attack on the Jewish cemetery in Charlottenburg, Berlin, that received national attention. There was also an arson attack on a synagogue in Potsdam, and desecrations of other synagogues in Regensburg, Dresden, and Celle, where Nazi posters were mounted.

**France**

In late 2000 and early 2001, France saw the largest number of officially reported anti-Semitic attacks in a decade, with numerous attacks on synagogues as well as Jewish cemeteries. The Stephen

Roth Institute noted that these attacks included arson and petrol bomb attacks against synagogues and Jewish schools. In Trappes, a suburb of Paris, the synagogue was razed to the ground; worshipers were stoned outside synagogues in the Pantin and Bondy suburbs of Paris and in Nice; a sniper shot a rifle into the Great Synagogue in Paris during the Yom Kippur service; and there were attacks on Jewish property, such as the torching of a Jewish bakery in Strasbourg and a Molotov cocktail attack on a Jewish restaurant in the mixed Arab-Jewish Belleville neighborhood of Paris.

The hatred in France appears to be so rampant that almost anything can trigger it. For example, on October 25, 2000, at a movie theater at Rosny, when a rabbi appeared on screen in the film *Double vie,* youths shouted, "Death to the Jews; dirty Jews; the Jews into the sea; you rule us over there, we'll rule you here; we'll lynch you; we'll burn you."[10]

During the week of October 2, 2000, threats and insults were made by telephone at the synagogue at 3, rue Gresset. An unidentified voice said, "Bunch of dirty Jews." One morning during Slichot services on Yom Kippur, an incendiary bottle was thrown into this synagogue.

Attacks on synagogues in France are quite common. For example, on October 7, 2000, the Bagnolet synagogue was burglarized. On October 8, 2000, Molotov cocktails were thrown during services at the synagogue in Clichy sous Bois. On October 10, 2000, stones were thrown, followed by anti-Semitic insults, at the Henri Murger synagogue. And someone sprayed tear gas during services at the synagogue at Julien Lacroix.

It is not only the synagogues that are in danger. No visibly Jewish place is a refuge for Jews. Attacks have been launched against Kosher restaurants (Rue Manin on October 13 and 14, 2000). Computers and money have been stolen from Jewish schools (Tipheret Israel school in Sarcelles on July 28 and 29, 2001). Jewish cemeteries have been desecrated (Trappes on October 8, 2000). Even private apartments are not safe. For example, on May 5, 2001, one hundred Mezuzot were torn from the doors of an apartment building in Créteil and burned.

The streets are not safe for (obvious) Jews either. For example, on October 10, 2000, a person wearing a chai pendant was physically abused and struck by a North African-looking person beside the Pyrenées metro station. On October 12, 2000, a man wearing a kippah was struck on the skull with glass bottles by a group of four Arabs and an African at impasse Montplaisir.

Particularly disturbing are the many attacks on young Jewish students, such as the violence directed at a school bus from a private Jewish school in Garge le Gonesses on December 22, 2000. Two men threatened the bus driver with a blunt instrument. Following this, the aggressors smashed a window of the vehicle and made anti-Semitic remarks. (One of these aggressors was detained by the police.) On October 4 and 5, 2000, Jewish students were physically abused when classes let out at the Ohr Yossef school. And on October 6, 2000, students at the Ténoudji Jewish school in Saint Ouen were insulted and had stones thrown at them.

The rise in anti-Semitic violence that began in France in 2000 continued into 2001, reaching unprecedented heights. Four hundred separate attacks were reported for the period of fall 2000 and spring 2001 alone, compared to 146 reported for all of 2000. Official reactions were relatively muted. The Stephen Roth Institute hypothesizes that the government avoided prosecuting these crimes in order not to offend the Muslim electorate before the April elections.

In January 2001, two Jews were stabbed in Strasbourg, and North African youths attacked an amateur Jewish soccer team in Bondy, a Paris suburb, with clubs and iron bars, hospitalizing one player.

In 2002, such occurrences only became more common and their intensity was exacerbated. On January 21, 2002, in Sarcelles, Val d'Oise, a school bus transporting six children to the Sinai Jewish school was attacked by a group of seven or eight youths, who threw a stone weighing about two pounds that shattered a window and injured a six-year-old girl. According to Le Monde, on the night of March 31, 2002, the Or Aviv synagogue in Marseilles was entirely destroyed by fire caused by arson. On April 28, 2002, in Sarcelles, Tipheret Israel, a Jewish day school in the suburbs of Paris, was set on fire, and a warehouse at the school was destroyed.[11]

Additionally, anti-Semitic graffiti has been on the rise. For example, on April 10, 2002, in Marseille, anti-Semitic graffiti and pictures of swastikas were found on Jewish-owned shops; and on April 12,

2002, in Cronenbourg, anti-Jewish graffiti and pictures of swastikas were found on about twenty gravestones and a cemetery wall in the Jewish cemetery.

In January 2003, the council of L'Université Paris 6 adopted a resolution calling on the European Union to suspend academic ties with Israeli institutions. On January 7, 2,500 demonstrators gathered on campus to protest this resolution. There were also approximately fifty pro-Palestinian demonstrators behind the university gates who shouted anti-Israeli slogans and called Sharon a "murderer." They were protected by a police cordon. The atmosphere was tense. At the end of the rally, roughly thirty young pro-Palestinians required a police escort to leave the neighborhood.[12] University president Gilbert Bereziat said the university would "never" cut off ties with Israel.[13]

In other events, liberal rabbi and peace supporter Gavriel Farhi was stabbed in his synagogue in Paris by a masked individual who shouted "Allah is great" in Arabic. On Monday, January 6th, the rabbi's car was torched. Former French prime ministers Lionel Jospin, Alain Juppé, Edouard Balladur, and Laurent Fabius visited the rabbi in a show of support; U.K. prime minister Tony Blair also sent a message.[14]

The Israeli government released figures that showed that the emigration of French Jews to Israel reached record heights of 2,326 in 2001.[15]

On February 27, 2003, the BBC announced that Luc Ferry, France's Minister of Education, acknowledged that "some 445 racist and anti-Semitic incidents (bullying, mocking, vandalism, and so on) were recorded in French state schools in the autumn term alone [of 2002]." Ferry said that "anti-Semitic insults of a new kind were becoming a feature of everyday life." He announced that teachers would no longer be allowed to "turn their heads when Jewish students were being harassed." A tougher line is being advised, one that includes expulsion or legal action.[16]

## United Kingdom

In 2000, the United Kingdom saw a 50 percent increase over the previous year in the number of anti-Semitic incidents, with 405 events reported. Of these, 51 were non-life-threatening physical assaults, but there were two life-threatening ones in October, including the stabbing of a twenty-year-old rabbinical student on a Stamford Hill bus in North London. Eleven percent of the total British Jewish population live in Manchester. The city has always had a high level of street crime, but the report says that while break-ins were down, physical assaults on Jews were up (fifteen total).

Vandalism of communal property constituted 13 percent of the total (seventy-three incidents) compared to twenty-five incidents (9 percent) in 1999. In the most serious incident, during two days in June, more than five hundred gravestones were smashed at the Federation of Synagogues' cemetery in Edmonton, North London.

The largest proportion of incidents were acts of abusive behavior against individual Jews. There were 196 such incidents, compared to 127 in 1999.

During the month of October, 2000, there was an unprecedented number of demonstrations by Islamic groups in London, Manchester, and elsewhere. Some of the slogans were virulently anti-Jewish, as well as anti-Israel, such as the following: "Jewish occupiers—kill them when you see them," "Global death for Israelis," and *"Khaybar Khaybar ya yahud, jaysh Muhammad sawfa ya'ud"* or "Khaybar Khaybar, Oh Jews! The army of Muhammad will return."

Unidentified individuals issued a printed "warning to all Jews" not to show any support for Israel or "you will become a part of the conflict." Muslim Internet discussion boards posted calls to "publish a list of important Jewish personalities" and the "need to use militant groups all over the world against Jewish and Western targets." Others called for a stop to demonstrations because "we should concentrate on strategy for jihad on the Jews."

On July 11, 2002, in Swansea, Wales, the Swansea synagogue was desecrated by vandals with Nazi graffiti, including a swastika and the phrase "T4 Jewish c*** from Hitler." A three-hundred-year-old Torah scroll was damaged and another was burned. The building was also covered in a flammable material; however, attempts to burn it down were unsuccessful. Earlier, on May 6, 2002, in London, following a rally in support of Israel, a boy wearing a shirt with a Star of David was attacked by three youths and hit on the head with a baseball bat.[17]

The distinguished Irish poet Tom Paulin, a lecturer at Oxford (the same Paulin who, in 2002, was first invited, then disinvited, then reinvited to speak at Harvard), told the Egyptian *Al-Ahram Weekly* that he understood "how the suicide bombers feel," that "attacks on civilians in fact boost morale," that Brooklyn-born Jewish settlers "should be shot dead. [. . .] I think they are Nazis, racists. I feel nothing but hatred for them," he said. Saying that he "never believed Israel had a right to exist," Paulin also described it as an "artificial, [. . .] ahistoric" state and accused the Europeans who allowed its creation of bearing "a very heavy responsibility." In February 2001, Paulin published the poem "Killed in the Cross-fire" in the *Observer.* It read, "another little Palestinian boy/In trainers jeans and a white tee-shirt/Is gunned down by the Zionist SS."[18]

Paulin's and the demonstrators' licentiousness in likening Israelis to Nazis is depressingly typical. The *Guardian*'s Rod Liddle reported that a British lecturer working at the University of Tel Aviv received the following response when he sought to obtain a position back at home: "No, we don't accept any applicants from a Nazi state."[19]

According to the Stephen Roth Institute, most of the anti-Semitism in the United Kingdom "emanates from militant Islamist and other Muslim groups."[20] However, many white, Christian, neo-Nazi and Holocaust denial groups and leaders are also highly visible. Although the number of incidents declined from 405 in 2000 to 310 in 2001, there is a "marked tendency toward more violent attacks on the Jewish community." Nearly a third of the anti-Semitic incidents in 2001 occurred within a six-week period immediately following 9/11.

A total of 310 anti-Semitic incidents were reported; 98 occurred between September 12 and October 31, 2001. These incidents included physical assaults (one life-threatening), insults, property desecration, Holocaust denial conferences, and the dissemination of anti-Semitic propaganda. Conversely, recent antiracist laws, anti-terrorism legislation and enforcement, conviction of neo-Nazis, and various court cases may have contributed to an overall decline in anti-Semitic incidents.

## Italy

On March 31, 2002, in Modena, Italy, anti-Semitic graffiti and swastikas were found on the synagogue, and two arson threats were received by telephone. On July 17, 2002, in Rome, forty graves were desecrated in the Jewish section of the historic Verano cemetery in a nighttime attack on the ninth day of Av, Tisha B'Av, a traditional Jewish day of mourning. The perpetrators partially opened one coffin, smashed headstones, and ripped off parts of gravestones with Hebrew writing and Star of David decorations.[21] These were only two of the reported one hundred cases in Italy during a fourteen-month period. However, on April 15, 2002, a group of progressive Italians, led by the intellectual and journalist Guiliano Ferrara, who is my friend, carried out a pro-Israel march.

## Belgium

In the fall of 2000 there was an attempt at arson at a Brussels synagogue. In addition, the Anderlecht monument to Jewish martyrs was defaced. On September 28th, during Friday prayers at two mosques in Brussels, worshipers were urged to take revenge against the Jews for their treatment of the Palestinians. Various Muslim religious and cultural authorities condemned the anti-Jewish attacks.

There were also several serious incidents in October. A Jew was hospitalized after being severely beaten by a group of Arabs near a Brussels synagogue. And on October 15th, four Molotov cocktails were thrown at the Sephardi synagogue in the Schaerbeek quarter of Brussels. In addition, in Brussels stones were thrown at a synagogue, smashing several windows. Anti-Semitic slogans were smeared on the Holocaust memorial, and a large swastika was drawn on the main entrance of the Maimonides synagogue. A window of a Jewish library in Antwerp was also smashed.

Stephen Roth suggested that the perpetrators of these acts were possibly Arabs and Muslims but cautiously noted that "in November posters with the slogan 'Israel—Murderer!' bore the signature of Intifada Européenne, [which] appears to have succeeded the Anti-Zionistische Aktie, a neo-Nazi group which was active at the end of the 1990s in Belgium and in the Netherlands."[22]

More recently, on April 3, 2002, in the Jewish quarter of Antwerp, a pro-Palestinian demonstration with two thousand participants included vandalism (cars were torched, shops were sacked, and an Israeli flag was burned).

### Romania

On May 18, 2002, in the small town of Falticeni, Suceava, Romania, a synagogue was found vandalized. The perpetrators called themselves the Anti-Semitic Battle Front. They broke windows, stole scrolls, and wrote "Heil Hitler" and "Death and Gas Chambers to the Jews" on the walls. Half of Romania's Jewish population lived in this town before World War II. Only fifty Jews remain.

### Russia

Although there were many incidents in Russia, the most widely publicized incident occurred in Moscow on May 27, 2002, when a woman was injured by an explosion when she tried to remove from the Kiev Highway a booby-trapped road sign that read "Death to Jews."

### Switzerland

Switzerland also saw its fair share of hate. On February 25, 2002, in Geneva, swastikas and anti-Semitic graffiti were found on a memorial to Holocaust victims. A nearby synagogue was also pelted with beer bottles and street lamps.

### South Africa

South Africa is not a part of Europe, of course, but it has the most Jews (85,000) of any country on the African continent and has many European connections. While the overall incidence of anti-Semitism has been low, nevertheless—perhaps due to the anti-Semitic and anti-Zionist UN Conference in Durban, South Africa, and to the global rise of anti-Semitism—various anti-Semitic events did occur. In September, 2001, for example, an old Jewish doctor in Cape Town was beaten by three men in keffiyahs. The men reportedly said, "You Jews are the ones making trouble in the Middle East." The windows of a Johannesburg synagogue were smashed, and a Jewish cemetery near Cape Town was vandalized.

According to the Stephen Roth institute, Shaykh Ebrahim Gabriels, president of the Muslim Judicial Council, which was once seen as moderate, has made a number of anti-Semitic statements.

In October 2001, for example, he led worshipers in a chant: "The Jew will hide behind a tree," which would itself say, "There is a Jew hiding behind me. Come and kill him." In July, the largely Indian-supported *Lenasia Times* carried a letter referring to "those murderous barbarian Jews."

On October 13th, the *Eastern Province Herald* carried an anti-Semitic letter written by Nasrudeen Campbell, who said that the United States and the Jews were "the ultimate coward terrorists" who had "killed millions of people the world over," all because of "their satanic lust and passion for monetary and land gain."[23]

There were numerous anti-Semitic rallies during the World Conference Against Racism at Durban and after the 9/11 attacks on the United States. In December, Ahmed Cassim, founder of the Muslim fundamentalist group Qibla (or Kibla), told an Al-Quds day rally in Cape Town that "the final solution for the Jews," that is, the creation of "the Zionist Terrorist State," had "become . . . possibly its final nightmare." During the Durban conference, Jews participating in a parallel forum for nongovernmental organizations were continually molested. A planned march by ten thousand pro-Palestinian demonstrators on the Durban Jewish Club forced the evacuation of the premises. In addition, a press conference as well as a meeting of the Anti-Semitism Commission were both disrupted by pro-Palestinian demonstrators and had to be ended.[24]

## European Intellectuals and Academics on the March

The new anti-Semite is not only an illiterate or underemployed Muslim immigrant from North Africa or the Middle East who has joined a mob to torch a synagogue or to beat up Jews in Europe or North America. The new anti-Zionist or anti-Semite is also an Egyptian physician or journalist, a Saudi Arabian prince, an Iranian cleric, a North American college student or his esteemed professor, or an Islamic terrorist in Indonesia, Africa, Chechnya, Lebanon, Iraq, or Syria. The new anti-Semite can also be a European Nobel Prize winner, an international scholar, an activist, a journalist, or a poet.

On October 7, 2002, Avi Becker suggested in *Haaretz* that "a campaign of incitement is under way under cover of intellectualism." He went on to note that there is a clear "symbiosis" between the anti-Semitic violence in Europe and the atmosphere in intellectual circles and in the media. I agree.[25]

The new anti-Semitism is a joint enterprise being carried out by heavily propagandized mobs and by the leading ideologues of the day. Academics and intellectuals have either remained silent, justified the violence by blaming Israel and the Jews for all evils, or actively sought to punish Israeli academics and intellectuals for Israeli military and political policies.

For example, in 2002, European academics sponsored a petition to boycott and defund Israeli academics. (By default, Israel is considered a part of the European bloc because the Arab and Muslim world has refused to allow Israel formal status as a Middle Eastern country.) In the signed petition (initiated by Steven Rose, professor of biology at the Open University, United Kingdom), European academics called for a moratorium of support (that is, no grants and no contracts) until Israel "abide[s] by UN resolutions and open[s] serious peace negotiations with the Palestinians."[26]

Signatories of the petition are from Austria, Belgium, Bulgaria, Britain, Cyprus, Denmark, Ireland, Finland, France, Germany, Greece, Iceland, Israel, Italy, the Netherlands, Norway, Portugal, Spain, Sweden, and Switzerland. Some signatories are Arab, some are Jewish—some are even Israeli. Yet it makes little sense to punish individual Israelis or Jews for their government's decisions. Should we boycott all Europeans for Europe's treatment of the Jews?

Another unnerving European boycott was initiated by a single individual via e-mail from a scientific institution in Norway. An Israeli scientist, Evelyne Zeira, sought to receive clones of pig cells for research destined to aid in muscle cell problems of anemic Palestinian children. In response to Zeira's request, the Norwegian institution wrote:

Due to the present situation in the Middle East I will not deliver any material to an Israelitic [sic] university. My institution, as well as most universities in Norway, have recently sent protests against the Israelitic military action on the West Bank to the Embassy of Israel in Norway and to the Department of Foreign Affairs. . . . I find it impossible for me to deliver any material to an Israelitic university. Best Regards[27]

Equally unnerving: the Finnish government refused to supply gas kits to Israel. According to the Board of Deputies of British Jews (BOD), these kits would enable Israel to quickly analyze and identify gas and allow doctors to counteract a gas attack against the civilian population. Yet despite the defensive and remedial nature of the gas kits, Finland chose to express its disapproval of Israeli policy in this way.[28]

On April 13, 2002, the leading British medical journal *The Lancet* published an editorial that accused Israel of "carnage" and condemned "Israel and the Palestinians alike (for having) terrorized each other's children." The editorial pretended to even-handedness by blaming both sides—whether or not both sides were actually to blame. *The Lancet* quotes Peter Hansen, Commissioner General of the UN's Relief and Works Agency for Palestine Refugees: "We are getting reports of pure horror . . . in the name of human decency the Israeli military must allow our ambulances safe passage." *The Lancet* did not quote anyone—certainly not a physician—who tried to save or treat any Israeli civilians who died or were wounded by Palestinian terrorists. While *The Lancet* also condemned the international community for having failed to apply the "pressure necessary to ensure that the law is upheld," in my view, *The Lancet* also failed its own scientific mandate by publishing biased political propaganda as if it were neutral and objective.[29]

In October 2002, British academic publisher St. Jerome Publishing decided to stop selling books and periodicals to Bar-Ilan University due to Israel's activities in the territories. This is the same publisher that publishes the journals run by Egyptian-born

British academic Mona Baker, director of the Centre for Translation and Intercultural Studies, Manchester, who fired two Israeli academic advisors from her journals' board.[30]

## Unilateral European Anti-Semitism

In March of 2003, the director of the ArtMalaga gallery in Spain refused to stage an exhibit by Haifa artist Patricia Sasson. "We absolutely refuse to work with any person related with Israel, as we are in total disaccord with its segregationist policy and we certainly hold an anti-Semitic attitude to any person related to that country." This collective punishment is incredible and unsettling, especially because there are almost no Jews left in Spain.[31]

In addition to these various boycott and divestment drives, individual Europeans have also begun to ostracize individual Israelis. For example, Israeli journalist Arik Bender was denied lodging at the four star Lakeland Cottages in Killarney, Ireland, on political grounds. Brian O'Shea, the cottages' owner, told Bender that he would not be welcome because "of Mr. Sharon's treatment of the Palestinians."[32]

According to BOD, Pat Hennessy, the Irish ambassador to Israel, subsequently and personally apologized to Bender, a "thousand welcomes" campaign was launched in County Kerry, and Sandra McDonald, owner of Crutch's Hillville House Hotel in Castlegregory, requested that postcards be sent to Bender in care of her hotel. BOD's Fiona Macaulay noted that the "religious bigotry" displayed by O'Shea "must be deeply embarrassing to the Irish government who actively promote Ireland to Israelis as being a desirable and open tourist destination."

In March 2002, the *Union Européenne de Football Association*, Europe's governing body for the administration of continental soccer competitions, announced that due to the increasing violence in Israel, it was suspending all European competition matches in Israel until further notice. This means that all scheduled Israeli home matches had to be hosted outside of Israel—and at Israeli expense.[33]

This decision came at a time when soccer revenues worldwide were disastrously low. In protest, the BOD noted that "both European Youth Football and European Championship basketball were still being played in Israel."[34]

## The Media

In addition, as we have noted, the European media have displayed a marked bias in favor of the Palestinians and against Jews and Israel. Perhaps we might say that the media have refused to deal with the complexity of the situation and have instead closed their minds and chosen sides. In his column entitled "Who Goes There?" Alain Finkielkraut wrote:

> Camus said: "To misname things is to add to the misery of the world." People who unconditionally support the Palestinian cause with their eyes closed are not pacifists. They accept terrorism and give it the odious name of resistance. This pacifism is the first lie. The second lie is the words used by Jose Bove in speaking of Israeli army actions: "roundups," "internment camps," "watchtowers"— that is to say, words that imply a comparison with Nazism. Finally, the worst are the declarations of the antiglobalization leader made on television, according to which the attacks, the anti-Semitic violence in France, were perhaps the fault of the Mossad. . . . In place of a Star of David, the twenty-first century is sewing a swastika on our chests.[35]

According to *New York Times* columnist Thomas L. Friedman:

> The anti-Semitism coming out of Europe today suggests that deep down Europeans want Mr. Sharon to commit a massacre against Palestinians, or they want to describe what he did in Jenin as a massacre, so that the Europeans can finally get the guilt of the Holocaust off their backs and be able to shout: "Look at these Jews, they're worse than we were!"[36]

Three editorial personalities—sociologist Edgar Morin, European Member of Parliament Sami Nair, and author and senior lecturer at the University of Paris Nanterre Danièle Sallenave—jointly published an essay in the pages *of Le Monde* titled "Israel-Palestine: The Cancer," which demonized Prime Minister Sharon, nazified Israelis, and denied the singularity of the Holocaust:

> It is the knowledge of having been a victim that allows Israel to become the oppressor of the Palestinian people. The word "Shoah" singularizes the victimized fate of the Jews and makes all others banal (those of the gulags, the Tsiganes, the enslaved Blacks and the Indians of America), and comes to legitimize colonialism, apartheid and ghettoization for the Palestinians.[37]

The European media have been eager to accept accounts of Israeli war crimes without verification. They have continuously held Israel accountable for Palestinian terrorism, and justified suicide bombing as a function of Palestinian "despair."

For example, in 2002, *Le Monde* ran an article entitled "Suicide Attacks: The Palestinians' Weapon of Despair," by a reporter who had investigated the circumstances of the bombers.[38] Also in 2002, former British secretary of defense Lord Ian Gilmour wrote in the pages of the *Observer* that suicide bombing was a direct result of Palestinian despair "induced by the Israeli army killing more than 1,400 Palestinians in 18 months."[39]

The British press in particular seemed eager to accept accounts of Israeli war crimes without verification. In 2002, in its April 17th lead editorial, the *Guardian* wrote that the Israeli Defense Force's behavior in Jenin was "every bit as repellent" as Osama bin Laden's attack on New York.[40] On April 15th, A. N. Wilson, literary editor of the *London Evening Standard*, wrote in the *Standard*, "We are talking here of massacre, and a cover-up, of genocide."[41] On April 16th, *London Times* correspondent Janine di Giovanni wrote, "Rarely in more than a decade of war reporting from Bosnia, Chechnya, Sierra Leone, Kosovo, have I seen such deliberate destruction, such disrespect for human life."[42]

Freelance reporter Tom Gross scrutinized the sources on which those making these claims had relied. For example, Gross revealed that four different newspapers had a single source—*one man*—on whom they relied for evidence of genocide, massacre, and war crimes in Jenin. Gross writes, "The British media appear to have based much of [their] evidence of 'genocide' on a single individual: 'Kamal Anis, a labourer' (*Times*), 'Kamal Anis, 28' (*Daily Telegraph*), 'A quiet, sad-looking young man called Kamal Anis' (*Independent*), and referred to the same supposed victim—'the burned remains of a man, Bashar' (*Evening Standard*), 'Bashir died in agony' (*Times*), 'A man named only as Bashar once lived there' (*Daily Telegraph*)."[43]

Yet, this was not what Palestinian sources told the Arab language media. Palestinians speaking to Arab media representatives spoke not of a massacre but more accurately of embroiled fighting in pitched battles.

For example, the Jordanian weekly *Al-Sabil* reported that Sheikh Abu-Al-Hija said, "The Mujahideen managed to besiege nine Zionist soldiers inside one of the houses, and attacked them using hand grenades and bombs until the entire house went up in flames with the soldiers of the occupation inside. Witnesses said that the occupation forces extracted the soldiers charred and burned."[44]

Thus, HonestReporting.com awarded the British media its Dishonest Reporting Award for 2002. Honestreporting.com noted that the British media were dishonest in three ways. First, "by allowing unfounded rumors to be reported as factual, the media has helped create a false Palestinian mythology over the battle of Jenin," which will make true reconciliation more difficult. Second, even after the truth was clear, "countless residual references to a massacre were made," demonstrating the inability of the media to let go. Finally, the media "continues to rely on Palestinian spokesmen who have spread falsities in the past."[45]

## Chapter Six

# The Betrayal of Truth, Part Two

## The Intifada in North America

Nothing in North America can compare to the sustained, intense campaign against the Jews in Europe or in Israel-Palestine. However, according to the Stephen Roth Institute for the Study of Contemporary Anti-Semitism and Racism, forty states and the district of Columbia reported 1,434 anti-Semitic incidents committed in 2001 by both right- and left-wing groups and individuals. That same year, 1,424 incidents were recorded in Germany, whose population is between one-third and one-quarter that of the United States. There are 5.2 million Jews in the United States; thus Jews constitute approximately 1.8 percent of the total population.

Right-wing, white-supremacy groups, including the World Church of the Creator, the National Alliance, Christian Identity, Aryan Nations, the Liberty Lobby, the Ku Klux Klan, the National Socialist Movement, the Holocaust deniers, and various neo-Nazi skinhead and militia groups, regularly demonstrate against Jews, spread anti-Semitic and anti-Zionist propaganda on the Internet and through hate rock and hate rap music, use Israeli flags as doormats, brandish swastika flags, give the Nazi salute, chant racial slurs at demonstrations, blame Israel for 9/11, and urge that America bomb Israel, not Iraq. In 2000, at a demonstration in Washington, D.C., placards said, "No Blood for Israel," and protestors chanted, "No more terror, no more war, no more being Israel's whore." These groups are national and international, but are headquartered in East Peoria, Illinois; Hillsboro, West Virginia; Schell City, Missouri; Dallas, Texas; Sandpoint, Idaho; Harrison, Arkansas; and Minnesota, California, Arizona, and elsewhere.

Louis Farrakhan's Nation of Islam, the New Black Panther Party (NBPP), and the Nation of Aztlan are pro-Palestinian, pro-Muslim, anti-Israeli, and anti-Jewish. For example, in a 2001 television address, Malik Zulu Shabazz of the NBPP described America and Israel as the "number one and number two terrorists right now on the planet," and described Zionism as "racism, colonialism, [and] imperialism." Shabazz also insisted that the root cause of 9/11 is America's support for Israel.

According to the Stephen Roth Institute, in 2001 there were 878 acts of anti-Semitic harassment (intimidation, threats, assaults, and shootings) and 556 acts of vandalism (arson, cemetery desecrations, violence against synagogues and other Jewish institutions, and other kinds of property damage) perpetrated in forty of the fifty-three American states. Anti-Semitic incidents markedly decreased in New York and California but markedly increased on college campuses. Eighty-six incidents of campus anti-Semitism were reported for 2001.

Right-wing groups insert anti-Semitic propaganda into newspapers; they call this "night riding." They have also mounted anti-Semitic Internet Web sites, or "hate sites," and have created violently anti-Semitic and anti-black video games with such names as *Ethnic Cleansing*, *Run the Concentration Camp*, and *Shoot Blacks*. According to the Stephen Roth Institute, "Holocaust denier Gary Lauck (Nebraska) offers several games, including one set in Auschwitz where the player is challenged to shoot 'Jewish' rats racing between canisters of Zyklon B and a Star of David."[1] Lauck served a jail term in Germany for "inciting racial hatred and anti-Semitism."

In 2001 and early 2002, a number of American anti-Semites were sentenced to local or federal jails and ordered to pay fines. In one instance, Richard Baumhammers received five consecutive death sentences for the murder of five people, including Jews, African Americans, and Asian Americans in Pittsburgh, Pennsylvania.

On March 5, 2003, Democratic Congressman James Moran of Virginia told a church forum that "if it were not for the strong support of the Jewish community for this war with Iraq, we would not be doing this." According to a Reuters Report, Moran "went on to suggest that Jewish leaders could prevent war if they wanted to." Moran subsequently apologized for his "insensitive remarks."[2] Early in March of 2003, one-time presidential candidate and CNBC commentator Pat Buchanan published a piece in the American Conservative. He wrote:

> We charge that a cabal of polemicists and public officials seek[s] to ensnare our country in a series of wars that are not in America's interests. We charge them with colluding with Israel to ignite those wars and destroy the Oslo Accords . . . We charge them [American neoconservatives; read: Jews] with deliberately damaging U.S. relations with every state in the Arab world that defies Israel or supports the Palestinian peoples' right to a homeland of their own. We charge that they have alienated friends and allies all over the Islamic and Western world through their arrogance, hubris and bellicosity . . . They charge us with antisemitism. False. The truth is, those hurling these charges harbor a passionate attachment to a nation not our own that causes them to subordinate the interests of their own country and to act on an assumption that, somehow, what's good for Israel is good for America.[3]

On March 13, 2003, Secretary of State Colin Powell announced that U.S. policy and its war against Iraq "is not driven by any small cabal . . . (nor is it) engineered by Israel or American Jews;" rather, it is "driven by our own national interest."[4]

In 2003, Gary Tobin, president of the Institute for Jewish and Community Research in San Francisco, released the findings of an International Communications Research survey of 1,013 randomly selected adults between the ages of 18 and 34. The survey, titled "Anti-Semitic Beliefs in the United States," by Tobin and Sid Groeneman, also asked some other questions, and yielded some surprising results:

Nearly one-third of Americans (32 percent) were concerned that a Jewish president might not act in America's best interests if they conflicted with Israel's interests.

Democrats tend to be more anti-Semitic than Republicans. For example, Republicans are less likely (12 percent) than Democrats or independents (20 percent each) to view Jews as caring only about themselves.

Thirty-seven percent of Americans agree that Jews were responsible for killing Jesus Christ.[5]

In Tobin's view, "Much of anti-Israelism is thinly veiled anti-Semitism—anti-Semitism in disguise." However, according to Tobin:

We cannot ignore the flip side of this story: Jews are accepted in America by large numbers. . . . Indeed, it is not insignificant that about 50 million plus Americans, or 24 percent of our sample, do not hold even one anti-Semitic belief.[6]

The issue of Israel and the Palestinians is also very hot on North American campuses and in demonstrations. College students and their professors are calling for boycotts and divestment, and taking sides, often in profoundly uncivil ways. Sometimes campus riots occur.

The Anti-Defamation League Web site has collected a group of photographs of banners carried by anti-Zionist protestors in the United States.[7] Protestors in Washington, D.C., San Francisco, and New York held up signs equating Israel with the Third Reich, and burned Israeli flags. On one pro-Palestinian march in Washington that took place on Hitler's birthday (April 20, 2002), protestors held up a sign that read "First Jesus, Now Arafat. Stop the Killers." The same day another banner read "Freedom Fighters, Not Suicide Bombers!" Another mock Israeli flag replaced the Jewish star with the swastika. A month later, another march on Washington saw one protestor hold up a sign that read, "Sharon and Hitler are the same. The only difference is the name."

A trend of violence toward Jews is also occurring in Canada. According to the *Jerusalem Post,* more than three hundred anti-Semitic incidents took place in Canada in 2001–2002. The *Post* editorial "Hatred in Canada" noted that "our synagogues have been the targets of arson attacks, Jewish day schools have received bomb threats, and there have been numerous property crimes and hate propaganda directed against Jews and their institutions."[8] The article also mentions the horrible atmosphere on many campuses, including Concordia University. The situation is so dire that on December 17, 2002, one hundred well-known Canadians signed an ad in the *Globe and Mail* that read, "An increasing number of students in universities and colleges say that they fear reprisals if they challenge prevailing pro-Palestinian, anti-Israel views. If they argue that Israel has the right to exist, they are often greeted with threats, even physical assault."

The *Jerusalem Post* editorial also noted the verbal attacks on Jews by Saskatchewan Indian leader David Ahenakew, who called Jews a disease and justified the Holocaust. He apologized only after much pressure was applied. Finally, a Jew was murdered early in 2002 in Toronto merely because of his identity. According to the CBC news Web site, the victim, David Rosenzweig, was a Hasidic Jew and easily identified as such; he was stabbed to death at an Israeli-owned pizzeria by two men with shaved heads.[9]

## Boycotts and Divestment Campaigns

The divestment movement calls for an end to U.S. aid to Israel and demands boycotts of Israeli products and services. The movement generally claims that it is akin to boycotting South Africa, and that because Israel is presumably in violation of UN resolutions and is violating human rights, all business and investment in Israel should be ended. Yet once again these movements are blind to the complexities of the conflict. They have one, higher standard for the Jewish state, while they utterly fail to critique or boycott many other states that violate human rights.

The so-called progressive divestment campaign has been undertaken in extremely bad faith. Similar campaigns have not been undertaken against countries such as Saudi Arabia, Iraq, Turkey, Nigeria, North Korea, and China, where the human rights abuses are far greater. Alan Dershowitz has suggested the following:

> Let Harvard choose nations for investment in the order of the human rights records. If that were done, investment in Israel would increase dramatically, while investments in Saudi Arabia, Egypt, Jordan, Philippines, Indonesia, the Palestinian Authority and most other countries of the world would decrease markedly.[10]

Divestment campaigns are active on at least seventeen campuses. Additionally, a statement urging divestment was adopted on February 17, 2002, on another seventeen campuses.[11]

Thus, approximately thirty-four American campuses have launched divestment campaigns. Fortunately, not all people involved with these universities support this movement. On September 17, 2002, Harvard president Larry Summers denounced the divestment campaigns in a speech given in Cambridge, as did Columbia University president Lee Bollinger in a statement that read "I want to state clearly that I will not lend any support to this proposal. The petition alleges human rights abuses and compares Israel to South Africa at the time of apartheid, an analogy I believe is both grotesque and offensive."[12]

• • •

Similarly, certain Jews have decided to renounce their right of return to Israel. On August 8, 2002, a letter titled "We Renounce Israel Rights" and signed by forty-five individuals appeared in the British daily the *Guardian*.[13] The letter asserted that its authors "are Jews, born and raised outside Israel who . . . wish to renounce this unsought 'right' of return." The Web site of the Divest from Israel Campaign has begun accepting signatures from Jews wishing to renounce their right of return to Israel.[14] The site does not disclose how many such signatures they have obtained.

Of course such campaigns ignore the reality that Israel has saved countless Jewish and non-Jewish lives. In addition to Jewish Arabs from Ethiopia, Yemen, Egypt, Syria, Iraq, Iran, and North Africa, more than a million Jewish and a half-million non-Jewish Russians have emigrated to Israel and been granted asylum there; more than one million Arab Israelis (both Muslim and Christian) are also Israeli citizens.

• • •

The Boycott Israeli Goods Web site is coordinating information for persons wishing to participate in a boycott of goods made in Israel. It also lists American companies that do business in Israel for the purpose of allowing sympathizers to boycott them as well. The site recently announced that Gaslight Productions, a British film production company, was withdrawing its film "*Sunday,*" about the events of Bloody Sunday in Derry, Ireland, from the prestigious Haifa film festival in support of the boycott.

A San Francisco food co-op recently posted a notice saying that two of its departments had voted not to sell Israeli products.[15] This co-op's committees apparently reached this decision after a great deal of internal debate.

## Campus Violence

The New McCarthyism on campus consists of the anti-Israeli and pro-Palestinian point of view. No other view will be tolerated. If one ventures a reasoned opinion that does not conform to this politically correct view, one risks contempt, hostility, and economic and physical repercussions.

Although North American violence against Jews hardly compares to that in Europe, it is still important to recognize its existence. The Anti-Defamation League noted that one of the more

pressing problems in campus anti-Semitism was the sneaky inser-
tion into student newspapers of "stealth ads" that denied either the
scale or the truth of the Holocaust, particularly by notorious Holocaust denier Bradley Smith, who is based in San Diego and is director of the Committee for Open Debate on the Holocaust.

By the end of 2000, rising tensions on campus led to increased
anti-Israel demonstrations. Jeffrey Ross of the Anti-Defamation
League notes that most of this was peaceful and legal; however, a
significant amount of it "crossed the line."[16]

In November 2000, hundreds of violent protestors forced Bibi
Netanyahu, former prime minister of Israel, to cancel his speech
at the University of California in Berkeley—ironically, the home of
the free speech movement. (Orwell was right: not all pigs are
equally entitled to free speech.)

On a single night in March 2001, at Birmingham University in
Alabama, twenty-five swastikas were drawn on campus buildings.
That same spring, the Hillel building at the University of Califor-
nia, Davis, was set on fire and fliers promoting the fraudulent
Protocols of the Elders of Zion were distributed at the University
of California, San Diego. In October 2001, Arab students at New
York University distributed articles by David Duke and Noam
Chomsky. According to Nat Hentoff of the *Village Voice*, Duke's
thesis was this:

> The primary reason we are suffering from terrorism in the United
> States today is because our government policy is completely sub-
> ordinated to a foreign power: Israel and the efforts of worldwide Jew-
> ish Supremacism.[17]

In the San Diego State campus newspaper, the *Daily Aztec*, a
writer reiterated the fallacy of Mossad culpability and Jewish com-
plicity in the attacks of 9/11. It was in this climate that Bradley
Smith was again able to place stealth ads in twenty-five campus
newspapers, which called for revising the history of the Holocaust.[18]

On April 9, 2002, a member of the Colorado Campaign for Middle East Peace called a Jewish student a "kike" at a University of Denver anti-Israel rally. The same day, campus police at the University of California, Berkeley, arrested seventy-nine pro-Palestinian demonstrators who stormed a Holocaust Remembrance Day commemoration. According to the *Village Voice*, someone also smashed the glass door to the Jewish student center with a cinder block and wrote "Fuck Jews" on the center's recycling bins.[19] The university subsequently suspended the Students for a Free Palestine organization, pending an investigation.

The same day, an anti-Israel rally at San Francisco State University (SFSU), staged as a follow-up to the anti-Israel rally of the previous day, featured posters of soup cans that read "Made in Israel" and listed the contents as "Palestinian Children Meat." A photo of an eviscerated baby was labeled "slaughtered according to Jewish Rites under American license."[20]

On April 15, 2002, a Palestinian student at Illinois State University asked a Jewish student to sign a pro-Palestinian petition. When the Jewish student asked if the petition mentioned suicide bombings, according to the Anti-Defamation League, "the Palestinian student walked up to him and said the petition talked about how to blow the Jewish student's head off."[21]

On Hitler's birthday, April 20, 2002, someone threw a rock through the front window of the home of an Israeli couple living near a University of Illinois campus and vandalized their car.[22]

• • •

On May 10, 2002, I received a report from Laurie Zoloth, director of Jewish Studies at San Francisco State University. In the report, she described a near-riot that occurred on campus on May 7, when Jewish students held a pro-Israel peace rally.[23]

Zoloth described a campus in which daily she had to walk past "maps of the Middle East that do not include Israel, past poster after poster calling out 'Zionism = racism,' and 'Jews = Nazis.'"

Zoloth experienced this as akin to the Weimar Republic. Then she and her students encountered the Brown Shirts. In response to a Hillel student-sponsored pro-peace, pro-Israel demonstration, pro-Palestinians began chanting for the death of the Jews, and pushing, shoving, and cornering some real Jews.

According to Zoloth, an "angry, out of control mob surrounded the peaceful Jewish students screaming 'Go back to Russia,' 'We will kill you,' 'Hitler did not finish the job.'" Zoloth could not get the campus police to maintain the promised separation of one hundred feet, nor would they make any arrests, because "that would start a riot." Zoloth responded that a riot was already in progress. Ultimately, the campus police had to escort the cornered Jewish students to safety.

I sent Zoloth's report to a colleague who teaches in California's State University system. My colleague, who shall remain anonymous, described Zoloth as a "manipulative liar" who was never in any real physical danger and who had exaggerated the danger in order to attract even more private Jewish funding for her underenrolled Jewish studies program at a public institution.

I could not make this up. Listen to my colleague's words: "As repugnant as they were, the Hillel students did have the right to brandish Israeli flags and posters . . . . [H]owever, they must have known that this would be seen as a provocation in the context of the Israeli actions on the West Bank."

Thus, support for the Jewish state, which is the liberation movement of an oppressed and persecuted people, is in this professor's view equivalent to supporting that state's every policy. If this is so, then brandishing a Palestinian flag would be equivalent to supporting the corrupt, repressive, and terrorist policies of Arafat and the PLO.

Unexpectedly, I called an old, dear friend from the sixties, Barbara Joans, a California-based anthropologist. She told me she was about to go to New Orleans, where she understood that American Anthropological Association members had "proposed ten different resolutions against Israel."

"Are there really ten?" I asked.

"Yes, definitely," she said. "I plan to stand up and fight against each and every one of them. Often I am successful. I can shame these armchair cowards with their never having been beaten up by the police as I was, never having gone to jail, as I did, never having had to pay the smallest price for their ideals."

On a hunch I asked her if she had heard about what happened at SFSU.

"Heard? I was there," she said. Joans described a terrifying scene indeed, confirming what Zoloth had written up.

"The Jewish kids were very young and very brave. They were beaten up and they were running away. The pro-Palestinians were chanting 'Death to the Jews,' not death to Israeli military policy." Then she paused and said something important: "These were not marchers who happened to attack people who had provoked them or who had attacked them first. These were *attackers* who were marching."

We have come full circle from Copenhagen 1980 to America 2002.

• • •

On September 9, 2002, Bibi Netanyahu was scheduled to speak at Concordia University in Montreal. One thousand Palestinians and their supporters gathered. They screamed vitriolic hate at, taunted, spat at, chanted, and physically and verbally harassed all those who had come to hear Netanyahu speak.

The police canceled the event, having decided that they could no longer guarantee Netanyahu's safety. Rioters physically assaulted some of the people hoping to attend the event, smashed a plate glass window, and tossed furniture at the police. The protestors trashed the university. Ultimately, the riot police used tear gas and pepper spray to disperse them. However, the police did not intervene when the mob attacked individual Jews and their supporters.

Two days later, on September 11th, noted Palestinian and PLO spokeswoman Hanan Ashrawi gave a keynote speech at Colorado College in Colorado Springs titled "September 11: One Year Later." Although some Jews lodged nonviolent protests, no one stopped this apologist for suicide terrorism from speaking.

Inexplicably, early in 2003 the Canadian government and its Customs and Revenue Agency announced plans to close Canadian Magen David Adom (Israel's Red Cross). This Israeli institution treats Jews, Muslims, and Christians, is not a political organization, and has nothing to do with the Israeli-Palestinian conflict.[24]

In January of 2003, Middle East expert Dr. Daniel Pipes was allowed to speak at York University in Toronto—but only in a "curtained off section of a basketball court, where the audience was frisked beforehand." One hundred police, some on horseback, were there to keep the campus peace. And because Pipes is pro-Israel, a "detective from the Hate Crimes Unit was dispatched to explain the hate-speech statute to him."[25]

On February 24, 2003, the African-American Cultural Center at Yale sponsored the poet Amiri Baraka in a reading and discussion of his poem "Somebody Blew Up America." The event polarized the Jewish- and African-American students on campus. The inviters defended Baraka's appearance as a matter of "free speech," and as a statement in opposition to "censorship." The protestors saw Baraka as someone who engages in "hate speech" that borders on racist anti-Semitism. According to James Kirchick, a student columnist for the *Yale Daily News*, what shocked him was not what Baraka said but the wildly enthusiastic way in which Yale's students responded to his words. According to Kirchick, Baraka, upon spotting Kirchick's "skeptical expression, loudly declared that I had 'constipation of the face' and thus required a 'brain enema.'" In the pages of *The Forward*, Kirchick writes:

> What has been most frustrating for myself and other Jewish students
> is the task of convincing our non-Jewish colleagues that Baraka's

conspiracy theories rise above the level of mere criticism of Israel, and into the territory of antisemitic blood libel.[26]

In March of 2003, two hundred "peace" protestors at York University blocked traffic, trashed a table where students were handing out leaflets documenting Saddam Hussein's human-rights abuses, and pushed, kicked, and insulted easy-to-identify Jews, calling them "fascists," "Nazis," and "oppressors." Reportedly, there is always fresh graffiti in the washrooms: "Jews are a disease." According to *The Globe and Mail,* "the faculty at York has long been dominated by old-hippie radicals, whose causes these days are peace and Palestine." Thus, such professors do not identify this behavior as abusive, intimidating, fascistic, and racist.[27]

## North American Intellectuals

A politically correct madness seems to have hijacked most North American universities. A steady stream of anti-Israel courses, conferences, demonstrations, petitions, debates, books, and articles have—almost overnight—come to characterize campus life.

But this has been under way for a long time. And the truth is that I and many other well-intentioned professors may have had a hand in this. This is not what I had envisioned when, in 1969–1970, I pioneered courses in women's studies and lectured on the psychological effects of discrimination and violence on oppressed, colonized, and racially despised peoples. However, hard-core (mainly armchair) leftists and sexual and ethnic identity politicians have tried to link their long-standing and long-inactive opposition to American imperialism, racism, and sexism to whatever struggle garners the most headlines and foundation funding. Thus, many American professors, university-connected social justice activists, and public intellectuals have written against Israel in rigorously self-righteous and simplistic ways.

Like their European counterparts, many—too many—American intellectuals and academics are passionately secularist, pro-socialism, anti-religion, pro–affirmative action, pro-prostitution, pro-pornog-raphy, anti–death penalty, pro-abortion, and anti-war—unless, of course, the armed struggle is being waged by revolutionaries against the colonial, capitalist state. (By the way, I both share and oppose some of these views.)

Most American professors cannot compete with the vitriol and invective unleashed by their European counterparts in Paris or Lon-don. Nevertheless, the ugly anti-Jewish and anti-Zionist mood on campuses is given cover by the views of writers who are lionized in the pages of liberal and leftist magazines, week after week, month after month, year after year.

For example, in 2001, Susan Sontag was the twentieth recipi-ent of the Jerusalem Prize and only the second female prize winner since its inauguration in 1963. Israeli and Jewish feminists tried hard to persuade her not to accept the award as a way of protesting Israeli military and political policies. *Nation* columnist Alexander Cockburn wrote a column pressuring Sontag not to go to the award ceremony.[28] Sontag claimed that she did not have enough informa-tion to weigh in on these issues and would not enter the debate. On May 9, 2001, Sontag went to Jerusalem and accepted the award. However, she also chose to criticize Israel—but not the terrorist sui-cide bombers—in her acceptance speech. Some people walked out in disgust; some stayed and cheered.[29]

On July 4, 2001, in the pages of *Nation* magazine, Cockburn approved of Sontag's performance; however, he lamented that Son-tag had not gone further in her denunciation of Israel. She had dared to praise then-Jerusalem mayor Ehud Olmert as "an ex-tremely persuasive and reasonable person." "This," Cockburn wrote, "is like describing [Serbian war leader] Radovan Karadzic as a moderate in search of multiconfessional tolerance."[30]

• • •

Noam Chomsky is a linguist at the Massachusetts Institute of Tech-nology. He is best known for his views on imperialism, colonialism, the Jews, and the Middle East. He has supported Holocaust deniers like Robert Faurisson and campus campaigns to divest in Israel. He is a master of Orwellian linguistics; thus, he refers to the Gaza strip as "Soweto like"[31] and compares Israel's desire for peace with that of "Hitler, who also wanted peace on his terms."[32] In a 2002 speech at Harvard, Chomsky again pointed out that the Israelis, like the Nazis, consider their extermination efforts to be counterterrorism.[33] Also in 2002, Chomsky wrote:

> Not surprisingly, the guiding principle of the [Israeli] occupation has been incessant humiliation. . . . Thirty years ago, Dayan advised the Cabinet that Israel should make it clear to refugees that "we have no solution, you shall continue to live like dogs, and whoever wishes may leave." When challenged, he responded by citing Ben-Gurion, who said that "whoever approaches the Zionist problem from a moral aspect is not a Zionist." He could also have cited Chaim Weitzman, first president of Israel, who held that the fate of the "several hundred thousand Negroes" in the Jewish homeland "is a matter of no consequence."[34]

These quotes attributed to Dayan, Ben-Gurion, and Weitzman do not sound right or in context to me—but in my opinion even if they are, Chomsky does not reliably present an account of two peoples in a tragic battle for the same homeland. He is universally lauded for his uncompromising ideological views in which capitalism, imperialism, colonialism, and Zionism are presented as the four horsemen of the Apocalypse, and in which the Palestinians and other oppressed peoples are noble innocents who can do no wrong.

Chomsky is the kind of leftist who, on the one hand, faults America for having an imperfect democracy but who, on the other hand, utterly forgives its total absence in Islamic countries. According to social scientist George Jochnowitz, in Chomsky's book *9/11*, Chomsky equates the 1998 American bombing of the al-Shifa pharmaceutical plant in Sudan (which, arguably, might have killed tens of thousands of people by depriving them of needed medicine), with the combined Russian and Chinese planned famines which killed nearly one hundred million of their own peoples. Jochnowitz writes:

> If the people of Sudan are indeed dying because they can't get drugs, that is the fault of the Sudanese government, an insane regime that allows slavery and is waging a war against non-Muslims. . . . (Sudan, China, North Korea all declined U.S. offers of food and medicine) . . . Despots are more committed to their oppressive systems than they are to their own people—a fact that Chomsky does not seem to understand.[35]

Chomsky seems to hate America and Israel more than he hates bin Laden or Islamofascist terrorism. According to Jochnowitz, Chomsky views 9/11 in a negative light only because he believes that the attacks may have helped Israel and hurt the Palestinians. Chomsky attempts to justify bin Laden's terrorism: it is "caused" by poverty, humiliation, and rage which, in turn, are "caused" by America and Israel. Chomsky blames the current world crisis almost entirely on the Israeli mistreatment of the Palestinians and not on the aggressive and intolerant Talibanesque military agenda of al-Qaeda and of fundamentalist regimes. For this, he is lauded, glorified, and followed by leftists around the world. Chomsky describes *America* as being "among the most extreme religious fundamentalist cultures in the world." Jochnowitz writes:

> This is the great mystery of the left. Leftists are totally silent about the excesses of radical Islam. They are equally silent about the fact that Israel allows dissent . . . and has an annual gay pride parade . . . the most fundamentalist of Americans does not believe in executing women who have been raped although such things happen in Islamic states.[36]

Palestinian-American Edward W. Said, a prestigious professor of English and comparative literature at Columbia University, is by far the most well-known and influential of all the North American intellectuals who oppose Israel and the Jews. At a Gaza symposium in March 1999, Said gave a lecture on contemporary geopolitics. The Arabic-language daily *Al-Quds Al-Arabi* reported that Said said that "the persecuted Jewish people has turned into an occupier."[37] *Al-Ayyam* reported that he said, "Israel's continued confiscation of the land is my living nightmare." He referred circumspectly to Israel *per se* as those lands "occupied in 1948."[38]

Writing in the *Nation* on May 6th, shortly after the Israeli Defense Forces invaded the West Bank town of Jenin, Said decried the "propaganda machine" of the "mainstream U.S. media," which has made "unavailable, or blocked or spun out of existence" the "evidence" of what Said obviously believed had been a massacre. He accused Israel of "systematically attacking ambulances and aid workers."[39]

The fact that we now know this did not happen in Jenin has not led Said to reevaluate his position.

Finally, on September 30, 2002, Said published a piece in the Arabic-language daily *Al-Hayat Al Jadidah* in which he compared the plight of European Jews under the Third Reich to that of Palestinians under Israeli occupation. Said wrote of Arafat that

> if there is no point in looking for equivalence, there is a value in seeing analogies and perhaps hidden similarities, even as we preserve a sense of proportion. . . . Arafat is now being made to feel like a hunted Jew by the state of the Jews. There is no gainsaying the fact that the greatest irony of his siege by the Israeli army in his ruined Ramallah compound is that his ordeal has been planned and carried out by a psychopathic leader who claims to represent the Jewish people. I do not want to press the analogy too far, but it is true to say that Palestinians under Israeli occupation today are as powerless as Jews were in the 1940s.[40]

Were Jews or Zionists blowing Nazis up in the 1940s or hijacking airplanes or crashing planes into tall buildings? Did I miss this?

Ironically, Said's friend Christopher Hitchens (a writer I much admire who, since he quit the pages of *Nation* magazine, has been referred to in left circles as the "late" Hitchens) had obviously not read Said's nazification of Israelis. In the September 2002 issue of *Vanity Fair*, Hitchens wrote:

> one sign of modern anti-Semitism is the obsessive, nasty need of some people to compare Israel to Nazi Germany. It would actually be good if all sides dropped this outrageous analogy, which is designed to cheapen something, namely the Shoah, or Final Solution, the memory of which must not be abused.[41]

## More Feminist Anti-Semitism

And then—we have my people: American feminists, most of whom are also left, liberal, progressive, and secular; some are also Jewish.

Most feminist magazines, newspapers, and spokeswomen have continually, routinely, and loudly condemned Israel as a colonial, apartheid, and misogynist state. Many feminists have claimed they are pacifists and have always condemned the United States for its violent invasions of other countries, including Afghanistan; oddly enough, these same feminists rarely oppose the murderous terrorism of the Palestinian liberation movement, members of which they consider to be "freedom fighters."

For some time some feminist marchers have waved the Palestinian flag and worn Arab headdresses in various demonstrations. (They don't have it right, though, because they wear Arab male keffiyahs. Were they marching anywhere between Cairo and Kabul, they'd be wearing burqas, headscarves, veils.) Feminists have signed petitions in favor of boycotting Israel, including the boycott of Israeli academics, many of whom are also feminist academics.

American feminists have condemned one nationalist struggle (the one being waged by Jews) and backed another (the one being waged by the Palestinian people) and they have done so *as feminists*. Like everyone else, academic and intellectual feminists have not seemed reluctant to render passionate opinions on matters about which they have no special expertise; they already "know" that the Jews and the Zionists are to blame: for killing the Goddess and for right-wing anti-abortion Christianity, the slave trade, capitalism, American foreign policy, and of course for oppressing the Palestinians.

As feminists, they are no longer as concerned with the "occupation" of women's bodies worldwide as they have been with the Zionist occupation of Palestinian lands. From 2000 on, every feminist listserv group that I've been on has been inundated with petitions against Israel and with anti-Zionist propaganda. The Internet atmosphere has been highly charged, tense, hostile, and heartbreaking, and the discussions have been decidedly unfriendly toward anyone who dares to question this exact party line. It's almost as if the feminist world has become a wholly owned subsidiary of the PLO.

It is my impression—please correct me if I am wrong—that in the last three years many feminists have either consciously or unconsciously muted their critiques of Arab and Muslim misogyny—as if they were once more pseudofighting the Algerian war and determined not to mention Algerian fundamentalism until the French colonizers are good and gone. Every feminist knows that the women of Algeria did not get their freedom once the French got out; on the contrary, their situation under Islamic fundamentalism has become perilous and terrible.

Please understand: I am not in favor of colonialism merely because the colonized are misogynist as hell; I am in favor of feminists learning from history when it comes to women's freedom. Whether we like it or not, some of the consequences of imperialism, Christianity, and colonialism were very positive for Third World women, just as some consequences were very negative.

These very same feminists (so keenly aware of Palestinian suffering) have failed to condemn the terrorist attacks against Jewish civilians in Europe and Israel—not even when nearly half the dead and wounded have been women and children; nor have they condemned the physical violence against and intimidation of Jews on various American campuses. International feminists have not organized contingents of human shields to ride the buses in Tel Aviv and Jerusalem, or to live in endangered "politically correct" kibbutzim whose historic and current priority is peaceful coexistence with their Palestinian neighbors.

What some feminists have done is to misapply feminist concepts in the service of demonizing Israel. For example, Andrea Dworkin, whom I personally had had funded to join me on her first-ever trip to Israel and whose work I have in the past championed, wrote the book *Scapegoat: The Jews, Israel, and Women's Liberation* in which she made the analogy between Israelis and "pimps" and "johns," who treat the Palestinians as the "prostitutes" of the world. (I could not make this up and it gives me no joy to share this information with you.)

The one feminist academic conference on women and war and peace in Palestine-Israel, which took place in America in 2002, had a keynote speaker who fully equaled Dworkin's metaphoric hyperbole. Ruchama Marton, an Israeli Jewish psychiatrist, likened Israelis to "batterers" in a marriage. Guess who is the "battered wife?" None other than the Palestinians.

Are the Israelis and Palestinians married? Is the feminist view of marriage that it is like the Israeli-Palestinian conflict? When one says this—instead of talking about West Bank settlers stealing olive trees or shooting peaceful Palestinians at point-blank range or denying the Arab citizens of Israel equal rights—one is both misusing hard-won feminist knowledge and rendering the specifics of Palestinian Arab suffering invisible. Such an inflammatory and vulgar misuse of ideas is worthy of Joseph Goebbels, not of supposedly independent-minded feminists.

I once decried the influence of Jacques Lacan upon the feminist academy and said that those who championed him had degutted the radical politics of feminism. Alas, I said the same thing when gender studies replaced women's studies, and when queer studies replaced them both. (At least I am consistent.) But even I could not have anticipated the Palestinianization of women's studies on the American campus.

On Monday, January 27, 2003, a day before President Bush's state of the union address, a letter-advertisement appeared in the *New York Times*. It was signed by many prominent feminists (whom I know and admire), and by others, including politicians, antiracism activists, and celebrities. I was not surprised that Noam Chomsky, Edward Said, Ramsey Clark, Angela Davis, Bernardine Dohrn, Daniel Ellsberg, Mumia Abu-Jamal, Jesse Jackson, Cornel West, Ani DiFranco, Susan Sarandon, Jane Fonda, and Eve Ensler had signed.

Please understand: I strongly support the free expression of ideas, especially if they are dissident and pro-peace ideas at a time when war is imminent.

My objection: the letter states that "peoples and nations have the right to determine their own destiny," but I strongly doubt the signers were thinking about the Jews, Israel, or even America. Why? Because they did not single out North Korea, Saudi Arabia, Algeria, Iran, Iraq, Cambodia, Guatemala, Argentina, Bosnia, China, or Rwanda for grievous military abuses and human rights violations; they singled out only America and Israel. They wrote:

> In Our Name, the Bush administration, with near unanimity from Congress, not only attacked Afghanistan but arrogated to itself and its allies the rights to rain down military force anywhere and any-time. The brutal repercussions have been felt from the Philippines to Palestine, where Israeli tanks and bulldozers have left a terrible trail of death and destruction.[42]

They do not mention the suicide bombings of Israeli civilians, nor do they mention the long history of Palestinian airplane hijackings and suicide bombings.

They claim that, in America, "dissident artists, intellectuals, and professors find their views distorted, attacked, and suppressed." Excuse me? We have seen, rather, how pro-Israeli and pro-American ideas have been attacked and suppressed on campuses. And they do not mention the much graver and more pervasive imprisonment, torture, and execution of artists, intellectuals, and professors in Islamic countries.

Finally, the signatories write, "We draw inspiration from the Israeli reservists who, at great personal risk, declare 'there *is* a limit' and who have refused to serve in the occupation of the West Bank and Gaza."

As of January 29, 2003, such Israeli reservists numbered exactly 520 and represent about .000086666 percent of the Israeli population. Why is the American and feminist Left identifying with such a small group? Clearly, given the recent Israeli election, Israelis do not. Further, there are only two female names on the list of 520 reservists. Why are feminists not "listening" to what Israeli *women* soldiers have to say?

I am not saying that these reservists are not motivated by high principle, and I am sure their decision not to serve was a wrenching and courageous one. On December 31, 2002, the Israeli Supreme Court ruled that they could not refuse to serve.[43] Perhaps these brave refuseniks are thinking politically about Israel's long-term future; but perhaps the Israeli government is thinking about Israel's survival today, this week, this month. Both concerns are important.

## The Betrayal of the Ideologues

The American and European Left have made a marriage in hell with their Islamic terrorist counterparts. The same Left that has still never expressed any guilt over its devotion to communist dictators who murdered millions of their own people in the service of a Great Idea has now finally, fatefully joined the world jihadic chorus in calling for the end to racist Zionism and to the Jewish apartheid state.

Psychologically, what both groups share is extraordinary rage turned outward toward others, a refusal to look within, an overwhelming need for group approval, an inability to think as individuals, an adolescent in-your-face rebelliousness and uncivil behavior toward certain authorities—but coupled with an adolescent, slavish adoration of certain other authorities, a desire for cathartic violence, for the ecstasy of mob action, and the most uncanny and frightening ability to scapegoat and burn Jews precisely because leftists have not been able to achieve their desired new world order. If some abstraction can't be achieved, then the Jews must pay.

The politically correct thought police have prepared the way for American students and professors to view all Third World people as noble and oppressed—not as imperfect human beings with their share of both heroes and corrupt and despotic oppressors.

Thus, the American and European Left have failed to note that the perpetrators of 9/11 were well-educated, well-funded Arabs with a terrorist worldview not too different from that of the Taliban. Likewise, the politically correct thought police have taught the media that all Israelis are evil, and that America and global capitalism are the new Evil Empire.

The uprisings against global capitalism have reflexively and thoughtlessly tacked on the anti-Jewish, pro-PLO agenda to their cocktail parties on the barricades. Thus, in a demonstration against McDonald's, you will see placards reading "Queers for Palestine." In Palestine and in the Arab Islamic Middle East, real homosexuals are tortured and murdered and must flee for their lives, as must girls and women whose sexual purity is suspect. Demonstrators are no longer being encouraged to make distinctions, to undertake fair, deep, nuanced analyses of reality.

One of the reasons that radical Islamic fundamentalism has had such appeal is due to the enormous poverty and hopelessless experienced by so many in the Islamic world—a world in which Islamic leaders and most Westerners live like royalty. Among those who are starving and without hope, our Western ideas of democracy, modernity, and progress merely elicit bitterness, since such ideas do not seem to include them; also, despite our higher standards of living and educational opportunities, Westerners indulge in immoralities that are envied, feared, and forbidden. Islamic fundamentalists often provide the only educational opportunities for the sons of the poor, charity for widows and orphans, and a heightened and meaningful collective reality to their followers.

To the extent to which Western intellectuals really do care about global injustice it is to their credit that they champion the cause of the downtrodden; not to their credit is their simplistic misidentification of the root cause and cure for poverty and inequality.

Intellectuals, academics, journalists, and scientists are no more important than other people in society. However, they do teach our children and advise us as experts. We assume they know the truth and also what's best for us as a nation or a species. Academics exercise great influence. If *they* believe that anti-Semitism or anti-Americanism is politically and intellectually respectable, they will transmit this view to the coming generations and such views may prevail for a century or more.

## Chapter Seven

# Is Anti-Zionism the New Anti-Semitism?

Such a question: But dear reader, this is the key, and most important, question. Am I only a paranoid Jew who sees Nazis behind every bush, am I hysterically misinterpreting any criticism of Israel as an attack on all Jews everywhere? Am I reacting to legitimate political analysis as heinous anti-Semitism? Am I exaggerating the danger that Jews and Israelis are facing?

I don't think so.

The question deserves a serious and thoughtful answer, so let's begin with the State of Israel.

QUESTION: *Is Israeli policy ever wrong?*

ANSWER: *Yes, it is.*

Let us remember that Israel is only fifty-five years old. Compared to most other new countries in the Third World, Israel has made the most remarkable progress, both culturally and economically, and in terms of human and civil rights. Israel is not perfect; no country is or can be. Like the United States, it has a long way to go. But it stands head and shoulders above its Arab and Islamic neighbors, who surpass Israel in land mass, valuable natural resources, and population.

Israel has accomplished miracles, given the ashes from whence it arose and its mandate to rescue and shelter Jews from every continent, many of whom have arrived from all of the Arab lands in the Middle East and from Islamic North Africa, but also those who have come from Iran, Afghanistan, India, and South Africa, and from Europe, South America, and Asia, with nothing but the clothes on their backs. Post-1948, Jews have also come from North America, Europe, Russia, South Africa, and Australia.

The first, second, and third waves of Zionist pioneers (1880s–1920s) beat back the deserts, planting and cultivating a modern garden that stands beside the rocky wasteland occupied by Arabs, for whom life was never meant to change or improve, and most of whose religious and secular leaders do not want to join the modern or Western world. Ultimately, Arab and Islamic leaders want cell phones, movies, cars, and military weapons—but they want this without having to abolish slavery, without having to develop literacy, freedom of thought and expression, political democracy, or freedom for women.

Tiny newcomer Israel almost immediately extended its hand to less developed countries who wanted Israeli agricultural and small business technology, medicine, science, and so on. Such projects were well under way long before the Six Day War against Israel in 1967, and they continued long after the Yom Kippur war against Israel in 1973. My dear friend Mina Ben-Zvi trained women in many Third World countries, especially in Africa and Asia, in her capacity as the director of Haifa's Mount Carmel Center or the International Training Center for Community Service.

Can you imagine what an enormous accomplishment this is, given that Israel is about the size of the state of New Jersey and has been under continuous siege since its beginning? Charles Krauthammer, writing in the *New Republic*, puts it well:

Israel was our sovereign Island from which we were exiled and the claim to which we never renounced; unlike the colonizers of, say, Australia, South Africa and North America, we are returning to—not creating—our patrimony. And the argument from necessity—that a people savagely persecuted and denied refuge in every corner of the globe needs at least one place of its own—was made fifty years ago, tragically and definitively, in the wake of the Holocaust. Moreover, the last fifty years of rebuilding the land with Jewish labor and genius, and of defending it with Jewish blood, have made denials of the Jewish claim unworthy even of reply. No one asks Australia to justify its right to breathe. The time for justifying Israel's is long past.[1]

## Fundamental Flaws

I am not a simple-minded apologist for the state of Israel or for individual Israelis. How could I be? I was once married to an Israeli—need I say more? He was a Sabra (native Israeli) in reverse—sweet in the beginning, on the "outside" of our relationship; hard and unforgiving at the end, on the "inside."[2] Such behavior is typical of the Middle Eastern sons of Abraham, and it constitutes cruel and unusual punishment for the women and children who are condemned to suffer it. I had a very similar experience with my first husband, whose European sophistication and charm could not hold its own against the forces of repression and misogyny that ruled his Afghan Muslim heart and mind.

Israel is not a feminist paradise. Because of the peculiarities of its origin as a Jewish state, and also because of the structure of its parliamentary government, in which minority coalitions are essential in order to create a functional government, a very small minority of ultra-Orthodox ideologues have been able to wield an influence on secular affairs far beyond their actual numbers. (With the 2003 election of an Israeli political party that is committed to secularizing the state, some of this may change.) Nevertheless, Israel is a theocratic state, which means that the state holds individuals—women especially—captive to a sacralized misogyny. I personally have opposed this by co-leading a successful campaign to permit women to pray together at the Wailing Wall, which you may read about in my book *Women of the Wall: Claiming Sacred Ground at Judaism's Holy Site*, which I co-edited with my dear friend Rivka Haut.[3]

The majority of Israelis are and have always been secular and antireligious and have resented and opposed the stranglehold on their personal lives that living under right-wing Orthodox rabbinic rule has meant for them. The majority of Israelis would prefer a separation of synagogue and state.

But injustice toward women or injustice toward non-Orthodox and female Jews is not what gets Israel in trouble in the eyes of the world. Israel is mainly judged by how it treats its Israeli Arab *citizens* and how it treats Palestinians who live in what has increasingly become an occupation on the West Bank and in Gaza.

Jews are used to disagreeing with one another. Two Jews require three synagogues and read four magazines of opposite opinions, or so the joke goes. Thus, most left-wing Israelis and left-wing American Jews are the first to criticize the Israeli government and the settler movement. And many religious Jews of all denominations have been denouncing the second-class citizenship of Israeli Arabs for a long time; many have denounced the inevitable cruelties of an occupation.

Many Israelis (alas, they have few counterparts on the Palestinian side) have denounced the Jewish West Bank settlers as dangerous criminals. They do not see them as Israel's saviors, as the country's only "human shields." They view them as endangering Jewish and Israeli survival. (The settlers in turn view such left-wing Israelis as responsible for the delusion of the Oslo peace talks, which in their view led to the Rosh Hashanna/Al-Aqsa Intifada that has killed and wounded thousands of Israelis.) Many Israelis have also denounced and resented the financial support that settlers have received from the government, often to the detriment of other Jewish Israelis, and definitely to the detriment of non-Jewish Israelis. Listen to the words of an American-born Israeli woman who has lived in Israel for more than thirty years:

> I was once a radical but now I'm an anarchist. I'm doomed with everyone else no matter what I believe. Right-wing settlers are not that different from Palestinian terrorists. They are both zealots, ready to use force; they see themselves in each other, and they hate what they see. I did not go to Israel to live in a version of South Africa. I know it's not the same as South Africa but it's supposed to be very

different. If Israel can't be a *tikkun* [a healing corrective] for the rest of the world, it does not deserve to exist.[4]

As a Jew, this woman does not believe that Israel deserves to exist if it is not better than other countries. Another Israeli denounces the hard-hearted government policy that funded Jews but not Arabs:

> I remember Yamit [a town in the Sinai]. The government offered Jews a spanking new town right next to the most bedraggled set of shacks for the Bedouins. There was literally a fence between the Jews and the Arabs at the beach. The children used to shake the fence for coins. Raggedy farming villages, with some goats, a donkey, right next to this modern town.[5]

So, let's first discuss Israel's mistakes in terms of its own Israeli Arab citizens (who are also "the Palestinians") and the Palestinians who live on the West Bank and in Gaza.

## Israeli Arabs as Second-Class Citizens

Although Israeli Palestinian Arabs may privately admit that their lives as second-class citizens in Israel are far better than the lives of their counterparts all over the Arab world, they remain second-class Israeli citizens in Israel proper. (I am not yet talking about the West Bank and Gaza.) This means two very different things. First, those Palestinians who did not flee Israel in 1948, who chose to remain, were granted Israeli citizenship, which most value and will not give up. They vote in Israeli elections, have elected some of their own representatives to Parliament, travel on an Israeli passport, go to Israeli hospitals, receive the same medical care that Jewish Israelis do. However, Israeli Arabs were not granted equal citizenship. This is unforgivable, an understandable but huge mistake.

Unequal citizenship for Israeli Palestinian Arabs means the following: the Israeli government has never allocated an equal amount of money for Arab community development, so many Arab village roads remain unpaved, and electricity and water sources remain compromised. In addition, until recently, the government subsidized Jewish-only communities where Arabs did not live. The Israeli Supreme Court recently ruled that this is unjust and illegal. Communities who discriminate against home buyers or renters on the basis of religion or nationality are now violating the law of the land.

At the same time, the government has not allowed Arab farmers to grow certain crops that it has allocated to Israeli kibbutzim (collective settlements), and it has not assisted Arab farmers in the distribution of their crops, on which their survival depends.

Israeli Palestinian Arabs are not conscripted into the Israeli Defense Forces, but they may volunteer. Most do not, either because of antipathy toward the Israeli state or because they are afraid both of Israeli mistreatment and of Arab charges of disloyalty, which often carry a vigilante death penalty. Arabs have served in the Israeli army, but they have not risen to the level of major positions. (Members of the Druse religion have occupied high ranks and have tended to be loyal to the Jewish state.) This means that the many benefits that flow from army service are not available to most Arabs. These benefits include access to a substantial array of educational, housing, and civil service opportunities, as well as access to lifetime friendships and networks that begin with one's army experience.

If you are a student at Hebrew University, for example, most of the scholarships have been earmarked for Jewish army veterans and not for Arab Muslim or Arab Christian students. Arabs may attend, but at their own expense. If you speak only Arabic and are dressed as a traditional Arab, you might very well feel "different," even undesired, on beaches and in other public places in Israel proper. There have also been isolated instances in which Jewish thugs have attacked Arabs. However, this is the exception, not the rule—even during the latest spate of nonstop suicide bombings of Israeli civilians.

The main reason that Israel has denied basic and equal rights and opportunities to its Palestinian Arab citizens is because Israel has been at war for the last fifty-five years with a vast Arab Islamic "nation" that does not want Israel to be there, to live in peace with its neighbors, or to survive. Nevertheless, this unequal treatment is against the ethics and morality of the Torah, which commands us to treat the stranger at our gates, the widows, and the orphans just as we treat the high priest.

Consequently, this mistreatment is despicable and unjust, and must be corrected. However, immoral and heart breaking as it may be, it does not mean that Israel is an apartheid, racist, or colonialist state, committed to the genocidal extermination of the Palestinian people. Nor does it justify the violence unleashed against Israel by all the Arab nations over the past one hundred years.

Are Israelis racist in terms of skin-color prejudice? Some are, but many are not. As I've noted, Jewish Israelis come in many colors: black, brown, olive, yellow, and white. Thus, Israel has not constructed an apartheid state based on racial differences or on concepts of racial purity and impurity. Their policies are a direct result of security concerns and have everything to do with the reality of terrorism and nothing to do with race.

In the past, white European Jewish Israelis received preferred treatment—not necessarily because they were white but because they were the standard-bearers of Western culture. While there has always been a continuous, indigenous Jewish population of many colors in Israel, the Jewish refugees from Arab lands did not come to Israel in the late nineteenth or early twentieth centuries. They tended to come after the establishment of the state in 1948. Jews from Arab lands (and from India and Iran) have increasingly become more dominant, more politicized, in Israel. Because they have personally suffered persecution at Arab hands, they are not inclined to trust or believe Arabs. They also tend to be both very poor and very religious.

Unlike between white South Africa and black South Africans, Jewish Israel has wanted to befriend Arabs in the region. It has not wanted to insinuate Arabs into its infrastructure as a permanent subclass of laborers. (Israel has in the past employed Arab labor for less money than they would have to pay a Jewish Israeli laborer, but for more money than an Arab could earn in his or her village. This is a morally agonizing situation but is not unique to Israel.) Palestinians on the West Bank and in Gaza should long ago have been employed by Arab countries or seriously funded to create the infrastructure for a future state. They were not. Israel employed them. This was not a good idea, but every country on Earth does likewise. The Palestinians allowed themselves—the Arab countries forced them—to become almost utterly dependent on Israel as an employer and on the United Nations as a social service provider.

## Crisis on the West Bank and in Gaza

The thorniest issues, most painful confrontations, and most murderous incidents in Israel may be due to the settlements in which Jews have moved into already inhabited territories and created their own homes and fortified enclaves. As I have previously suggested, the roads and borders through and around these settlements are possibly—probably—now essential for Israel's safety. I mourn this fact, it gives me no joy, but I have concluded that Israeli control of the borders, checkpoints, and roads right down to the sea and to the river in the West Bank and in Gaza is precisely what has allowed Israel to repel the thousands of attempted suicide bombers and mass weaponry from entering Israel proper. Please realize that I am not a military insider and expert. I always marvel at all those who think they know what Israel should do but cannot read a military map of the region and have not seen a day of battle.

The Israelis elected Ehud Barak in 1999 in the hope that the Palestinians would finally be willing to trade land for peace with the Jews. Arafat's corruption and murderous terrorism coupled with his absolute refusal and inability to end the terrorist reign of Hamas, Hezbollah, Fatah, Islamic Jihad, and the Al-Aqsa Martyrs Brigade has made it impossible for the Israelis to unilaterally withdraw from the West Bank and Gaza. Some Israelis have wanted to do this, but they are now also talking about building a fence clear up to the sky to separate themselves from the Palestinians.

Most Israelis now understand that they cannot live together in peace with the Palestinians who have been penned up in refugee camps for fifty-five years and brainwashed into blaming Jews and Israelis for all their many sorrows. And the desperate Palestinians, deserted by the entire Arab and Islamic world—except as cannon fodder and propaganda to be used against Israel—are climbing over fences, risking death, merely to be able to work secretly in Israel so that they and their families will not die of starvation.

While the Arab-Islamic world has been willing to use the Palestinian people and youth for more than fifty-five years and in the most cynical of ways in order to destroy a *pre-1967* Israel, from an ethical, financial, and public relations point of view, the Israeli settlements are an utter disaster. The cost of protecting the settlers and of their preferential treatment has been decried by left-wing and progressive Jewish critics of Israel, and demonized by the rest of the world. Most Israelis do not want to occupy and administer a highly hostile and pitifully impoverished Palestinian population. It is too costly and too dangerous. But the experts all speak at once and all disagree on what to do about this.

Some Israeli journalists and activists might tell you that Ariel Sharon is no better than Yasser Arafat. They blame the right wing for having produced the assassin who killed pro-peace prime minister, Yitzhak Rabin. They blame the right wing for voting Netanyahu and Sharon into office. They condemn the policies of occupation—even as they increasingly concede that the Arab world does not seem to want peace with Israel. For example, according to Amos Elon:

> The vast settlement project after 1967, aside from being grossly unjust, has been self-defeating and politically ruinous. "We've fed the heart on fantasies,/the heart's grown brutal on the fare," as William B. Yeats put it almost a century ago in a similar dead-end situation in Ireland. The settlement project has not provided more security but less. It may yet, I tremble at the thought, lead to results far more terrible than those we are now witnessing.[6]

However, contemporary (1980–2003) right-wing Israeli military tacticians are not fronting for Israeli private corporations who are after natural resources to colonize and plunder. There are none on the West Bank. If Israeli generals were after gold, they would long ago have taken over the oil wells in Saudi Arabia and Iraq. Some may now be thinking about forcing the Palestinians out of the West Bank and Gaza, but not for corporate or personal gain; rather, so they can have a better way of militarily protecting the heart of Israel.

## The Israeli Army

Until the Palestinians can create a nonviolent, nonterrorist leadership, what is Israel to do? Invite their enemies into their living room so they can be continually blown up?

In response to really Big Lies, one can only tell the truth. Thus, contrary to what you may have heard, over and over again, the Israeli army is one of the most civilized armies in the world. Soldiers do not routinely target enemy women for rape or gang rape, nor do they kidnap them and sell them as sex slaves. Other standing armies do this all the time. Israeli soldiers do not confiscate property and valuables for personal use. Israeli soldiers have not targeted civilians to shoot or blow up in response to the enormous provocation of the Intifada of 2000.

On the contrary: as I have noted, the majority of the Palestinians who have been killed in the last three years have been armed (male) soldiers and (male) suicide bombers. The majority of the Israeli dead have been civilians, and an overwhelming number of these have been women and small children.

Have individual Israeli soldiers been jumpy, edgy, stupid, cruel? I am sure they have. They are human beings—*male* human beings armed with guns and with a good dose of fear and rage. Have some Israeli soldiers been unnecessarily cruel to Palestinians at checkpoints? Have they looked the other way when settlers destroyed or stole from Arab olive groves? Have they sometimes brutalized Israeli Jewish dissidents who were trying to protect peaceful Palestinian farmers? Possibly, probably, definitely—but given that this is war, I believe that Israeli soldiers have acted with restraint. They are not hacking Palestinian limbs off as Hutus did to Tutsis in Rwanda, nor are they torturing and slaughtering them as Bosnian Serbs did to their Muslim Albanian adversaries. Israel has not annexed the West Bank and Gaza as China has annexed Tibet, nor is Israel arresting and imprisoning huge numbers of Palestinians as China has done to Tibetans, Christians, dissidents, and so on. In the matter of the (non)massacre in Jenin: twelve Israeli soldiers died because they did not enter Jenin in a tank or bomb Jenin from the sky. They entered single file and were blown up in an ambush in which the streets were booby-trapped. To date, a total of twenty-three Israeli soldiers died during the Israeli invasion of Jenin.

In terms of frustrating and humiliating waits at checkpoints, plus the absence of food, water, jobs, housing, and hope, we might say that the Palestinian Authority (a terrorist entity whose leader has been siphoning off cash meant for the Palestinian people into his own private bank accounts) has been unnecessarily cruel to its own people by refusing to negotiate in a nonviolent manner and preferring to use bombs and terror.

Men can be dangerous, men with guns even more so; but men with guns who are under attack and fighting for their lives defending their homes and their honor are capable of anything. We may say that this describes both Israeli and Palestinian soldiers—yes?

In my opinion, now that we have reviewed the history of the wars against the Jews and the current Intifada against the Jews as a worldwide phenomenon, we are finally prepared to understand who our new anti-Semite really is.

QUESTION: *Is anti-Zionism really anti-Semitism and anti-Judaism?*

ANSWER: *Yes, it is.*

There is no difference whatever between anti-Semitism and the denial of Israel's statehood. Classical anti-Semitism denies the equal right of Jews as citizens within society. Anti-Zionism denies the equal rights of the Jewish people its lawful sovereignty within the community of nations. The common principle in the two cases is discrimination.[7]

Today's new anti-Semite hides behind the smoke screen of anti-Zionism. He or she knows that it's immoral, unfair, and inaccurate to hate and blame the Jews, but because they really do hate and blame the Jews, they have found that anti-Zionism is a popular and politically respectable way to do so. Anti-Zionist views were not always synonymous with anti-Semitism. A little historical background is now in order.

## History of Anti-Zionism

### 1900–1948

In the past, both Jews and non-Jews criticized the concept of Zionism as the solution to the persecution of Jews in exile. Most non-Jews are unaware that a significant percentage of Jews throughout the twentieth century were not Zionists and in fact opposed the idea of a Jewish state. For example, assimilated and secular German and French Jews found both Zionist nationalism and religiosity repugnant and "primitive," and remained loyal to the lofty ideals of the Enlightenment and of the French Revolution—even as they endured pogroms and were driven into exile, or into the gas chambers. Many German-Israelis, beginning with Martin Buber, continued to oppose Ben-Gurion's and Herzl's vision of a *Jewish* state and of a Jewish *state*.

Many European Orthodox Jews also resisted Zionism as a concept because, in their view, Jews were not meant to find a haven in Israel until the Messiah came. Many Jewish and non-Jewish revolutionaries in Russia also denounced Zionism as a solution to the Jewish Question and cast their lot with the future proletariat under totalitarian Marxism. And in America, many Jews actively opposed Zionism and the idea of a Jewish state, particularly the assimilated German Jews of San Francisco and New York. Several modern Jewish intellectuals and writers, most notably Hannah Arendt, also wrote extensively in opposition to Zionism.

Most Jews in Arab and Islamic lands dared not show any support for the concept of Zionism. Indeed, between 1947 and 1956, when the state of Israel first came into being, Muslim and Arab governments expressed their hostility toward Zionism by promptly fining, jailing, killing, or exiling the same Arab Jews who had clearly opposed the Zionist venture and affirmed their primary identities as (second-class) citizens of Yemen, Morocco, Algeria, Ethiopia, Egypt, Syria, and Iraq.

The fact that most Arab Jews said they were not Zionists made no difference; they were Jews—that is all that mattered. Those Al Qaeda terrorists who executed journalist Daniel Pearl executed a *Jewish-American*; they did not know whether he was a Zionist. Historically, for 2,300 years, Jewish communities were collectively punished for the alleged crimes of Jewish individuals and for the crime of being Jewish; post-1948, Jewish communities and Jewish individuals were also punished for the collective Jewish crime of Zionism—which is, after all, the liberation movement of an oppressed people. Jews and their well-wishers hoped that a Jewish state would finally grant human and civil rights to Jews—rights that they had never been granted in any non-Jewish country.

Of course, some Jews also hoped that Israel would be a model country—one that would treat both its Jewish and non-Jewish citizens and neighbors in ideal and precedent-setting ways. In some ways, Israel has done just that. It has absorbed impoverished multiracial and multicultural Jews from all over the world—Yemen, Ethiopia, Morocco, Iran, India, and Russia—and created a modern democratic country in a miraculously short period. It has also absorbed half a million non-Jewish Russians and more than one-and-a-half million non-Jewish Arabs. It has done so despite constant terrorist attacks and despite major wars against it.

Islamic and Arab governments understood that Zionism was the liberation movement of an oppressed people, but they viewed infidel Jewish sovereignty in their midst as abhorrent and unjust. Christian Europe had perpetrated the Holocaust; why didn't Christian Europe offer the Jews a sovereign state somewhere in Europe, as penance for the magnitude of its crime? Why should an already colonized Islamic Arabia have to pay the price for the sins of Christianity in the West?

I must again stress that there are many sane, kind, peaceful Muslims who are not terrorists or fanatic fundamentalists; if they are secular or progressive—certainly if they are feminist—they are being held hostage by Islamic terrorists, whom most dare not oppose. In addition, the greatest bravery (some might say willingness to die) currently exists among certain Arab and Muslim intellectuals, artists, and political dissidents. They know they can be flogged to death, gang raped, clapped into solitary confinement, or placed under lifelong house arrest, have their limbs amputated or be stoned to death—and still they speak out. Hassan Yousefi Eshkavari, Saad Eddin Ibrahim, Faraq Fouda, Norma Khouri, Aung San Suu Kyi, Naquib Mahfouz, Taslima Nasrin, Muhammad Jamil Bandi Rozhbayani, Salman Rushdie, Ezatollah Sahabi, Nawal el Sadawii, and Hussein Bahar al-Uloom all come instantly to mind, but there are many others who have been killed, imprisoned, taken hostage in a variety of ways, and on trial or in state custody waiting to die for having spoken the truth in any one of a dozen Islamic countries.

But in my experience most Muslim non-terrorists are regrettably also anti-Jewish and anti-Zionist. Perhaps some Muslims are pro-Jewish—but if they are, they are quiet, very quiet, about it. They do not hold positions of public power. None are pro-Zionist. Let me also note that rebellion and resistance are psychologically foreign to Saudi-Wahabi fundamentalist Islam, which absolutely opposes individual, human, and women's rights, which are viewed as abominable Western conceptual imports. Marxist and fascist secularists like Saddam Hussein share bin Laden's hatred of the West. Both have quite happily used Western modern communications and weaponry to further their anti-Western aims; they have not turned to Western capitalism, science, medicine, or the arts to empower their own peoples, but rather to further repress them and to establish ever more reactionary regimes, which inevitably leads to even more conformity and despair.

Let us agree that Jews and Christians have routinely been persecuted under Islamic rule. Let us remember that the Islamic Middle East also suffered the Christian Crusades, and was colonized by Islamic Turkey and subsequently by Britain and France. By the end of World War II, both Soviet Russia and the United States were competing for control of the region and were alternately desired, feared, and resented. Both the Arabs and the Europeans habitually blamed and scapegoated the Jews for the sins of both the colonizer and the colonized.

Pre-1948, if a person did not believe that Zionism would solve the age-old problem of Jewish persecution, or if a Jew did not personally want to live in Israel, neither that view nor that choice necessarily constituted anti-Semitism. Fierce ideological battles were taking place between Marxists and nationalists, between secular assimilated people and people of faith, and between colonizers and the colonized, in which anti-Zionist positions were not necessarily anti-Semitic. This is actually surprising because most people were also anti-Semites. Such deep, long-lasting prejudices do not disappear immediately or even quickly.

In this same period (1900–1948), Jews continued to disagree with each other on many issues. They did not want to suffer the inevitable collective punishment for the "crimes" committed by Jews with whom they happened to disagree. Assimilated and secular Jews were outraged by religious and Zionist Jews, whom they viewed as giving Jews a bad name. Similarly, religious Jews felt that in leaving the Orthodox faith, secular, assimilated, and non-Orthodox Jews would bring about a terrible disaster upon all Jews.

None of these views were necessarily anti-Semitic. They are theological, psychological, and intellectual differences, which, however rigid and intolerant, tend to cause people to suffer enormously.

There have always been self-hating Jews, that is, Jews who have internalized anti-Semitic beliefs; but such Jewish anti-Semitism did not cause pogroms, confiscation of property, exile, or the Holocaust. A Jew who held negative views about other Jews often blamed the Jewish victim for Jewish disasters and also tried to distance himself or herself from other Jews in the hope that in so doing he or she would be distanced from Jewish misfortune. This did not help matters, but neither did it cause them. Jewish *kapos* (who carried out the will of the Nazi camp commandants and guards in Nazi concentration camps) and Jewish heads of Judenrats (Jewish councils) in Europe were not criminally liable for the crimes of Nazis. Perhaps they were morally liable, but that is another discussion.

## 1949–1999

Critiquing the Jewish state has never been proof that the critic was an anti-Semite. In addition to its non-Jewish critics, as we have seen, Israel also had its share of Jewish critics. Jews are a nation of kings and priests. Therefore, Jews wanted to see their own ways reflected back to them by the Jewish state, and they turned savage if they failed to see their own ways glorified.

Many anti-Zionist and antireligious Jews in Israel wanted Israel to be more European, cosmopolitan, "sexier." They wanted more American-style freedoms and consumer goods. Many Israeli secular idealists had been hoping for Paris and promiscuity, lambs cavorting with lions in Jerusalem-on-the-Jordan. Even though Israel was the only democracy in the Middle East, to its Israeli Jewish critics that was not enough, because it was also an Orthodox theocracy; there was no separation of synagogue and state.

Conversely, Orthodox Israeli Jews were horrified by the pagan values of most Israelis and of many Diaspora Jews (especially women), who wanted to work on Saturdays, wore skimpy clothing, were sexually promiscuous and intellectually independent, and did not observe the strict rules of Orthodox Jewish life. In addition, many Jewish Israelis, including religious Israeli Jews, strongly opposed the second-class citizenship of Israeli Arabs and the Israeli government's position on the West Bank settlements.

These critiques of and disagreements with one's own sovereign government were not necessarily anti-Semitic. Such critics sought to improve the state of Israel; none envisioned killing large numbers of Jewish Israelis or abolishing the Jewish state. However, some Israeli critics did envision a secular, not a Jewish state. Others opposed a Jewish state on earth.

From about 1953, when Russia stopped supporting Israel, until the end of the twentieth century, Islamic and Stalinist anti-Zionists who opposed Western (capitalist) values mounted a serious campaign against Zionism as a way of attacking Jews, the national liberation movement of the Jewish people, and the capitalist, democratic West. Such anti-Zionists and anti-Semites were joined by a growing number of European and American intellectuals and activists, mainly on the left but also on the neo-Nazi right. They falsely and simplistically equated Zionism with racism, colonialism, and apartheid as part of a propaganda effort to drive Israel and America out of the Middle East.

Public opinion, influenced by such propaganda, swiftly changed. For example, in 1967 in Tanzania, British-born Israeli law professor Frances Raday (who argued the Women of the Wall case in the Israeli Supreme Court) was involved with New Left activism. When Israel was attacked by four Arab armies, the New Leftists viewed the Jewish state as the only democracy in the Middle East and the Jews as a much maligned and persecuted minority—the dispossessed of the Earth. In six days, wrote Raday, "the tune changed. Israel was an outpost of American imperialism and as long as Israel continued to exist, the Arabs would never be able to fulfill their economic, political, and cultural potential."[8] A Tanzanian colleague of Raday's, Guyanese historian Walter Rodney, said, "This is not a war between left and right or between imperialists and anti-imperialists. This is a tragic conflict between two dispossessed peoples struggling for survival on the same small tract of land."[9] Raday noted wryly, wistfully, that Israel had been criminally blamed merely for insisting on survival, and the Palestinians had been valorized for doing so.

It's painful to acknowledge this but the United Nations was, unbelievably, the headquarters for this anti-Jewish and anti-Israeli propaganda campaign. It first condemned Zionism as racism in 1975, under the auspices of a large block of countries that were anti-United States, and allied with or felt misplaced sympathy for their Third World Arab brothers. It did not matter that Zionism was a refuge for the remnant of world Jewry. It mattered only that the state was composed of Jews, many of whom had Western, modern values, and that the Jewish state was supported by Russia's Cold War enemy, America. Actually, for years Israel was also in part a socialist country, for which it rarely got any credit. Like Jews in the Diaspora, Israel was both left wing and right wing at the same time.

## 2000–2003

As we have seen, we have now entered a new era of global anti-Semitism. The continued scapegoating of Israel and of European Jews by multiple groups simultaneously, the systematic shedding of Jewish-Israeli civilian blood, has reached a dangerous, contagious level. Even as civilian Israel is attacked literally every day, anti-Zionists and anti-Semites deny that this is so and falsely accuse Israel of atrocities that it has not committed.

Let me be clear: the war against the Jews is being waged on many fronts—militarily, politically, economically, and through propaganda—and on all continents. In my opinion, anyone who denies that this is so or who blames the Jews for provoking the attacks is an anti-Semite. Anyone who falsely accuses Israel of committing atrocities and massacres it has not committed is an anti-Semite. Anyone who cannot talk about Israel's mistakes, failures, and imperfections without demonizing Israel is an anti-Semite. I am sorry to say that these days some anti-Semites are also Jews and Israelis.

For years many Europeans resented being blamed for the Holocaust—more so if they or their parents and grandparents were Nazi perpetrators or collaborators. For centuries Islamic Arabia persecuted its own Jewish citizens; imagine their outrage when those very citizens found refuge from such persecution in a nearby Jewish state, one that Muslims also viewed as a Western infidel intrusion.

I am forced to conclude—it is as plain as the nose on my face—that the new anti-Semite is an anti-Zionist, that is, someone who is willing to deny a national refuge to only one group in the world—the long-oppressed Jews. They assume that every other group on Earth deserves its own nation, no matter how barbaric its leaders and citizens may be.

## Diaspora Jews

Some Diaspora Jews view it as their responsibility to continually criticize, expose, and thus "improve" the behavior of other Jews. Perhaps they think this is how God intended the Jews to "bless" the world. Perhaps they are right. They *are* right. But what if they are also wrong? What if they are endangering Jewish survival by special pleading the case of Jew haters and killers? Thus, what are we to make of those Jews who, for the last three years, have spent all their energies endlessly criticizing the Jewish state—but have not criticized the Palestinians for terrorism or the Arab and Islamic nations for using the Palestinians as a permanent wedge against the Jewish state, and for abusing their own Arab and Muslim citizens?

My friends, many Diaspora Jewish leftists have shown absolutely no concern when Jewish Israeli civilians or Christian missionaries or American embassy personnel have been blown up or maimed for life; nor have they shown much concern for attacks on Jews outside of Israel. As the current siege has continued and worsened, a few such progressives have begun to mention—quietly, as an afterthought—that innocent Jews are also dying, that terrorism is, after all, violence, too. (In other words, while the occupation is a form of violence, so is the terrorism that opposes it.)

Perhaps many Jewish leftists *are* concerned about human life—including Jewish and Israeli life—but one would not know it because they do not take out ads protesting the loss of Jewish or American life to terrorism, nor do they deliver speeches about it. Their ads, petitions, lectures, and demonstrations are mainly against American capitalism and militarism (in Afghanistan and in Iraq), against the Israeli occupation, and on behalf of Iraqi civilians. They do not seem to understand that the Saudis are capitalists too.

Perhaps Diaspora Jewish leftists *are* terrified, but I fear that many are more afraid of appearing "too Jewish" than about the clear and present danger posed by anti-Western and anti-Israeli terrorism. I fear that some Diaspora progressives are more afraid of losing their positions, reputations, funding, and social networks—were they to support as well as criticize Israel—than of Jews losing their lives and all peace of mind to anti-Semitism.

American and European leftists have continued to impose a 1920s–1960s doctrinaire, socialist-communist style of thinking on twenty-first-century problems. Thus, if the Taliban are stoning women to death in Afghanistan, the political correctniks blame the American empire for having funded them, and blame it again for trying to correct its mistake. Theirs is a politics of blame, guilt, masochism, inaction, and symbolic theatrics. Few risk their own lives in war-torn countries and few engage in deeds of loving-kindness toward the victims of violence. Telling governments what to do is their favorite pastime. Once it was mine, too.

I feel honor-bound to acknowledge that many leftists and feminists, beginning with the National Organization for Women, the Center for Reproductive Rights, the National Coalition Against

Domestic Violence, and the Center for Constitutional Rights (CCR), have all been "right" about many issues, including some that I have been involved with myself. I am referring to the championing of the rights of women and children in flight from persecution and in need of sanctuary; the rights of torture victims, including women who have been systematically raped in war, to prosecute their torturers, both criminally and monetarily; and the rights of prisoners in general and those on death row in particular.

Just because the Left is wrong on the issues of Israel, the Jews, and terrorism does not mean that they are wrong on all issues.

Thus, although I have shared many of the same ideas, I have not always actively identified with or worked with those American and European leftists and feminists who refuse to acknowledge their own sexism, anti-Judaism, and anti-Zionism. (Of course, neither can I identify with or work with those who oppose freedom for women.) Long ago I learned to avoid the various antiwar and antiglobalism demonstrations with their ugly undercurrent of Israel-bashing. Their anti-Semitism is no longer under cover; it is right out there, fueling every march, petition, and demonstration. I am glad to see that another generation of Jews has just begun to learn this same lesson but unhappy that anti-Semitism has forced its hand.

I feel entirely differently about *Israeli* Jews who criticize the Israeli government. They have the right to speak, whether I happen to agree with them or not. They alone have the right to topple their government or back it to the hilt. And Israelis are very divided. For example, I have had many conversations with my most excellent colleague Deborah Greniman, editor of the journal *Nashim*. She lives in Jerusalem, ground zero in Middle Eastern terms. She understands that anti-Semitism is dangerous, that the forces of Islamic Jihad do not want peace with Israel, and that Israeli and American peaceniks have been blinded by their own anger at Israel, have completely forgotten Jewish history, and have underestimated the Islamic hatred of Jews. Still, Greniman insists that the occupation is "killing us from within, both physically and morally." She writes:

> I believe we simply cannot live—physically and morally—with the occupation, so if we value our lives, we had better figure out how to live without it, from both an ideological and a security point of view. . . . We are becoming like South Africa—except that the Palestinians are meaner as an enemy than the black Africans were against the whites. They are mean, and they bring out the meanness in us (they would surely put it the other way around). I see no long-term survival for Israel if we keep the territories. Who knows if we can survive at all?[10]

## Railers, Ranters, and Racists

When someone is railing against Israel, I wait to see if they are also willing to visit their perfectionism on any other people or nation. For example, do they also rail against the Muslim Turks who genocidally slaughtered the Christian Armenians; the Bosnian Christian Serbs who genocidally slaughtered Albanian and Croatian Muslims; the Indian Hindus and Muslim Pakistanis who slaughtered each other and who continue to do so; the Hutus who genocidally slaughtered the Tutsi in Rwanda; the Iraqis, Iranians, and Turks who genocidally slaughtered the Kurds; the Christian and Muslim Nigerians who in the last four years have slaughtered ten thousand people in God's name; the Muslims who for centuries have persecuted both Christians and Jews and continue to do so; and so on?

In other words, are anti-Zionists all-purpose "railers" or are they just anti-Semites and anti-Jewish? Do they ever mention the reign of Palestinian terrorism in the same breath that they condemn Israel's right to defend itself?

The new anti-Zionist and anti-Semite may be Jewish or non-Jewish; he or she may also be Israeli. He or she may be fervently religious or ardently secular. He or she may be a Christian or a Muslim, a European, an Asian, a North American, or a South American. In addition, the new anti-Semite might be a secularist-idealist who rejects the Zionist state—not only because it has mistreated the Palestinian people and its own Arab citizens, but because it has failed to enact a messianic ideal. According to certain ideologues and idealists, if Israel cannot deliver a miraculous, messianic, multiethnic, multiracial, cosmopolitan, supertolerant state, then it does not deserve to exist.

I do not pay attention only to what a person says about the Jews or about Zionism. I also note their mood, tone, facial expressions, and nonverbal behaviors. Do they seem to be overly enjoying themselves when they say they are not anti-Semites, they are only anti-Zionists? Do they overly protest their love for the Jews by condemning the Jewish state? Do they sound smug, overly righteous, a bit sly? The new anti-Semites do not sound cool, calm, or sad about the Jewish troubles; rather, they sound jubilant, triumphant, gleeful, coarse, vulgar, energized, exalted. They sound like white American racists sound when they talk about African Americans, like they are having a really swell time indulging their prejudices.

"Well, the Jews have been asking for it," a left-wing peer of the British realm told a British journalist. "And now, thank God, we can say what we think at last."[11] Barbara Amiel (aka Lady Black), wife of British international newspaper magnate Conrad Black (aka Lord Black of Crossharbour), exposed a London political salon hostess for having said "she couldn't stand Jews and everything happening to them was their own fault."[12] When others balked at her comment, the *salonista* said "Oh, come on. You all feel like that." Amiel also reported what the French Ambassador to London, Daniel Bernard, had said, namely that "those people" are leading the world into World War III and that all contemporary evils could be traced to "that shitty little country, Israel."[13]

Many British newspapers blamed Amiel for having exposed her friends and class intimates. British journalist Tom Gross noted that "in England today, the crime is not actually being anti-Semitic, but rather condemning someone for their anti-Semitism."[14] Gross quoted one reporter as predicting that Amiel and her husband would soon have to "decamp" to Manhattan. Another journalist reported that Amiel was now "unwelcome in polite society."[15]

Barbara Amiel is welcome in my home anytime.

In addition to noticing a sly glee and a thrilling coarseness, I also note whether an anti-Zionist is hard-hearted. One can render an intellectual or even a theological argument against the idea of a Jewish state and against specific Israeli government policies, but one cannot say that the Jews do not deserve freedom from persecution, or dismiss Jewish persecution as unimportant or imaginary. One cannot blame the Jewish victim—and whoever does so is an anti-Semite.

Do the new anti-Zionists and anti-Semites seem to enjoy the idea that the Jews might once again have no home? Does this idea give them pleasure? Are they so totally blinded by Jewish imperfection that they cannot feel any sympathy for Jewish civilians who are being killed and wounded in terrorist attacks?

People do not generally foam at the mouth when they talk about the persecution of Christian minorities in Islamic countries. They are sad, sober, practical. They do not say that the state of Saudi Arabia cannot continue to exist given the evil actions of its leaders. People don't go around saying that Rwanda does not deserve a nation state given its genocidal tendencies, nor do they say this about any other nation that has persecuted both its minorities and its neighbors far more savagely than Israel has ever done.

Some anti-Zionists and anti-Semites express their views very boldly, with rage, indignation, and moral righteousness; they do not sound gleeful, vulgar, or jubilant. They are not enjoying a sly and private joke behind closed doors. They are seriously overstating their case in public and in countless demonstrations. They are willfully distorting the facts. They are filled with animosity. In their eyes, Israel's virtues earn her no credit and her crimes are absolute.

There is something immoderate, unbalanced, erotic, and almost psychotic about how they present their views. (I am talking here about their psychological demeanor, their affect, not about the substance of their views.) They also glare, bristle, growl, and quiver with emotion. Some yell. Their irritable, insatiable anger is a dead giveaway.

For example, was Leon Trotsky, the Russian revolutionary, anti-Semitic? Richard Pipes, reviewing Solzhenitsyn's most recent book about Russia and its Jews in the pages of the *New Republic*, tells us this story.[16] Trotsky was once approached by the chief rabbi of Moscow during the Russian civil war to help Jews in Russia who had been victimized by pogroms. "I am not a Jew," he angrily replied. "I am an Internationalist."

Is Trotsky entitled *not* to help the Jews, not to put the Jews first, without being called an anti-Semite, or without being called disloyal to his race, religion, culture? From his point of view, he *was* helping the Jews, and all humanity, with his internationalist vision. The fact that he turned out to be wrong does not necessarily prove that he was an anti-Semite. Yet his gratuitous cruelty and anger betray something. Trotsky might have said, "I can help a little, not much, but here's what I can do." To turn on a rabbi who is begging for the lives of his people tells us something else.

The anger is a giveaway.

## The Anti-Semitic Jewish Woman

For years I have attended a number of synagogues in both Brooklyn and Manhattan. All pride themselves on being politically correct. Thus, most members remain adamantly, aggressively, super-concerned about the plight of the Palestinians and consumed with hatred for Prime Minister Sharon. During this latest Intifada, they barely and only reluctantly spoke about the murdered and wounded Israelis.

In one synagogue, in order to keep the peace, the rabbi carefully, dutifully announced pro-Palestinian and anti-American marches as "peace" marches and remained relatively quiet in public about any pro-Israel marches. I understood he wanted to keep his job, but this was still very disquieting and disappointing. One day I committed an unforgivable crime in that synagogue. After services I stood up and said that the United Nations had just voted to condemn Israel. I said nothing else. I was not yelling or crying or emotionally demonstrative in any way.

Afterward, a woman whom I did not know came up to me and began haranguing me at close quarters. "I know who you are," she said darkly, menacingly. But she had obviously confused me with Ariel Sharon. Her rage was enormous, totally unexpected, frightening; she was quivering with it. I thought she would hit me. I stood there, white-faced. This was the level of rage I'd encountered long ago when I'd debated people about abortion—and when I'd worked on locked psychiatric wards. I did not want to engage in such a hateful dialogue in a synagogue and on a Shabbos (Sabbath).

I absorbed all her vicious words until I could bear them no more and then I tried to appease her by reminding her that I was still a Jew, still a progressive, not the devil, not her enemy. She would have none of it, and after having her say she stormed off. I stood there, a little faint. A friend passed by. She stopped, touched my elbow, asked me if I was all right.

"No," I said. "I am definitely not all right."

A few weeks later I found myself at a Passover seder at a friend's Manhattan home. I was seated opposite a young French Jewish woman. We talked about Italian and French writers. My crime this time was mentioning, with admiration, a well-known European intellectual who had decided to leave the communist party and who was, in addition, a strong supporter of Israel. Woe! She turned out to be a communist party member whose command of English was painful to the ear. For a full fifteen minutes she skewered both this man and Israel as if his defection from the communist party was brought about by Zionists like me. She grated on nonstop, against Israel and against anyone who would dare support the "criminal, Zionist state."

Please understand: she did this during a Passover seder. My guard was down. I felt violated, as if I'd been dealt a blow to the stomach while at prayer. It's hard to say whether I suffered more from her training in interpersonal brutality, her lack of respect both for the occasion and for her elders (that's me, because I am more than thirty years her senior), or from the harshness of her accent in English.

She was young, smart; perhaps we could try to "hear" each other. I asked her to step away from the table with me, not to fight but because I did not want to engage in a public debate with her. My heart was heavy with grief on the subject of Israel and terrorism. I had no easy answers, certainly no doctrinaire answers. For another fifteen minutes I tried to talk with her about the tragic history of the Jews, about Israel's longtime commitment to semi-socialism and democracy, about the various superutopian pro-peace projects that Israelis have engaged in. Her mind was closed, as was her heart. Nothing any Israeli had ever done was right; the country itself was a crime against the Left.

I left the seder early.

I am not saying that such women are not entitled to express themselves or that I even disagree with everything they have to say. Over the years I have probably made some of their same points. What struck me in each instance was their level of anger: righteous, vicious, merciless. I might almost say it was a pathological level of anger, but I think it is something else as well: these women have been politically energized, empowered, to express their anger mainly on this subject and mainly against other Jews. The very women who might be angry about sexism or about human rights atrocities everywhere else in the world are eerily silent on all subjects save one: Israel's wrongdoing.

In the 1960s, Albert Memmi, a Tunisian-born Jew who lived in exile in Paris, wrote a number of mournfully elegant books about Jewish (male) self-hatred and anti-Semitism. Permit me, in his honor, to say a few words about female Jewish self-hatred and anti-Semitism.

Many progressive Jewish women, both here and in Israel, seem obsessed with the Palestinian point of view. (It seems to be a new form of Orthodoxy.) It reminds me, just a wee bit, of the women who used to march outside the Museum of Natural History protesting the experiments on animals but who refused to march for abortion rights or against rape. I believe that their rage against the oppression and frustration in their lives and against patriarchy in general is being unconsciously transferred onto Israel in particular. All wrongs are Israeli; all rights are Palestinian. American Jewish feminist pacifists are romanticizing or at least justifying fundamentalist terrorism; they reserve their pacifist standards only for the Jewish state.[17]

Of course, both Jews and women have been underdogs for so long that whenever a battle exists, both Jews and women tend to root for the underdog. But at some point, for reasons not entirely clear and which may amount to a form of group madness, a good number of American Jewish feminists stopped fighting for women's rights in America and began fighting for the rights of the PLO as if their own lives utterly depended on waging this other kind of Jihad. Had they given up on themselves, or was this a blind bid for the most-politically-correct-of-them-all prize? Was this a classic assimilationist tactic, or were they truly trying to practice Jewish religious ethics in a secular way? I am not sure, but I agree with Jacques Givet, author of *The Anti-Zionist Complex*, when he says:

> That there should be Jews to challenge the existence of Israel and indulge in lengthy public self-questioning on this theme represents warped thinking, a breach of faith, and a human tragedy. And this is a unique phenomenon; no Algerian, Cambodian, Chilean, Czech (and now, Afghan) exile, however bitterly opposed to his current government, questions his country's right to exist. . . . The language of anti-Semitism and anti-Zionism—blatant, insinuating, grotesque or vulgar—is monotonous enough, testifying more to the existence of a psychological malaise than to any originality of thought.[18]

What does a Jew, a female Jew, do when she is faced with a conflict between her desire to lead her one precious life and the reality that her tribe and species are under siege? Some Jewish women marry and multiply as quickly as possible so that Hitler will not have the last word, to make up (not that this can ever be done) for the missing six million. Some Jewish women refuse to be limited by misogynist tribal demands and insist on identifying themselves primarily in other ways.

A Jew can pretend to herself that she is not really Jewish, or rather, that she is the "right" and only acceptable kind of Jew (assimilated, antireligious, anti-Zionist, pro-peace, pro-PLO), and therefore does not and should not have to deal with anti-Judaism or anti-Semitism. It is not her problem, and if and when it becomes her problem, clearly it is the fault of the other, "bad" Jews who are stubbornly, stiff-neckedly refusing to melt away among the nations—to fit in, get along, disappear. The Jewish problem is not, God forbid, Christian or Muslim anti-Semitism. Not at all. What plagues Jews are—other Jews. *Jews* get other Jews into trouble. They are either too rich or too poor, too pushy or too passive, too clannish or too internationalist, too Zionist or too anti-Zionist, too—Jewish.

I write this mournfully, sarcastically.

## Worse Than Nazis

Perhaps some American Jews, both men and women, hope that if they are the "right" kind of Jews and if they are the first to condemn the "wrong" kind of Jews they will be the remnant saved. Perhaps they are annoyed and angry that the Jewish Problem continues to plague even them—the first among internationalists, yiddishites, secularists—alrightniks. They blame the nearest Jew, not the more distant and powerful anti-Semite. How different is this from the psychology of the most assimilated and wealthy of Jews in pre-Nazi Europe, in Germany in particular?

The problem is not confined to Americans on the Left or to anti-Semitic European intellectuals; it also exists in Israel among what is left of the Left. Recently, one Israeli Jewish feminist announced that if she were prime minister for a day she would get rid of the Israeli military entirely, which in her view would then stop the violence.

As Yoram Hazony, the director of Jerusalem's Shalem Center, has argued, many of Martin Buber's Israeli academic children and grandchildren—his heirs—have rejected Herzl's and Ben-Gurion's vision of a Jewish nation state. Most are anti-Zionists or post-Zionists. In *The Jewish State: The Struggle for Israel's Soul,* Hazony describes how a one-hundred-year difference of opinion became a bitter and enduring feud between German-Jewish philosopher Martin Buber and the two Zionist leaders. Buber's arguments against the Zionist enterprise, both politically and religiously, ultimately found firm and enduring adherents among Israelis. Thus, in Hazony's view, many of the leading Israeli academics, intellectuals, and artists have gradually come to condemn the Jewish state. Faults and failings have now been called crimes. A cruel and self-destructive cynicism, contempt, irony, despair, and detachment have come to signify intellectual greatness and academic tenure ability.

According to Hazony, in 1958, Buber said that "the belief in the efficacy of power embraced by so many Jews in his generation had been learned from Hitler." In the 1970s and 1980s, Israel's most influential philosopher, Yeshayahu Leibowitz of Hebrew University, called the Israeli armed forces "Judao-Nazis" and declared that "Israel would soon be engaging in the 'mass expulsion and slaughter of the Arab population' and 'setting up concentration camps.'" Hazony's thesis, eloquently argued, is shocking and simple, namely, that some Israeli scholars have "denied the legitimacy of a sovereign Jewish state . . . (indeed) a systematic struggle is being conducted by Israeli scholars against the idea of the Jewish state, its historic narrative, institution, and symbols."[19]

In the fall of 2001 I published an article in the Israeli newspaper *Haaretz* in which I begged Jews to display some evenhanded compassion for the civilians on both sides. I was hotly attacked by a leader of the Israeli Jewish feminist peace movement. She said, "We expected better from you. This is some betrayal."

Thus, for quite some time I was almost alone in my views among progressive circles. Most feminists, including Jewish feminists, did not feel as I did. Their sense of injustice most profound was strictly reserved for the Israeli settlements on the West Bank and for the failure of Israeli society to integrate its Arab citizens. They lived and breathed the politics of a foreign country far away, a country in which they were not citizens, did not vote or pay taxes. (I did too.)

This particular crowd blanked out on the terrorist acts against Jewish civilians. They absolutely did not understand that the Islamic and Western-intellectual hatred of Jews on the Arab street had been brewing for more than a century, and that contemporary Islamic terrorism—the kind first practiced on Israelis, now on Americans—was a clear and present danger, a collision of worlds. It took most of them more than two years of nonstop terrorist attacks on Israel to begin to say that perhaps—but only perhaps—Israel's failures did not justify such horrific attacks against civilians.

About a year into this latest Intifada I unexpectedly met a friend of mine on the street. This man is nothing if not informed about Israel.

He said, "Last year I thought you were becoming a right-winger. Now, I think, What are you, some kind of prophet?"

We laughed and groaned and stood in the sun together, savoring our conversation.

"What the hell comes next?" he asked.

"Nothing good," I said. "But I am glad that we are now both seeing the same thing, that I am not alone."

The new anti-Semite says, "The Zionists are a criminal gang. They should be shot. They are far worse than the Nazis," and so on. She does not say, "What a tragedy that anti-Semitism has returned, and how disappointing that Sharon and Arafat have both failed to make peace." Instead, she insistently, obsessively, likens Israel to the Third Reich, as if doing so neutralizes or cancels the significance of the Holocaust.

For years European anti-Semites resented being made to feel guilty about their role in the Holocaust. Having their proud Orwellian snouts pressed into their own barnyard shit is precisely what they experienced as "Jewish aggression." Characterizing the (less than perfect) Jews as Nazis is one way an anti-Semite can fight back. If the Jewish Israelis are as guilty as the Nazis, then the Holocaust never happened, or because it happened only to Nazis, it therefore doesn't count. Everything is equal or the same; therefore nothing has any meaning. (This is also known as false moral equivalency.)

The new anti-Zionist and anti-Semite does not distinguish between Jews and the Jewish state and finds both objectionable in the same way that Nazi-era or Christian-era propagandists found individual Jews objectionable. The new anti-Semite treats Zionists and Jews as if they are one and the same, and what's more—what's crucial—views Zionists as far worse than the Third Reich ever was.

•  •  •

In my opinion, one cannot claim to be an antiracist and in the same breath condemn Zionism. One cannot claim to be an anticolonialist and condemn Zionism. Israel was the very first *formerly* colonized state reclaimed by the United Nations, which determined that the Jews had a prior right and deserved to live there. The Jews were viewed as Israel's original inhabitants (since 1250 BCE) whose land had been occupied, first by Babylonia, then by Greece, Rome, Persia, the Christian Crusaders, the Mamluks, the Turk-Ottomans— and finally by the European powers.

In 1948, when colonial Britain formally withdrew from Israel-Palestine, the land was considered a legally sovereign land. The United Nations deemed the Jews a "people," a group that had the legal right to self-determination in its sovereign land.[20]

I would therefore argue for linguistic caution, preciseness, and narrowness when describing Israel and specific Israeli policies. I know this is hard for ideologues, who much prefer to think in metaphoric, poetic, and ecstatic ways.

One can oppose a particular government policy or a particular leader. One cannot oppose the entire country. One cannot collectively punish an entire country for the mistakes and sins of its leaders. In fact, this is precisely the point that so many European and American intellectuals have made vis-à-vis an invasion of Iraq. These same people have turned a blind eye to the terrorist invasion of the Jewish people both in Israel and abroad.

One cannot say they are for peace and support terrorism—even terrorism against an occupier. Gandhi's message was to oppose the occupier nonviolently. He did not have suicide bombings in mind.

One cannot say one is pro-freedom or in favor of freedom fighters and support the Palestinian Authority. Arafat and his henchmen have shown that they are homicidally and fiscally murderous. However, one can oppose Arafat's specific policies and still uphold the idea of a Palestinian state, yes? This is precisely my point about opposing certain pro-occupation policies but not the right of the Zionist state to exist.

One cannot say that one is anti-American without impugning millions of good Americans—including the many honorable American citizens who regularly both support and oppose specific American policies and who seek to nonviolently uphold or change them.

Insisting that you are an anti-Zionist—but not, God forbid, an anti-Semite—endangers millions of Jews who live in Israel and everywhere else. Scratch the veneer of most politically correct anti-Zionists and you will find a virulent anti-Semite.

*Chapter Eight*

# What We Must Do

So, what is my solution to the new anti-Semitism? I have no simple answer. Who does? Who can lead us this time, once again, to the promised land and teach us how to stop the demonization and scapegoating of Jews that is taking place today, every day, twenty-four hours a day, seven days a week, all over the world? Who or what can loosen the madness that has gripped the world and that threatens to annihilate the Jews and the West?

It would certainly be presumptuous to say, I will. Perhaps only God can. Perhaps only all of us—all the good people of Planet Earth—can stand up to terrorism, fascism, and evil; perhaps only human beings can speak truth to power and in so doing expose Big Lies. Therefore, I do believe there are things we can and must do, both separately and together, to fight the new anti-Semitism. Allow me to offer a modest series of suggestions.

We'll begin at the heart of the matter.

## We Must Face the Reality About Israel

Is there anything easy or fast that can be done about the conflict between the Israelis and the Palestinians? Unfortunately, at this time it's hard to be optimistic.

Whether Israel should have become entrenched in the West Bank and Gaza, whether Arafat's Palestinian Authority should have accepted a less than perfect peace plan are hopelessly irrelevant questions. The damage has been done—by both sides—and an unforgiving tide of blood threatens to engulf the Jews, the Palestinians, and with them, the world. I agree with author Amos Elon: peace might have been far easier to achieve thirty years ago when there were very few Jewish settlers in the West Bank and Gaza and when Palestinians were not yet as radicalized, indoctrinated, humiliated, enraged, or occupied.[1]

However, on December 20, 2002, in New York City, Israeli Consul for Media and Public Affairs Ido Aharoni confirmed that Israel had repelled more than 27,000 terrorist attacks against it since the beginning of the Rosh Hashanna Al-Aqsa Intifada. The mind reels. I know: Israel *repelled* these would-be attacks, but only because they were able to control the shipment of arms and the entry of suicide bombers into Israel from the West Bank and Gaza. The PLO did not send 27,000 messengers who wanted to nonviolently negotiate a peace settlement. They sent suicide bombers.

Each bomber literally represents thousands more. Unlike the Cossacks and the Nazis, Palestinian and jihadic terrorists are willing to kill themselves in order to kill Jews and Americans. They are not taking their chances in battle. They are going in knowing that their mission means their death. The cost of their training and weaponry is minimal. This is a cheap operation for terrorists to mount. Al Qaeda did not have to buy and maintain planes in order to fly them into the World Trade Center and the Pentagon.

In 2003, a spokesman for the Israeli Defense Forces announced that they had prevented a total of 122 attacks in January and February of 2003 and that it was now stopping an average of fifteen suicide bombing attempts monthly. This is only possible only because Israel has cracked down on the West Bank and in Gaza.[2] According to Uri Dan, the bus bombing on March 5, 2003, was the eighty-seventh successful homicide attack against Israelis in approximately twenty-eight months. That means that about 3.1 attacks were successfully mounted against Israel each and every month of this latest Intifada.[3] For precisely such reasons, some Israelis are now reluctantly but seriously contemplating "transferring" the Palestinians out of Gaza and the West Bank. Others do not believe that even

Israeli security justifies doing so. They do not view the Israeli occupation of the West Bank and Gaza as an ethical or even politically realistic long-term solution.

Let me be clear: ultimately, most of the settlements will have to go. The alternative: the transfer of Arabs out of this land is morally unacceptable. But given the escalating reality of terrorism and the complex web of entrenched settlements, it's not realistic to think that Israel can easily or quickly just give up the territories, nor can it give up the pursuit of peace. Most Israelis I know want peace, not war, and are willing to trade land for peace. Some Israelis believe that peace can be won only by winning the war, at the edge of the sword. Clearly this is why most Israelis voted for Sharon in the latest Israeli election.

I have long viewed the Israeli Jews and the stateless Palestinians as similarly damned in the sense that both groups have been betrayed and abandoned by the rest of the world, and perhaps by their leaders as well (although I think this is more true of the Palestinians than of the Israelis). If only these two groups could band together: what an inspiration, what transcendent justice this would be. My friends: banding together solely on this basis is not enough. We are, at this moment, very different from one another.

For example, Haaretz journalist Ze'ev Schiff quotes a Palestinian leader who prefers to remain anonymous who analyzed the 2000 Intifada in this way: "While it's true that Palestinians have their backs to the wall, they nonetheless have notched up two major accomplishments. In the beginning, there was one dead Israeli for every 11 dead Palestinians, whereas today the ratio is 3 dead Palestinians for each killed Israeli. The second gain is Israel's abysmal status in world opinion."[4]

New York Times journalist Thomas L. Friedman, crediting Israeli journalist Danny Rubinstein, confirms that a similar disparity in "math" or logic does exist:

The equation goes something like this: Suppose Israel discovers that 10 Palestinians from Nablus are planning suicide attacks. Israel says:

If we can kill at least two, that will be progress, because only eight will be left. The Palestinians, by contrast, say: If you kill two, four more will volunteer to take their places and you will be left with 12. So for Israel 10 minus 2 is 8, and for the Palestinians 10 minus 2 is 12.[5]

As a Jew, an American, and a woman, I do not want to live under Islamic rule. I am sure that most Palestinians do not want to live under Jewish rule. As a human being, I do not want to live on the same block or in the same building as people who hate me and who keep trying to kill me. I am sure that Palestinians feel this way, too.

Conversely, I have been drawn to, and have loved, Arab Muslims, Arab Christians, and Arab Jews. I love their "stuff." I am in awe of all those Arab and Muslim physicians, lawyers, intellectuals, artists, clerics, and feminists who have risked torture and death by speaking the truth to despotic mullahs and heads of state. They deserve our support. Some say that for their sake, and for the sake of all those held hostage by reactionary Islam (but especially the women), the West should take a stand against terrorist Islam.

By the way, I do not view the rescue of prisoners undergoing torture as a "colonial invasion." Do you? As a feminist, I have long dreamed of rescuing women who are trapped in domestic and sexual slavery against their will with no chance of escape.

• • •

What is to be done? Whom do I beseech to save the Jews and to save all the innocent civilians of Planet Earth?

Israeli journalist Ari Shavit's longtime friend attorney Mohammed Dahla is a graduate of the Hebrew University Law School, the first Arab law clerk in the Israeli Supreme Court, and a legal advisor to the Palestinian Authority. Dahla reminds Shavit that Jewish Israelis are surrounded by three hundred million Arabs and a billion-and-a-half Muslims. In Dahla's view, the Israeli decision to create a Jewish democratic state was shortsighted and dangerous, as was its decision to rapidly, "arrogantly," build "European" cities in the Arab Middle East, post road signs in Hebrew and English, and rename Arab places and villages with Hebrew names. According to Shavit, Dahla concluded that

> There is no avoiding a struggle; there is no choice but to shake up the Israeli society. To make them understand that in the end, the solution will take a binational form: one state, democratic, between the river and the sea. A state in which the Jewish Law of Return will be complemented by a Palestinian right of return. . . . At the end of the day, it is the natives, not the immigrants, who have a supreme right to the country. . . . We are not like you. We are not strangers and we are not wanderers and we are not migrants. Therefore, no one can uproot us from [this land].[6]

Of course, Dahla does not mention that many Palestinians (they, their parents, and their grandparents, too) were actually born in Jordan, Egypt, Lebanon, and Syria.

Dahla does concede that the European Jews who survived Hitler's Holocaust returned rightfully under the "right of distress"; but he recognizes no other Jewish right of return. Dahla does not mention the two million or more Arab and Russian Jews who were also forced to flee their countries. Dahla envisions a single state in which Jews are a minority. He chides Shavit and the Israelis for not having approached Dahla (and others like him) as their one-and-only partner long ago.

> To live by the Jewish character of the State of Israel is to live by the point of the sword . . . and over time, you will not be able to live by the point of the sword. The world will change, the balance of forces will change, demography will change. In fact, demography is already changing. Your only guarantee is with me; your only way to survive in the Arab-Muslim world is to strike an alliance with me. Because if you don't do it, tomorrow will be too late.[7]

Dahla may have a point—but his point is our dilemma. Historically, Jews have always been persecuted, but they have always lived in so many places that a remnant always remained. Today, so many Jews are concentrated in so few places, and wherever we are, we are endangered. The Jews of France and of Argentina have begun to immigrate to Israel, where at least the Jews are armed. We are no longer barefoot and weaponless in concentration camps; we are armed to the nuclear teeth in the largest Jewish ghetto ever.

But Jews and Israelis do not want to spend their entire lives in perpetual military battle, or in feuds or revenge-killings, generation upon generation.

Would that this were not so, but we must be realistic about it. Here is how the daring and brilliant Italian journalist Oriana Fallaci puts it vis-à-vis the Islamic "invasion" of Europe and the Islamic terrorist threat:

> [I also accuse] us [in the West] of cowardice, hypocrisy, demagogy, laziness . . . the stupidity of the unbearable fad of political correctness. If we continue to stay inert, they [radical Islamists] will become always more and more. They will demand always more and more, they will vex and boss us always more and more. 'Til the point of subduing us. Therefore, dealing with them is impossible. Attempting a dialogue, unthinkable. Showing indulgence, suicidal. And he or she who believes the contrary is a fool.[8]

Fallaci understands that the price of war is always high—too high. She also understands that all wars are terrifying gambles (as are appeasement, nonaction, and ineffective action). Invading Iraq and deposing Hussein and his clique will not necessarily guarantee that stability, equality, democracy, modernity, human rights, or a favorable view of the West will flourish there or anywhere else in the Islamic Middle East, nor can it guarantee an end to the ethnic-religious rivalries and gender apartheid that exist in the Islamic world. She writes both daringly and chillingly:

Upheld by their stubborn optimism, the same optimism for which at the Alamo they fought so well and all died slaughtered by Santa Ana, Americans think that in Baghdad they will be welcomed as they were in Rome and Florence and Paris (in World War II). "They'll cheer us, throw us flowers." Maybe. In Baghdad anything can happen . . . the Soviets too were once cheered in Kabul. They too imposed their peace. They even succeeded in convincing women to take off their burqa, remember? After awhile though they had to leave. And the Taliban came. Thus, I ask: what if instead of learning freedom Iraq becomes a second Talibani Afghanistan?[9]

However, Fallaci castigates European leaders who oppose a war against Islamic terrorism; in her view, they do not remember or honor the Americans who died for European freedom in World War Two: 221,484 by her count. She concludes:

What if instead of becoming democratized by the Pax Americana the whole Middle East blows up and the cancer multiplies? As a proud defender of the West's civilization, without reservations I should join Mr. Bush and Mr. Blair in the new Alamo. Without reluctance I should fight and die with them. And this is the only thing about which I have no doubts at all.[10]

## We Must Focus on the Real Problems of the World

Our world faces enormous problems. Its obsessive focus on the Middle East—and on demonizing Israel—is a distracting luxury. It is also heartless, not only to Jews but also to the rest of the world. How much kinder and wiser the world would be if it were to focus its attention on the major problems that affect the majority of its people.

For example, there is the AIDS epidemic, which in Africa now has a female face. Forty-two million people are infected with HIV. In 2002, five million more cases were reported and three million people died from the disease. Current projections suggest that an additional 45 million will come down with the disease by 2010.[11] But there are other preventable diseases as well, such as various cancers, preventable malaria, asthma, and environmental and poverty-related illnesses. They cost only money to prevent.

By the way, war is a luxury the world can ill afford. For example, by the end of 2001, 22 million people were displaced by armed conflict in 150 countries, and there were 300,000 child combatants around the world.[12] The lifelong human suffering occasioned by war defies belief and simplistic financial calculation. There is no remedy to such trauma, and the costs to us as a species are literally incalculable.

Famine remains a major world problem. Every day 777 million people go hungry and two billion are chronically undernourished.[13]

Despite great progress in the twentieth century, more than one billion people remain illiterate, and UNICEF predicts an increase in the rates of illiteracy in the twenty-first century.[14]

Environmental disasters and the human ability to cope with them are ongoing problems, as is the destruction of the earth's resources. More than half of the world's population may be living in drought conditions by the year 2032. Unsurprisingly, the UN Environment Programme finds that there is a widening gulf between those who can afford to cope with ever-worsening environmental problems and those who cannot. Four billion people are subsisting on between one and two U.S. dollars a day. Weather-related disasters are increasing and some scientists say this is attributable to global warming. In the 1990s, 90 percent of those who died worldwide were killed in floods, windstorms, and droughts.[15]

From my feminist point of view, the fights against female genital mutilation, rape, incest, domestic violence, sex discrimination, and forced pregnancy, and for maternal and infant child care, are crucial and costly battles. I am talking about subsidizing the fight against another kind of occupation, namely, that of women's bodies.

According to a recent UN report prepared solely by Arab and Islamic intellectuals, the most grievous problems in the Arab world are caused not by others—not even by Jews!—but by the Arab nations themselves. While the experts (who include Saudis, Jordanians, Egyptians, Palestinians, Kuwaitis, and a former Arab League representative) note that "human development [for Palestinians] is all but impossible under Israeli occupation," for twenty-two Arab countries with 280 million people the Israeli-Palestinian conflict "has been a cause and a pretext for delaying democratic change." There is a "severe shortage of writing," and too many "religious books." The Arab world "translates about 330 books annually, one fifth of the number that Greece translates."[16]

In addition, according to the report, more than half of Arab women are illiterate, and the region's mortality rate is double that of Latin America and four times that of East Asia. (The Arab and Palestinian infant mortality rate under Israeli rule is much lower than it is anywhere else in the Middle East.) The report cites enormous gender inequality and the stifling of women at every level, which has resulted in utter stagnation within the Arab and Islamic world.

As for human rights abuses, most go unreported, and of those that are reported, most remain unregistered by the United Nations and by other international committees that spend most of their time condemning Israel. York University Professor of International Law Anne Bayefsky was commissioned by the United Nations to prepare a report on human rights abuses. Bayefsky's report condemned the irresponsible, theatrical, and prejudiced way that the United Nations deals with monitoring, registering, and resolving reported human rights abuses. Most of the 100,000 "sad tales of abuse at the hands of government or officially sanctioned thugs" that the UN receives each year simply remain unread.

[At] the annual Human Rights Commission session . . . The members were] able to agree on resolutions concerning only 11 of the 189 member states. . . . [I]n almost all cases commission members seek to avoid directly criticizing states with human rights problems, frequently by focusing on Israel, a state that, according to analysis of summary records, has for over 30 years occupied 15 percent of commission time. . . . There are fewer than 100 cases registered by this system annually. Not one has been registered from Chad or Somalia, for example, and just a couple from Algeria and Angola. The treaty body on women's rights, which has been empowered to receive complaints for the past year and a half, has still not registered a single case. . . . Nongovernmental organizations like Human Rights Watch and Amnesty International [are] the natural partners for such a high commissioner . . . but such organizations have . . . at times also shown a disturbing inability to sort worthwhile grievances from declarations of prejudice, as when the nongovernmental organizations forum at the United Nations conference against racism in Durban, South Africa, was turned into a platform for anti-Semitism.[17]

For those who believe that international bodies, such as the United Nations, can be—or have ever been—arbiters of peace, morality, and even-handedness, let us remember that the United Nations has never acted to prevent, halt, or punish ongoing genocide and other human rights atrocities. It did not do so in the former Yugoslavia (half a million dead) or in Rwanda (about two million dead). It did not stop the Khmer Rouge in Cambodia from killing half its people nor did it authorize or assist Vietnam when it finally sent in its army to remove the Khmer Rouge. The United Nations did not do anything to stop Saddam Hussein's Iran-Iraq war in which one million died nor has it done anything to stop the carnage in Chechnya.

## We Must Move Beyond Ideology

We have to move beyond ideology, beyond doctrinaire views, and develop the intellectual and moral habits of flexibility and openness. The situation is far too complex and tragic for simplistic slogans. It demands creative and individual thinking, courage, patience, and humility. I will beg you to honor the path of moderation and caution in all things. True believers and ideologues are dangerous—even when they're right, and perhaps more so then.

The twentieth century was the century of failed utopias, a century in which many millions of human beings were sacrificed to bloody, ideological gods. I am weary of doctrinaire ideologues and abstract armchair philosophers who are always fighting the last war. I am interested in realpolitick, in what is possible, in improving some things by an inch for some people. I will no longer take my marbles home and refuse to play if I can't win it all and on my terms, too.

Make no mistake: Western culture is under siege, and as imperfect as we may be, as I have previously noted, we are more democratic, modern, tolerant, and law-based than Islamic and non-Western countries are.

We must begin to educate everyone about how prejudice functions. Things are not either/or. Opposites often coexist; for example, we can both be attracted to and yet fear or be repulsed by someone else; we might allow them to exist but only "in their place," not in our place. Prejudice is complex, not simple. White racists do not "hate" dark-skinned people. They like them well enough if they know their place. Most men do not "hate" women. In fact, they will protect and cherish those women who know their place. Historically, Muslims accepted Jews "in their place," which meant in ghettoes and as second- or third-class citizens.

We must try to reject scapegoating as a psychological weapon. Simply because we find ourselves frustrated and angry does not mean that we can necessarily solve our problems by blaming someone else.

Two competing rights can coexist, when no one is wrong and no one is right. Perhaps we must learn to "sit with" a problem, for as long as it takes, until progress is made in a nonviolent way. Instead of warriors with bombs and chemicals, the world needs warriors of peace with wise words, patience, and faith to outlast the guns of war and the sands of time.

Many people refuse to question religious or political authority; others do nothing but challenge such authority all the time. But more and more people have come to understand that not all leaders are benevolent or even benign, that many leaders routinely sacrifice the majority and serve only a small elite, and that some leaders are incredibly mediocre, corrupt, deceptive, insane, and evil.

• • •

Ah, Chesler: have you forgotten all about the evils of empire, the sins of imperialism and colonialism, the fight against patriarchy? No, I have not, but my priorities have changed, my analysis has deepened; I have become more religious, less secular. I have not changed my mind about a woman's right to freedom and independence, but I've had my say about this. I do not like to repeat myself; I have moved on.

Now I see that Western intellectuals are leading the Islamic mob. The French—who gave us the Enlightenment—were first to do so. My conclusion: you cannot necessarily trust your professors and other intellectuals (academics and journalists) to tell you the truth. Therefore, you must learn to take what authorities tell you with more than the proverbial grain of salt. You must learn to think for yourself and always to read between the lines.

I personally mistrust any intellectual, academic, or journalist who engages in savage sound bites instead of thought, who views a debate as if it were a blood sport, who does not allow for the possibility that his or her opponents may be partially right and entirely honorable. If people must disagree with one another, they may do so firmly but respectfully. Mean-spiritedness has no place in human communication; it obscures by intimidation, it does not illuminate. It never opens the heart, which is the first step toward intimacy with God and with other human beings.

One must also keep an open mind. One's opponent may actually have a point.

Most people are not trained to think for themselves or as experts, nor are they trained to resist believing what others around them think. Therefore, perfectly nice people are easy targets for propagandists. Not to believe what a loved family member or a respected religious authority tells you is to risk being seen as disloyal; one may be ostracized for thinking independently.

I would like everyone on Planet Earth to be trained in independent thinking and intellectual disobedience. Ideology is often mindless, inflexible, cruel. But independent thought is a powerful virtue. Tyrants fear it. This is probably why the philosopher Socrates was sentenced to death. He infected the youth, dangerously, with a love of independent, rational, deductive thinking.

## The Jews Must Stop Fighting Among Themselves

Dare I say it? I must. I implore Jews to stop fighting with one another. Even if we disagree, we must try to do so respectfully, soulfully. I am psychologically very sensitive to Jewish self-hatred and anti-Semitism within the Diaspora. I fear it may very well function as a fifth column. I do not, however, think that other Jews are my main enemies. It is important for Jews to remember this. Even if all Jews saw eye-to-eye on everything, we would still have real enemies whose goal in life is to kill us and to drive a Jewish presence out of the Middle East.

There is an old joke about two Jews on a desert island who form four political parties. It's a cliché but painfully true that Jews are notorious for their contentious, internecine, parochial quarrels. It's a tradition that might have begun in Talmudic discussions, in "pilpuling" (hairsplitting) over the true meaning of some obscure phrase, word, letter, or punctuation mark in the Torah or Talmud. But it's gone too far. Jews must learn to unite, not splinter; to coalesce, not blow apart; to be more forgiving and tolerant and less rigid and rageful toward one another.

From now on I will try not to speak badly of other Jews or to dismiss their views in a hardhearted and contemptuous way. I will try to see God in them. I will speak softly with them—especially if I happen to disagree with them.

Thus, although I have criticized pro-PLO Jewish, left, and feminist views in this book, let me say that I also see merit in these views. There is something holy and Jewishly ethical about weeping for your enemy's downfall and pain. According to midrash, the angels began to sing as the Egyptians began to drown in the sea. God said, "My creatures are drowning and you're singing?" God's teaching stopped the angels midsong. The Bible tells us that as she sang a victory song, Dvorah, prophet and judge, also understood that Israel's mighty foe Sisera (whom Yael the warrior had just slain) was also his mother's son and that Sisera's mother would soon be weeping.

Beruriah, the second-century scholar and wife of the rabbinic sage Rabbi Meir, wisely advised, "Don't pray for the destruction of an evil person. Just pray for the destruction of evil."

Thus, those who caution Jews and Israelis not to hate or demonize all Palestinians, all Muslims, or all Arabs are following an honorable Jewish path—but so are those who believe that terrorism must be fought, not appeased.

## We Must Be Fair to Israel

A recent survey of 1,386 Jewish Americans found that after nearly three years of terrorist violence against Israelis, and post 9/11, American Jews have hardened their attitudes toward terrorists and toward the Palestinians. But even more important, American Jews have not deepened their sense of attachment to or involvement with Israel. American Jews see Israel as a dangerous place to visit. Most American Jews are "ambivalent loyalists" with no clear idea of what they or Israel should do. Younger American Jews are willing to visit or live in Israel; older American Jews are not.[18]

Thus, as we have seen in this book, many American Jews do not identify as Zionists; in addition, some strongly oppose the current government of Israel. Most American Jews are, above all, Americans, not Israelis, and would have a hard time living in Israel, even in times of peace and prosperity. Israel has developed a distinctly Israeli culture, one mired in poverty, contradiction, danger, and glory. Most American Jews (with the exception of young ultra-Orthodox idealists) have no reason and are not likely to ever leave America for Israel. Unlike the Jews in France or in Argentina, America has, so far, been good to the Jews.

But I hope that American and Diaspora Jews are willing to learn from Jewish history and that they will come to understand that they must not desert Israel, for Israel is our heart and soul and the best hedge we have against the out-of-control new anti-Semitism and, God forbid, against any future attempts to exterminate us as a people. Israel is also the heart of the Western world, its Holy Land, and what happens to Israel matters to people of faith everywhere. How Jews relate to Israel now will reflect on us forever. Actually, how non-Jews relate to Israel will also reflect on us all forever.

In Biblical times, non-Jews played a vital role in protecting the Jewish people; in doing so, they hastened the coming of the Messiah. Perhaps this tradition still holds true today.

Nevertheless, I must begin with the Jews. Each Jew must find a way to support Israel. There are many ways to do so. Each Jew must think of himself or herself as the most precious resource that Israel has at this moment, because it is true. Israel does not have oil but it has us as its goodwill ambassadors, truth tellers, goads, and conscience. Therefore, Jews have to do whatever we can to combat Israel's demonization and isolation, and to keep her people alive, whole, ethical, and in good enough spirits.

For example, in order to assist the failing Israeli economy, Diaspora Jews can purchase Israeli goods over the Internet and organize home or office-based parties where they can display Israeli products and sell them to their officemates, friends, and neighbors. Perhaps each synagogue and Jewish community center can do likewise on an ongoing basis. Perhaps over coffee and pastry one can also lead a discussion about the Big Lies that are being told about Jews and Israel, and engage people in thinking about what *they* can do.

Jews can send up to 10 percent of their income to Israel earmarked for the recovery of Israelis who have been wounded in this latest Intifada—or for Israeli military needs. This is a personal and political choice. Jews can also send money to Palestinian civilians who have been traumatized and wounded. Doing so in the name of the Jewish people is important.

Early in 2003, Germany announced its decision to stop all arms sales to Israel. Other European countries followed suit. In return, Israel cancelled its annual multimillion dollar contract with Germany for buses. Perhaps the Europeans and Muslims who have organized boycotts of Israeli products and services should themselves learn that boycotts can work both ways. Those who agree with such an approach might do two things: *start* buying Israeli, Italian, Canadian, British, American, and Japanese products and *stop* buying Evian water, clothing, and cosmetics from France; Godiva chocolates, watches, ski-equipment, or anything else from Switzerland and Belgium; cheese, coffee, and furniture from Norway, Sweden, Denmark, and Holland; melons from Spain; anything (cars, clothing) from Germany. Stop traveling to these countries as well. It is important to remember that the European Union gives $10 million a month to the Palestinian Authority, which is used to buy, import, and train Muslim terrorists and their weapons of mass destruction. For those who elect to follow this boycott: tell others what you are doing and why. Educate your friends, colleagues, and salespeople about your choices.[19]

Jews can develop and present antiprejudice, pro-Israel, propeace, and pro-justice programs in their communities, at their colleges and graduate schools, and at their professional conferences. Some American Jews may wish to work with American Christians and Muslims of faith on this; some may wish to develop programs with Palestinians. We must also continue to write letters to newspaper and magazine editors each and every time lies are told about the Jews and about Israel. We must also do so when lies are told about America and the West.

Jews can subsidize a family trip or organize a community trip to Israel. Upon their return home they may share their views and the words of Jewish, Christian, and Muslim Israelis with their communities. Israeli hotels are almost completely deserted and have been so for a long time. (I know: the Palestinians who live in dreadful poverty and who are also under siege have no tourist industry either, but I hope that by now you understand that this is not entirely Israel's fault.) In any event, Israelis are moved and restored when someone from abroad comes to visit. Being there in the flesh is important, both psychologically and as an expression of solidarity. Actually, friends who have visited Israel in the last three years have also described the people as so sweet and soulful that the visitor— who sought to uplift—came away uplifted.

At a time when Israel and the Jews are in danger, Diaspora Jews can decide to become Israeli citizens. Some say that the Jews of Israel will never again be as endangered as Jews were during the European Holocaust.

Jews can also offer their professional services to their Israeli counterparts for a time. Some professions may require fluency in Hebrew, others may not. Even a three-month stint might make a real contribution to morale and would provide the memories of a lifetime, and an honored place in the world to come.

Jews can "adopt" an Israeli family that has been traumatized and wounded by this latest Intifada. They can write letters and place phone calls; they can listen, be participant-witnesses, so to speak. We can "be there" even from afar. After all, we *are* family.

Jews may also invite Israelis to their homes and countries for some rest and recreation. Perhaps some of us can even exchange apartments with Israeli Jews for a month.

Jews can organize peace missions to the region. For example, those American Jews who honestly believe that "talking" will work—*must* work—must go and talk to both the Palestinian people and to their leaders. But of course they must also talk to the Israeli people and their leaders.

Jews can volunteer to be human shields, to put their bodies where their ideas are, to place themselves in danger in the hope that this will protect others who are more vulnerable and be a deterrent to military attacks, an appeal to conscience. This is very hard to do. It is dangerous. One would have to be very strong, fortified, politically and spiritually. Only long-time committed social justice activists, young idealists, and religious Jews may be able to do this.

Thus, a group that chooses to do this would make it known to the immediate world that they would be riding the Israeli buses, sitting at Israeli cafes, shopping in Israeli malls. Intellectuals especially might consider doing this, as might celebrities and dignitaries of all kinds. I wonder whether those Americans and Europeans who have been criticizing Israel for the last three years would consider doing this—along with similar kinds of nonviolent human shield work among Palestinian civilians.

By the way, in my view, it was bizarre that American and European so-called idealists flocked to protect Yasser Arafat in Ramallah in 2002, but not the people whom he has served so poorly. Thus, I am not recommending that anyone give cover to terrorists. I am talking about soberly sharing the ongoing fate of ordinary Palestinian civilians—*in the name of the Jewish people*.

Whatever I have suggested that Jews do—I wholeheartedly urge non-Jews to consider doing as well. Perhaps people of faith are the most likely to put their bodies where their principles are, but secularists have also done this. It would be wonderful if large groups of Baptists, Catholics, Jews, Buddhists, Muslims, and atheists came to the Holy Land, publicly mourned the lives taken by terrorism, and generated an international conversation.

I do not think such efforts have the power to stop a terrorist bomb from exploding, but they do have the power to keep good people connected, to keep a vision of love and peace alive.

## We Must Form Jewish-Christian Alliances

I also think that Jews must make common cause with the Christian left, right, and center, with whom we may disagree on other fundamental issues, in America and throughout the world. Jews must work with anyone and everyone who is willing to help us fight for Jewish and Israeli survival.

I believe that European and North American Christians have a historic opportunity to ally themselves with Jews and Israelis. Although I want such an alliance to exist and to endure, I still cannot minimize Christianity's past role in the persecution of the Jews. I can only hope and pray that enough Christians of good will are ready to protect us—precisely because of the Church's unholy role in the persecution of the Jews—and for God's sake.

Actually, a group like this exists: the International Fellowship of Christians and Jews. Their Stand for Israel program recommends that Christians become a "blessing to Israel," first by "praying for the peace of Jerusalem"; second, by "learning about the Jewish roots of Christianity"; third, by "walk[ing] the land of the Bible . . . [to] encourage the people of Israel and [to] reassure them they are not alone"; fourth, by fostering "solidarity with Israel by speaking out for her"; and fifth, by financially supporting immigration to Israel. They state:

> Christians have a moral obligation to stand in solidarity with Israel
> and be a blessing to her—to preserve Israel and to be a source of
> healing, reconciliation, and comfort to the Jewish people. This is
> particularly true in the aftermath of the Holocaust that destroyed six
> million Jews—one third of the nation of Israel—often at the hands
> of Christians and with little, if any, resistance from the Church.[20]

I am very moved by these words. These good people believe that Jews have an important role to play in matters both human and divine. In his Yom Kippur sermon of 5763 (2002–2003), Rabbi

Harold Kushner suggested that perhaps the "Jews are in fact different . . . and play the role for the world that the canary used to play for the coal miners. . . . We are the world's early warning system. Where there is evil, where there is hatred, it affects us first."[21]

I agree with him.

Kushner sees Jews as "a magnet for hatred," not because something is wrong with us but "because there is something terribly wrong with [those who hate us]." In his view, "[this] seems to be our fate." Kushner therefore recommends that Jews embrace our destiny and in so doing, experience satisfaction in leading a "spiritually serious life." In his view, living consciously as Jews will not necessarily make our lives easier, but it will "make our lives more meaningful because it will bless the world."[22]

## We Must Form Alliances with the Palestinians

Similarly, I hope that Israelis remain ever open to peace with the Palestinians, ever ready to assist them in the creation of a peaceful, modern, and democratic Palestinian state. Professor of International Studies Fouad Ajami writes that "histories can be remade and transcended" and calls upon the Palestinians to "choose a new, sober history" and renounce "the past."[23]

A handful of moderate Palestinians have called for the cessation of violence against Israel. We must honor their goodwill and bravery. Israelis must talk to them. For example, Sari Nusseibeh has made the following radical proposal:

> The Palestinians have to resurrect the spirit of Christ to absorb the sense of pain and insult they feel and control it, and not let it determine the way they act toward Israel. They have to realize that an act of violence does not serve their interest. This is a gigantic undertaking.[24]

In 2002, ten Palestinian leaders, including Nusseibeh, and 650 others signed a letter that appeared in the Arabic language newspaper *Al-Quds Al-Arabi*. They asked all those who "stand behind military operations which target civilians in Israel to reconsider their policy and refrain from recruiting young Palestinians for the purpose of mounting such military attacks. We strongly believe that actions of this type aggravate the current critical situation and augment hatred between the Palestinian and Israeli peoples."[25]

Still, I do not delude myself. Most Palestinians and most of the Islamic Arab leadership and peoples have so far shown no moral introspection or any desire for peace with Israel. As Israeli journalist Yossi Klein Halevi notes, "The Palestinians refuse to admit that a good deal of their suffering has been self-inflicted." In his view, the ten Palestinian leaders who signed the letter just mentioned were essentially rejecting suicide bombing as "ineffective," not as morally repugnant. He writes:

> Few Palestinians have challenged the historical revisionism now increasingly prevalent in Arab culture that denies the ancient roots of Jews in this land, the existence of the gas chambers and even Arab involvement in the Sept. 11 attacks. In my journey into Palestinian Islam, I encountered the profound Muslim ability to live daily life with a constant awareness of mortality—an awareness that can create humility, a prerequisite for reconciliation between enemies. Peace will come only through mutual introspection and atonement. Many Israelis went far in trying to understand Palestinian claims and grievances. To resume that necessary process among Israelis now requires a self-critical moral dialogue among Palestinians.[26]

## We Must Restore Campus Civility

As academics and intellectuals, we must model, set a standard for, an atmosphere of serious campus civility when the issues of racism, the Middle East, and the Jews are discussed. Civility must prevail when any issue is discussed, especially an incendiary one. I am not interested in censoring any view. I gain nothing by continued Palestinian statelessness or misery. However, I am interested in ensuring that our college and graduate students are free to express different views without being subjected to verbal cruelty, humiliation, ostracism, and physical danger.

In the past, I have debated opponents of abortion and fathers' rights activists on campus. There is a difference between a reasoned and respectful debate on abortion or child custody and one that is run by misogynist goons and thugs whose modus operandi include planted audience members who boo, jeer, and drown out what I have to say, who are trained to seize the microphone to ask one hostile question after another, and to accost me outside the auditorium in a picket line.

We must initiate very different kinds of campus discussions about Israel, the Jews, the Palestinians, Islam, the Middle East, and Islamic terrorism. In addition, I suggest that we organize town hall meetings on these subjects in every city and in each neighborhood. It is never too late to begin. I would like to see antidemonization textbooks and curricula in religious and public grade schools. I am suggesting that we

- Speak truth to power both within the academy and within our communities.

- Educate ourselves, others, and the coming generations about the nature of prejudice, the long history of anti-Semitism, what terrorism is and does, the conflict in the Middle East, and the nature of the new anti-Semitism.

- Talk to the media. Don't stop. Write letters. Continue to rebut the anti-Semitic propaganda.

## We Must Fight the Big Lies

As I've just said, we must speak truth to power. We must expose the Big Lies in an ongoing way. This is risky. People who expose naked emperors are subject to both ridicule and danger. Being a whistleblower has serious consequences. However, if enough people do it—and keep on doing it—the tide will begin to shift, if only slightly. Also, given the gravity of the situation, heroism is our only alternative.

We must not allow slander to pass unremarked. Whenever we hear a racist remark, we must challenge it. We may do so patiently, firmly, even lovingly. Most of us have not been present when an actual lynching has taken place, but we are situated everywhere within a culture that gives tacit approval to prejudice. Our silence is taken as approval, our passivity or indifference signals that we will do nothing to stop the atrocities or to punish their perpetrators.

We the people must demand that our clergy and political leaders refuse to look the other way or to collaborate with anti-Semitic propaganda and deeds of anti-Semitic violence. Those who spray swastikas must be found and prosecuted. Those who attempt to burn down synagogues or threaten Jews must be found and prosecuted. Those who beat up Jews must be prosecuted to the full extent of the law. Those who produce libelous propaganda must be exposed, criticized, even sued, which may limit their ability to tell dangerous lies.

Thus, we must tell our friends, students, neighbors, leaders, and opponents that, contrary to propaganda, the Jews and the Zionists do not control America, the banks, or the media; Zionists are not responsible for 9/11 or for the misery in Arab and Muslim countries. Israel is not a racist, colonialist, or apartheid state. The worst human rights record belongs not to Israel but to those countries that are either attacking or demonizing Israel.

We must say that what *is* true is that Israel has been overly scrutinized, demonized, and sanctioned for more minor crimes while other countries that routinely commit far graver atrocities have not been noticed at all.

It is important always to remind people that Israel is the only democracy in the Middle East; that given the danger and incredible stress of daily battles, Israeli soldiers have behaved with more restraint than most professional armies would under the circumstances; that the Jews have always been persecuted, that they are entitled to a homeland just as every other group on Earth is.

A 2003 survey of 1,013 randomly selected Americans between the ages of 18 and 34 found that 34 percent of these young Americans believe that the "Jews have too much influence on Wall Street"; 34 percent also believe that "Jewish control of the media distorts the news"; and 37 percent believe that Jews were "responsible for killing Jesus Christ." Let's address these Big Lies right here and now.[27]

BIG LIE 1:  *The Jews control Wall Street.*

This reminds me of a Jewish joke. A little old Jewish man is sitting on a park bench reading *Mein Kampf*. He has a stack of Ku Klux Klan newspapers by his side. "What, have you lost your mind?" his friend exclaims. "No," he replies. "When I read the Jewish papers they tell me that the Nazis are back and they're going to get me. The anti-Semites, they make me feel powerful. By them, the Jews control the banks, the newspapers, the movies, the world. By them, we got it all."

Wall Street is not owned by Jews. The Jews did not cause the current economic crisis and downturn in America. Al-Qaeda did that—as did many other market forces. Jews and Israelis were also killed on 9/11; no one warned them to stay away from work.

Here are a few facts and figures to disprove this particular big lie:

1. According to *Forbes*, the ten wealthiest international corporations are BP, DaimlerChrysler, Royal Dutch/Shell Group (Netherlands), Royal Dutch/Shell Group (UK), Toyota Motor, Mitsubishi, Mitsui, Total Fina Elf, Nippon Telegraph and Telephone, and Itochu.

    Not a single CEO at any of these corporations is Jewish. Thus, the Jews actually control 0 percent of the ten wealthiest international corporations in the world.

2. In America .006 percent of the five hundred top American corporations has a Jewish CEO. Again according to *Forbes*,

of the top ten highest-paid CEOs in America, only two appear to be Jewish.[28]

3. Among the wealthiest individuals in the world only 6 percent appear to be Jewish. Thus, 94 percent of the world's private wealth seems to be concentrated in non-Jewish hands.[29]

4. In 1999 the BBC reported that seven of the ten richest heads of state (who are not included in the *Forbes* list) were Arabs. This was true despite widespread poverty in their countries and "disastrously low" oil prices. In 1999, the Forbes list included Saudi King Fahd at $28 billion, Sheikh Zayed of the United Arab Emirates at $20 billion, Sheikh Maktoum bin Rashid Al Maktoum of Dubai at $12 billion, Iraqi president Saddam Hussein at $6 billion, Sheikh Hamad bin Khalifa Al Thani of Qatar at $5 billion, and late Syrian president Hafez Al-Assad at $2 billion.

5. Many wealthy Saudis, including Saleh Kamel and Khalid bin Mahfouz, have been accused of using their considerable wealth to fund terrorist operations. Both Kamel and Mahfouz deny any wrongdoing, but in October 2002 Mahfouz's charity *Muwaffaq* was identified by the U.S. Treasury Department as an Al Qaeda front. In addition, Rafiq Al-Hariri's son Saad heads a consortium that includes the bin Laden group.

BIG LIE 2: *The Jews control the media.*

As we have seen in this book, the Jews do not control the media; at times like this I wish we did! On the contrary, the Islamic, European, and left and liberal American media have quickly spread the wildest and craziest of rumors against the Jews. The media have not always been balanced or fair but often have used their position to argue the Palestinian and Arab case against the Jews. They have continued doing so even after 9/11.

For example, the Islamic media recently turned the Russian forgery *The Protocols of the Elders of Zion* into a forty-part television series. In addition, they routinely and repeatedly present doctored footage, rank propaganda against Israel and the Jews, twenty-four/ seven. The European media have continued to present the Israeli nonmassacre in Jenin as a massacre. They have also continued to blame Israel for daring to defend itself against terrorism, and equated Israel's right to self-defense with the Palestinian and Islamic right to terrorist violence.

In America, CNN and NPR in particular, but many major newspapers as well, including the *New York Times* and *Los Angeles Times*, have often given more sympathetic coverage to the Palestinians than to the Israelis. These newspapers have underestimated the attendance at pro-Israel rallies, have given equal if not greater and more sympathetic photographic coverage to much smaller pro-Palestinian rallies, and have sometimes misidentified photos in favor of the Palestinians. For example, the *New York Times* once identified a Jewish man who had just been beaten by Palestinians and who had just been rescued by an Israeli officer as a Palestinian man who had just been beaten by the Israeli officer shown. It took weeks of letters before a correction was printed.

The major media worldwide are owned by ten companies. Only one company, Walt Disney, which owns 10 percent, is run by a Jewish CEO. This means that 90 percent of the media in the world (AOL/Time Warner, GE, SONY, News Corporation, and so on) are run by non-Jews.[30] By the way, most if not all of the Disney corporate affiliates are owned and run by non-Jews.

As to the print media in America, of the most influential print media (the *Los Angeles Times*, the *San Francisco Chronicle*, the *Washington Post*, the *Philadelphia Inquirer*, the *Boston Globe,* and the *New York Times*), only two (the *New York Times* and the *Boston Globe*) are owned and run by (highly assimilated and often anti- or non-Zionist) Jews. Were we to list the leading one hundred newspapers in America, I doubt we would find that more than a handful are owned or run by Jews.[31]

The majority of the print and electronic media in Europe are owned or run not by Jews but by the governments themselves, who in turn are also not owned or run by Jews. For example, the BBC is part and parcel of the British government. The *Times* is owned by Rupert Murdoch's News Corporation. France 2 is part and parcel of the French government. *Le Monde* is owned by Le Monde SA, which is itself owned by a large number of other companies.

In terms of the Middle East, outside of Israel Jewish control and influence are nonexistent. Most of the European media are regularly seen throughout the Islamic Middle East. In addition, al-Jazeera was originally intended to be a joint Saudi-BBC venture, but this plan fell through when the BBC insisted on editorial independence. Then Qatari Sheikh Hamad bin Khalifa al Thani ousted his father and started reforming his country. As noted earlier, al Thani is the ninth-richest head of state, with $5 billion. Al Thani wanted to form his own news organization. He snapped up the reporters and editors who had been sitting around since the Saudi-BBC venture failed. Most of al-Jazeera's reporters are either pan-Arabists or Islamists.

The Middle East Broadcasting Centre is run by an in-law of the Saudi king, while Lebanese Broadcasting Corporation International is privately owned, and certainly not by Jews.

Finally, IQRAA, a major media channel in the Middle East, is owned by Arab Radio and Television (ART), which was formed in October 1993 as part of the Arab Media Corporation (AMC), which is a partner of Arab Digital Distribution (ADD). ADD and AMC, its holding company, are backed by the Dallah al-Baraka group and Saudi Prince al-Waleed bin Talal. Dallah al-Baraka was founded by Saleh Kamel, who is also the founder of ART, of which Talal is a major shareholder.[32]

Dallah al-Baraka and Kamel were named in a $1 trillion lawsuit filed by the victims of 9/11—a complaint brought in an attempt to paralyze those businesses thought to be involved in funding terror organizations.

BIG LIE 3: *The Jews killed Jesus Christ.*

Please go back and look at Chapter Two, where I deal with this lie. The ancient Romans, who eventually were among the first Catholics, were the ones who ordered and carried out the execution of Jesus Christ. At the time, the Jews were occupied by the Romans and did not have the power to prevent a Roman execution. Over time, Catholics began to resent Jews for not converting to Catholicism, because this meant that the Jews, unlike the Catholics, refused to acknowledge that they had a vested interest in Christ's crucifixion and the redemption it meant. At an unconscious level, Catholics and Christians may have felt guilty about "profiting" from Christ's sacrifice. Thus they may have projected this guilt onto Jews and scapegoated them as Christ killers. This is precisely how the psychology of scapegoating works.

As I've noted, now is the time for the Church and for Christians of good will to rectify the past and come to the aid of the truth and of the Jews.

People need to be taught that everyone is prejudiced, but what we do—our deeds—matter more than our unconscious or even conscious biases. Further, people must be educated about how scapegoating functions, and about what role the media currently play in the creation of anti-Semitic propaganda.

Although we are under siege, Jews and Americans must make sure that we do not tell any Big Lies about the Palestinians or Arabs or wildly hate or punish good and innocent Muslims or Arabs because we are at war with some of the countries that they themselves have fled or in which they reside.

Finally, it is important to teach people that tragedies are complex, not simple; that we have an obligation to educate ourselves, to develop patience and creative intellectual capacities. We must learn to reject simplistic slogans and quick-fixes.

## We Must Honor Our Dreams of Peace

Despite (or precisely because of) how awful things are, the vision of peace among formerly warring neighbors is a very compelling one; it is also a quintessentially Jewish vision. How can Jews ever give up yearning for peace? And how can Jews (of all God's people) continue to humiliate and occupy the stranger in our midst? It is not worthy of us. As Jews, we must absolutely defend ourselves—but we must also continue to pursue peace and justice in this tear- and blood-soaked world, not only for humanity's sake but for God's sake as well.

Not all dreams come true on Earth or in one's lifetime. Nevertheless, dreams are important guides to have. We must always continue to work toward them. Repairing the world is a process and we are each a link in these parallel real-world and other-world chains of being, which are as entwined as our DNA code is. It would be foolish to reject an improvement as "too little" because it is not yet "what it could become."

We must not give up the dream of beating our swords into ploughshares, or the biblical vision of lions lying down with lambs. We can work toward such dreams, but along the way we must be realistic and practical.

Clearly, the vision of Jerusalem as a city of peace has not yet been realized. Some say this will happen only in the messianic future, at the end of time; others insist that the Messiah cannot arrive if we do not first do our part.

The Jewish sages have envisioned peace as one of the pillars of this world. Yet it is also a dream, and almost impossible to achieve on Earth. Peace is not unidimensional. It is composed of—it may literally and mystically consist of—truth (*emet*), justice (*zedek*), and lawfulness (*din*), which in turn require Bible study, service to God, and deeds of loving-kindness toward other people. Usually when one speaks truth to power there is no peace. But lying to keep the peace makes it impossible for lawfulness to enter the world. Administering justice may also provoke discord. Sometimes, a good deed as well as "true" justice requires tempering the law or bending the truth for the sake of kindness.[33]

The prophets tell us that Jerusalem is the center of the world and the world's source of both light and peace. Perhaps this is also why the world overly focuses on events here. When Jerusalem is at war, when the source of peace is not at peace, it affects the peace of the entire world.

I hope that this book will help us bring more light and more peace into the world.

# Questions and Answers

QUESTION 1: *Aren't Jews just imagining that people are out to get them, or at least exaggerating the danger they are facing?*

ANSWER: It is true that Jews tend to document, memorialize, litigate, and cry out to the heavens about their persecution, past and present. There is something almost unseemly about this, because so many other, equally worthy groups have simply been swept away by their misfortunes.

Nevertheless, although individual Jews may be as paranoid psychiatrically as all other people are, the facts confirm that the world has indeed been against the Jews as a group. As I have shown, for nearly three thousand years Jews have been persecuted and murdered by pagans, Christians, and Muslims. Arab and Palestinian terrorists have been shooting and bombing Jews in Israel since the beginning of the twentieth century.

Israel, the Jewish state, has been under daily or weekly attack from the moment of its birth. It has been attacked numerous times by multiple Arab nations, beginning with the war of independence (1948) and followed by the Egyptian blockade of the Suez Canal and of the straits of Tiran (1951–1959), the Six Day War (1967), the War of Attrition (1967–1970), the Yom Kippur War (1973), the Lebanon war (1982), the First Intifada (1987), the Gulf War (1991), and the current Intifada (2000).

During the Gulf War, Saddam Hussein targeted Israeli civilian populations with scud missiles. The CIA discovered that Hussein also planned to attack Israel with biological weapons but was unable to carry out his plan.

As I have documented in this book, the Intifada (uprising) against the Jews is now a worldwide phenomenon.

Nazi-level anti-Semitic propaganda, graffiti, and media and academic bias as well as violent acts against Jews and Jewish places of worship and burial are occurring simultaneously in Europe, Africa, Asia, all over the Middle East—and to a lesser extent in North America. Europe has also done a poor job of documenting and prosecuting such violence and anti-Semitic hate crimes.

A campaign to demonize, scapegoat, and ghettoize Jews has been fully launched and is under way. Islamofascists have been unexpectedly aided by Western academics, activists, students, and intellectuals who have called for boycotts of Israeli goods and products, and for academic divestment in Israel. Individual Israeli scholars have been fired from academic venues because of the policies of the Israeli government. Individual Israeli Jews have been told that if they look "too Jewish" on the streets of Europe, the governments will not be able to protect them from Islamic and anti-Jewish mobs. Individual Jews and Israelis have been disinvited or not invited to certain events and conferences. In one instance, a Norwegian medical researcher refused to sell certain medical materials to her Israeli counterpart; in another instance, Finland refused to sell the Israeli government gas mask kits. An Irish innkeeper cancelled the hotel reservations of an Israeli journalist. (The government and other hotels offered apologies.)

All this is clear evidence that the Jews are not imagining or exaggerating the new anti-Semitism.

The United Nations itself is not a credible or neutral and unbiased institution vis-à-vis the nation of the Jews. It spends too much of its time condemning Israel while ignoring many problems that the world faces. In 1975, the United Nations, led by Arab states and the Soviet bloc, had the temerity to condemn Zionism as racism (denying only Jews a right to self-determination), and it took them sixteen years to repeal this declaration. Despite this repeal, the recent Durban conference on human rights was devoted mostly to condemning Israel, renewing the UN's sentiment that Zionism is racism.

The United Nations has also made Israel the only country ineligible to sit on the Security Council, and it has denied Israel permanent membership in both the Asian bloc and the Western European grouping. (Israel resides only temporarily with the Western European group.). The UN has made Israel the object of more investigations than any other country, and the sole honoree of Emergency Special Sessions over the past fifteen years (while ignoring Rwandan genocide, the massacre of the Kurds, and ethnic cleansing in Yugoslavia, for example). Finally, the UN has failed to properly investigate Palestinian terrorism and instead tolerates rampant anti-Semitism, mostly perpetrated by the various special committees and Palestinian Units of the UN, who among other things organize the annual Palestine Day event.

QUESTION 2: *If the Jews have always been persecuted, what's new about anti-Semitism today?*

ANSWER: What's *new* about the new anti-Semitism is that for the first time it is being perpetrated in the name of antiracism, anti-imperialism, and anticolonialism. Because the charges of apartheid Zionism and American capitalist imperialism are being leveled by those who champion the uprising of the oppressed, what they say cannot, by definition, be racist. The new anti-Semites allege that they are not anti-Semites because they say they're not. Even George Orwell would be astounded.

Old-fashioned anti-Semitism was expressed in the name of ethnicity, Aryanism, white purity, superiority, and nationalism. Nazi-era Germans and Americans viewed Jews as racially and biologically inferior. The new anti-Semites do not view themselves as anti-Semites or racists because they view themselves as speaking out on behalf of all oppressed people.

What's *new* about the new anti-Semitism is the way in which visual and print propaganda are being purposely created and used to indoctrinate and manipulate people on a scale that was neither imaginable nor possible fifty years ago. Films are being expertly doctored and played over and over again, especially in the Islamic world, in order to brainwash the viewers against the Jews and the Israelis.

QUESTION 3: *But as a formerly persecuted and colonized people, haven't Israeli Jews identified with their tormenters, internalized their practices, and created a racist, apartheid state that oppresses the Palestinians?*

ANSWER: Although many Jews and Israelis are, understandably, traumatized by genocide, torture, war, and terrorism, neither they nor the Israeli army have metamorphosed into Nazis. Nor are they colonialists or imperialists bent on subjugating and underemploying a racially different people. Racially, both Jews and Palestinians are Semites.

If Israel is a racist apartheid country, why did it launch Operation Solomon in 1991 to airlift 14,200 black African Jews from Ethiopia within a twenty-five-hour period? If Israel is a racist apartheid country, why did it absorb dark- and olive-skinned Arab Jews from India, Yemen, Morocco, Tunisia, Algeria, Egypt, Iraq, Iran, Afghanistan, and so on, and provide these dark-skinned Jews with every conceivable social and educational service?

In terms of color, many Israeli Jews are white or light-skinned, but an equal number of Jews are black-, brown-, and olive-skinned Arabs, Africans, and Asians.

It is true that Israeli Arab citizens (who are also Palestinians) are second-class citizens. I have discussed this at length. This is reprehensible and must change. However, their second-class citizenship is not race- or color-based. It is probably not even culture-based, because many Arab and ultra-Orthodox Jews are as anti-Western and antimodern as their non-Jewish Arab counterparts. Israeli Arab second-class citizenship is due mainly to continuing Arab terrorism against Israel. And ironically, in many respects (infant mortality, employment, education, religious and intellectual freedom, and freedom from torture), Israeli Arab Muslim and Christian citizens fare far better in Israel than do their Arab counterparts in Islamic Arab countries.

It is also true that a small but increasingly vocal number of ultra-Orthodox right-wing "settler" and terrorist-traumatized moderate Israelis have grown angry, bitter, and mistrustful of the Palestinian capacity or willingness to live in peace with the Jews. Some support the concept of "thinning" or "transferring" the Palestinian population in Gaza and on the West Bank. Other Israelis find this idea—even in the service of security—horrifying and unacceptable. Most Israelis do want clear and well-defended borders. Some want a wall right up to the sky. The creation of a thirty-foot-high border wall is under way.

QUESTION 4: *But doesn't Israel allow only religious Orthodox Jews to live in Israel? Don't the Israelis discriminate on the basis of religion and religiosity?*

ANSWER: There is no doubt that ultra-Orthodox Jews have become politically powerful in the last twenty years—indeed, in greater proportions than their existence in the Israeli population. However, most Israelis are profoundly secular and resent the Orthodox control over their lives in terms of birth, marriage, divorce, and death. In addition, a growing number of religious Jews who are not Orthodox but Conservative, Reform, and Reconstructionist have been fighting for greater recognition, power, and perks.

However, Israel accepts all Jews (religious, nonreligious, antireligious) under the Law of Return. Also, while Jews do not encourage converts, they certainly accept them. Anyone can become a Jew. People of all colors and ethnic backgrounds have converted to Judaism. Discrimination against them (as converts or for their different ethnic or racial origin) is forbidden. Also, Israel has accepted a half million non-Jewish Russian spouses and children. About one and a half million Arabs, both Muslims and Christians, are also Israeli citizens.

Unlike its Arab and Muslim neighbors, who seriously discriminate against—really persecute—Christians and Jews and do not allow non-Islamic religious insignia or practices to be visible, Israel does not discriminate on the basis of race, color, ethnic origin, or religion.

But things are complex, not simple. Over the past twenty years the Israeli government has increasingly given economic incentives to the ultra-Orthodox and to settlers. Secularists, anti-Orthodox activists, and non-Orthodox religious Jews have opposed this. The Israeli Supreme Court has recently forbidden housing discrimination against Arabs and has ordered that women be allowed to pray at the Kotel (Wailing Wall) in our fashion despite enormous ultra-Orthodox opposition. (The government has appealed this decision.) In the 2003 elections, a pro-secular and pro-separation of synagogue and state political party (Shinui) became a force in the Parliament and will have to be reckoned with. The new minister of justice is the head of this political party.

For all these reasons (and many others), one may understand that the systematic singling out of Israel as a racist and apartheid state is itself a racist act.

QUESTION 5: *Is Israel a colonial and imperialist state?*

ANSWER: No, it is not. Zionist pioneers had no mother country and treasury behind them. They were not on a mission for land, gold, cheap labor, or oil, alas. They were trying to escape from ceaseless persecution among the nations, attempting to return home to the only land in which the Jews had ever had a sovereign nation.

Zionism was a movement for the national liberation of the persecuted and formerly colonized Jewish people. The creation of the state of Israel in 1948 was the very first postcolonized state ever created by the United Nations and the international community. The entire world agreed that after losing one third of their people in the Holocaust, the Jews finally had the right to claim self-determination. Such self-determination was not race based, nor was it specifically cultural or religious. Most of the early Zionists were antireligious, and most Israelis today follow that same path.

As to being a tool of Western imperialism: It was a long time before Theodor Herzl's Zionist movement found favor with any established Western political or financial power. As historian Paul Johnson writes, "everywhere in the West, the foreign offices, defense ministries and big businesses were against the Zionists."[1]

Western imperialism sought to seize and profit from the riches of the world (natural resources and cheap or indentured labor) by seizing them. On the face of it, Zionism does not further this end, for in its creation Israel necessitated that the British abandon a British colony.

QUESTION 6: *But Arabs and Palestinians have always lived in this region. Palestine was always an Arab Palestinian country, wasn't it?*

ANSWER: This is true and not true. Let's begin with a bad joke.

Prime minister Ariel Sharon and chairman Yasser Arafat finally sat down together to negotiate. Sharon opened with a "biblical" tale.

"Before the Israelites came to the Promised Land and settled here, Moses led them for forty years through the desert. One day, miraculously, a stream appeared. They drank and then decided to bathe. When Moses came out of the water, he found all his clothes missing.

"'Who took my clothes?' Moses asked. 'It was the Palestinians,' replied the Israelites."

"Wait a minute," interrupted Arafat. "There were no Palestinians during the time of Moses!"

"All right," smirked Sharon, "now that we've got that settled, let's start talking."[2]

The word *Palestine* comes from the Latin *Palaestina*, which the Romans derived from the ancient Philistines as a way of dissociating rebellious Jews from their own land, Judea.

At no point in the entire time since the Romans left was the area that the British had called Palestine ever an Arab Palestinian state or a sovereign Arab Palestinian entity. If peace negotiations ever produce an independent Palestine, it will be the first time in history that such a nation will exist.

In 1937, a local Arab leader, Auni Bey Abdul-Hadi, told the Peel Commission, which ultimately suggested the partition of Palestine, "There is no such country [as Palestine]! 'Palestine' is a term the Zionists invented! There is no Palestine in the Bible. Our country was for centuries part of Syria."[3]

When the distinguished Arab American historian Philip Hitti, a Princeton University professor, testified against partition before the Anglo-American Committee in 1946, he said, "There is no such thing as 'Palestine' in history, absolutely not."[4]

The representative of the Arab Higher Committee to the United Nations submitted a statement to the General Assembly in May 1947 that said, "Palestine was part of the Province of Syria" and "politically, the Arabs of Palestine were not independent in the sense of forming a separate political entity."[5] A few years later, Ahmed Shuqeiri, later chairman of the PLO, told the Security Council, "It is common knowledge that Palestine is nothing but southern Syria."[6]

Arab Jews had already been living in Israel for thousands of years (and had been exiled twice) before Islam arose in the seventh century. Some Arabs are Christians. Arab consciousness has not always been a nationalist one in the modern or Western sense. In the past, most Arabs identified themselves either as Muslims and as part of Islam, or as part of Christendom. Many Arabs also identified themselves in terms of their village, land, family, and clan.

By the end of the nineteenth century, Arabs who lived in what the British colonizers had called Palestine began to identify themselves as anti-British; previously, some had identified themselves as anti-Turkish. At the beginning of the twentieth century, as Jews began to immigrate to British Palestine, the Arabs who lived there also began to identify themselves as anti-Jewish and anti-Zionist. In other words, early in the twentieth century, Palestinian Arab consciousness was *against* colonial occupation, both Western (British and French) and eastern (Turkish). The Arabs—even those who lived in British Palestine—had not yet evolved a national consciousness as Palestinians or *for* Palestine.

Jews had been buying land from Arabs since the late nineteenth century, but had not acquired very much. By 1948, Jews owned no more than 4 percent of the land. They came into more land only as a result of the 1948 war they were forced to fight.[7] By the late 1920s, the earliest Arab Muslim leaders in British Palestine believed that the Jews were going to create a third Jewish commonwealth. They opposed it. They knew that the Jews had been there before; they did not want them to return. They fought against the new Jewish state, and lost. Some died in battle, others fled. Some chose (and were allowed) to stay; Israeli soldiers massacred some civilians or exiled them.

The Israeli government had no reason to trust and therefore could not afford to welcome the Arabs back to British Palestine or Zionist Israel. Perhaps the Israelis should have; perhaps the Israelis hoped that the Arab nations would absorb these refugees just as Israel would absorb an even greater number of Jewish refugees from Arab lands. In hindsight, it would have been wiser and more humane for Israel to have reabsorbed a larger number of Palestinian Arabs. At the time, the Arab world insisted that Israel accept every last hostile, disloyal, angry, and profoundly anti-Zionist Arab Palestinian refugee. Israel refused.

Many Palestinian Arabs spent the rest of their lives and gave birth to the next three to five generations in refugee camps somewhere in the Arab world—camps created by their Arab brethren, who refused to absorb them as citizens, partly because their terrorist ways were feared and partly in order to use them as a permanent fighting force against pre-1948 and pre-1967 Israel. In the refugee camps, a different kind of nationalism was born—one that defined itself mainly in terrorist terms. If the Palestinians could not live as others lived, they would kill the Jews until they could—or die trying. Fueled by rage and humiliation, these Palestinians did not fight against their Arab brothers who refused to take them in. They became the Arab world's permanent fighting force against the Jews.

Palestinian nationalism as we now know it became a major movement only after the Arab defeat in the Arab-initiated Six Day War of 1967.

On November 6, 2002, in a scathing Internet letter, Yashiko Sagamori, a New York-based information technology consultant, requested that those who believe that Palestine has a recorded history should ponder a few questions:

1. When was it founded and by whom?

2. What were its borders?

3. What was its capital?

4. What were its major cities?

5. What constituted the basis of its economy?

6. What was its form of government?

7. Can you name at least one Palestinian leader before Arafat?

8. Was Palestine ever recognized by a country whose existence, at that time or now, leaves no room for interpretation?

9. What was the language of the country of Palestine?

10. What was the prevalent religion of the country of Palestine?

11. What was the name of its currency? Choose any date in history and tell what was the approximate exchange rate of the Palestinian monetary unit against the US dollar, German mark, GB pound, Japanese yen, or Chinese yuan on that date.

12. Have the Palestinians left any artifacts behind?

13. Do you know of a library where one could find a work of Palestinian literature produced before 1967?

14. And, finally, since there is no such country today, what caused its demise and when did it occur?

If you are lamenting the "low sinking" of "a once proud" nation, then please tell me, when exactly was that "nation" proud and what was it so proud of?

And here is the least sarcastic question of all: If the people you mistakenly call "Palestinians" are anything but generic Arabs collected from all over—or thrown out of—the Arab world, if they really have a genuine ethnic identity that gives them [the] right for self-determination, why did they never try to become independent until Arabs suffered their devastating defeat in the 1967 Six Day War?[8]

For those who were good enough to refrain from fainting while reading Sagamori's monologue, let me say that obviously there is no question that the people who now consider themselves to be Palestinians, not Jordanians, Syrians, Lebanese, or Egyptians, are a people that has been rejected everywhere else in the Arab world, even in what some believe to be the Palestinian homeland: Jordan. In 1970, King Hussein of Jordan massacred his troublesome Palestinian terrorists and exiled the survivors. For a while, Beirut became their headquarters-in-exile. Their Lebanese hosts (with some assistance from the Israelis) drove Arafat and his forces out to Tunisia. But after a continued campaign of terror, Arafat returned to the West Bank to continue to terrorize Israel on a daily if not hourly basis.

The Palestinians have, unfortunately, outrageously, developed a hostile-dependent relationship with Israel. Palestinians expect Israel (not the Arab world) to liberate, compensate, protect, and uplift the very people who are waging a vicious war against the Jewish state. This would be funny were it not so tragic. Thus, during the latest Intifada, Israelis have sustained enormous civilian losses at Palestinian hands and in their name. This has not stopped the Palestinians from demanding gas masks from *Israel*—to protect them from a possible Iraqi attack. (The Palestinians were strong supporters of Saddam Hussein. They did not demand that Hussein spare the Israelis in order that he also spare his Palestinian allies.)

Because of the refusal of the Arab world to accept Israel in its midst and because of the Palestinian leadership's refusal and inability to halt the violence against Israel, Israel has, understandably, refused to continue to employ Palestinians. For military and security reasons, Israel has also made it difficult, sometimes impossible, for Palestinians to sell their agricultural produce. Of course, this is a tragedy. The Palestinians are dangerously impoverished. However, they are not demanding further subsidization from their Arab and Muslim brothers or from the United Nations. They *are* demanding employment from Israel. And the media often reports such Palestinian demands as if they were entirely reasonable.

QUESTION 7: *Why have Palestinian Arabs never been offered a state?*

ANSWER: The Palestinians have rejected numerous offers to create a state for them:

In 1937, the British Peel Commission proposed the partition of Palestine and the creation of an Arab state.

In 1939, the British White Paper proposed the creation of an Arab state alone, but the Arabs rejected the plan.

In 1947, the UN would have created an even larger Arab state as part of its partition plan. The Arabs rejected this possibility.

From 1948 to 1967, Israel did not control the West Bank. The Palestinians could have demanded an independent state from the Jordanians.

The 1979 Egypt-Israel peace negotiations offered the Palestinians autonomy, which would almost certainly have led to full independence.[9]

The Oslo process that began in 1993 was leading toward the creation of a Palestinian state before the Palestinians violated their commitments and scuttled the agreements.[10]

In 2000, at Camp David, then prime minister of Israel Ehud Barak offered Arafat a Palestinian state on 95 percent of the West Bank, all of Gaza, major portions of East Jerusalem, and the Moslem holy sites of the Old City.[11] Arafat rejected the offer with the encouragement of major Arab leaders. Afterward, Palestinians claimed that Israelis would still have controlled the highways and that autonomous Palestinian encampments would not have been contiguous and could have been militarily patrolled and controlled by Israel. Nevertheless, some Camp David insiders insist that there had been no definite blueprint on the table. President Clinton blamed Arafat for the collapse of the negotiations, saying, "I believe Chairman Arafat missed a golden opportunity to make that agreement. . . . [T]he violence and terrorism which followed were not inevitable and have been a terrible mistake."[12]

QUESTION 8: *If Arabs have always lived in the region, what claim do the Jews have to Israel?*

ANSWER: Jewish people base their claim to the land of Israel on at least six premises:

1. Jews had once lived there as a sovereign nation.
2. While in exile, the Jews prayed to and for Jerusalem and Israel three times a day.
3. In modern times, the Jewish people settled and developed the land.
4. The international community granted political sovereignty in British Palestine to the Jewish people.
5. Israel captured more territory in defensive wars.
6. God promised the land to the patriarch Abraham and to all the other Jewish patriarchs and matriarchs.[13]

There is no other land in the world associated with Judaism. Modern-day Israel is the ancient site of the Kingdom of David. From 1250 BCE to 587 BCE, or for 663 years, there was independent Jewish rule in this land. And despite colonization by numerous empires over many centuries, for at least 3,700 years there has been a continuous Jewish presence, culture, and language in this land. The capital, Jerusalem, is the most holy city in Judaism. The two ancient temples (of which only the Kotel, or outer western wall, remains standing) signify the place where God's presence once dwelled, and still does, among the Jewish people.

The Jews are not the conquering Brits and the Palestinians are not the Native Americans in this situation. It's the Jews who are the native, indigenous people. Imagine that instead of murdering all of the Native Americans, the European settlers had exiled them to Europe. Then, after continuous persecution culminating in a Holocaust against them, the international community recognized their need for their own country and agreed to grant them their homeland and recreate a sovereign nation for them—perhaps the equivalent of a small part of one American state. This is exactly what happened with Israel and the Jews. However, I am merely saying that the Jews have an equal, not a superior, claim to the land. Charles Krauthammer, writing in the *New Republic*, puts it well:

> Israel was our sovereign Island from which we were exiled and the claim to which we never renounced; unlike the colonizers of, say, Australia, South Africa and North America, we are returning to— not creating—our patrimony. And the argument from necessity— that a people savagely persecuted and denied refuge in every corner of the globe needs at least one place of its own—was made fifty years ago, tragically and definitively, in the wake of the Holocaust. Moreover, the last fifty years of rebuilding the land with Jewish labor and genius, and of defending it with Jewish blood, have made denials of the Jewish claim unworthy even of reply. No one asks Australia to justify its right to breathe. The time for justifying Israel's is long past.[14]

Modern Israel was created in the wake of the Holocaust as a place that would end Jewish statelessness, which was believed to be one of the causes of anti-Semitism and Jewish marginalization. It was also created in the wake of oppression, second-class citizenship, and the systematic and periodic mistreatment and murder of Jews around the world, both in Europe and in the Arab world. One of the founding principles of Israel is that it can offer Jews the right to return to the nation. The country is a project expressly and explicitly dedicated to Jewish interests. This is why many Jews the world over take an interest in the affairs of Israel.

Accordingly, Israel has absorbed more than two and a half million Jews from neighboring Arab and Islamic countries and from eastern Europe and the former Soviet Union. The immediate peril that these returning Jews were fleeing is testimony to the necessity of the state's existence.

In the former mandates for Palestine, the necessity for the existence of a Jewish state that could accommodate "substantial immigration" is explicitly recognized in UN resolution 181 of November 29, 1947. For legal purposes, this resolution was the creation of Israel. Further, Israel was admitted to the United Nations in 1949 and is recognized by most states.

QUESTION 9: *All right, so both Jews and Muslim and Christian Arabs have just claims to the same land or to parts of it. Still, isn't it true that there would be no Intifada if Israel was not occupying the West Bank and Gaza?*

ANSWER: Yasser Arafat launched his terrorist crusade against Israel in 1964–1965—two to three years before there were any settlements. In 1967, Israel was attacked by four Arab armies. Unexpectedly, Israel won its war of self-defense and came to occupy parts of Jerusalem where the ancient First and Second Temples once stood. Thereafter, the Palestinians stepped up their terrorist attacks. Settlers, both militant and idealistic, wanted to settle in the ancient land of Judea and Samaria—in Hebron, for example, where Abraham and other Jewish patriarchs and matriarchs are buried.

Perhaps the overly zealous Israeli settlers would have had no chance to do this if the Palestinians and the entire Arab world had stopped their attacks on the Jews and negotiated a genuine peace.

The term *occupation* more properly applies to foreign control of an area that was under the previous sovereignty of another state. The West Bank had no legitimate sovereign because Jordan had illegally occupied it from 1948 until 1967, as Britain had before that. Of course, the Palestinians did not terrorize their Jordanian hosts as they have Israel, nor did the entire world demonize Jordan for having massacred and exiled the Palestinans. Further, because Israel captured the territories in a war of self-defense, Israel cannot be placed in the same category with a country that initiated a war and then kept its newly conquered land.

Many Jewish settlers hate, despise, and fear the Palestinians. Some have committed outrages against Palestinian civilians, such as stealing their olive crops, intimidating them while they are tilling their fields, and shooting at them at point-blank range. In addition, the existence of Jewish settlements under siege has necessitated an unwelcome Israeli army presence there, which by definition has humiliated and enraged both Palestinian terrorists and civilians. Israel and the Palestinians (who represent the entire Islamic world) are at war. War is ugly. People starve. They lose their homes, jobs, health, and ways of life. People are also wounded and killed.

But it's a vicious cycle. Israel has also been forced to maintain a military presence in the territories due to the terrorism and violence that threaten Israeli civilians. Rather than blame the cycle of violence solely on Israel protecting itself, we should also focus on the Palestinian Authority and on ending the terrorism that emanates from the territories, and from Lebanon. Israel has been forced to endure terrorist attacks from Arafat's PLO, al-Fatah, and the Al-Aqsa Martyrs Brigade, and simultaneously from Hamas, Islamic Jihad, and Hezbollah.

QUESTION 10: *As to the settlements: Aren't they the real obstacle to peace?*

ANSWER: The Palestinians keep citing the settlements as an obstacle to peace, but many of these settlements would have been largely dismantled if Arafat had accepted Barak's offer. It is worth remembering that when Arafat first began his terrorist attacks against Israel in 1964, the entire West Bank, Gaza, and Old City of Jerusalem were under Arab control. Yet he and other Islamic terrorists still attacked Israel. That is especially true of Hamas and the other terrorist groups whose sole objective is the elimination of a Jewish state anywhere in the Middle East.[15]

Long before any Jews lived on the West Bank, the Arabs refused to make peace with Israel. Until 1977, only a few strategic West Bank settlements had been created but no peace was offered by the Arabs. In 1978, Israel was able to sign a peace treaty with Egypt despite the fact that there were Israeli settlements in the Sinai (which were removed as part of the agreement). In 1979, one year after peace with Egypt, Israel stopped building settlements in the hope that other Arab nations would then join the Camp David peace process; none did. In 1994, Jordan also signed a peace treaty with Israel and settlements were never an issue, even though settlements were growing at the time. Finally, the rapid growth of the settlements in the early 1990s had no impact on the Palestinians' decision to join the Oslo accords in 1993 or 1995.

However, many Israelis and others have valid criticisms of the settlements. Some consider the settlements to be a moral and public relations nightmare for Israel, and expensive and difficult to defend from attacks. This is because a great amount of money, equipment, and soldiers must be used to protect and maintain the settlements. Yet others view the settlers as a first line of defense for Israel proper and as a necessary military position from which to repel terrorist attacks. Although Israeli control of the West Bank and Gaza is what now allows Israelis to repel thousands upon thousands of would-be terrorist attacks, according to left-wing and pro-peace Israelis it is also possible that if such settlements did not exist, by now the need for terrorism might have diminished. They continue to call for a unilateral Israeli withdrawal from the West Bank and Gaza.

The real obstacle to peace is the Palestinians' inability to accept a state next to Israel rather than on top of it. Further, blaming the settlements is only an excuse to continue terrorism rather than make real efforts at peace. The matter of the settlements will surely be determined at legitimate peace talks. And if real peace were ever offered, I am sure that most if not all settlements would be disbanded. Yossi Klein Halevi made another key point when he said, "If settlement building is now concentrated in areas that the Palestinians themselves acknowledge will remain part of Israel in any future peace agreement, why the obsessive focus on settlements as an 'obstacle to peace'?"[16]

QUESTION 11: *Didn't Sharon himself start the Intifada when he visited the Temple Mount in 2000?*

ANSWER: By omitting certain background facts, and then downplaying or denying them, the European and then the world media were able to blame Sharon—and not the Palestinians—for the Second Intifada. Yet the May 4, 2001, Mitchell Report (named after former U.S. Senator George Mitchell, chairman of the investigatory committee set up to look into the cause of violence that began in mid-2000) clearly concluded that "[t]he Sharon visit did not cause the Al-Aqsa Intifada."[17]

The violence began the day before Sharon's visit, with two Palestinian suicide bomb attacks that killed an Israeli soldier who had been escorting a civilian bus in Gaza.

Since the failure of the peace talks in July, Israeli intelligence had known and the Israeli media had reported that the Palestinian Authority had been planning a return to violence. Imad Faluji, the Palestinian Authority communications minister, admitted months after the incident that the violence had been planned long before the Sharon visit; in fact, it had been planned since Arafat's return from Camp David.[18]

Sharon's September 28, 2000, visit had been announced several days beforehand and had received the approval of the Muslim authorities, specifically the Palestinian security chief, Jabril Rajoub. Sharon never attempted to enter any mosques, and his brief visit was conducted during the hours that the area is open to tourists. Upon his expected arrival (granted, accompanied by a large police escort), an equally large number of Palestinian demonstrators threw heavy rods and metal objects at him. Sharon's police escorts responded by firing rubber bullets. Twenty-five Israeli policemen were wounded over a period of a few minutes. Palestinian rioters were also wounded. No one died that first day.

The true desecration of holy places was perpetrated by Palestinian mobs, who, a day after Sharon's visit, threw large, sharp, heavy stones at Israeli soldiers and at Jewish worshipers praying below at the Western (Wailing) Wall. The Israeli soldiers responded. At day's end, seven Palestinians were dead and 220 wounded. In October 2000, Palestinian mobs also destroyed Joseph's Tomb, tearing up and burning Jewish prayer books, and attacked Rachel's Tomb with firebombs and automatic weapons. In addition, Palestinians have also been systematically digging up and destroying Jewish archaeological remains of the First and Second Temples.

By the second day of the Intifada, the official French media, Agence France Presse (AFP), told the entire French press corps as a matter of fact that "the violence was started by Ariel Sharon's visit to the esplanade of mosques which is home to the third most holy site in Islam." On October 1st, this view was repeated thirteen times by the agency, and on October 2nd, more than twenty times.[19] This view then spread across the planet.

Over the following months, AFP and most other media repeated this explanation at every opportunity; at the same time, it continued to fail to mention the Palestinian decision to return to violence, the Palestinian shooting of two Israeli Defense Forces soldiers, the Palestinian attack on Sharon, or the Palestinian attack on the worshipers at the Wailing Wall. The bulletins kept mentioning Al-Aqsa as "the third holiest site in Islam," but rarely mentioned that it was also "the single most holy site in Judaism."[20]

QUESTION 12: *Isn't it true that Israelis shot unarmed children and per-petrated a massacre in Jenin?*

ANSWER: We have all seen, time and time again, that horrible sequence of photographs taken from film made by a camera crew for France 2 in September 2000. In it we see little Mohammed Al-Dura huddled in his father's arms—first terrified but alive, then shot and dead. It's awful, and ever since this terrible event, Israeli soldiers have been branded irrevocably as child killers.

There's only one problem: the footage is real, the boy was trag-ically killed, but . . . according to a German television documentary that aired in March 2002, "it is not possible to determine with absolute certainty that Palestinians shot the boy, but the extensive evidence points, with high probability, to the fact that *the Israelis did not do it* [my emphasis]."[21]

Israeli shooters were all stationed in low places, the boy was shot from above. The documentary charged that France 2 did not release all the video footage in its possession—film that shows the extent of Palestinian shootings in the same area.

Meanwhile, the boy is dead. This accident is an unspeakable tragedy. In fact, we don't know who did it, but hey, who cares; the Israeli army has been blamed, found guilty, and sentenced to infamy around the world, regardless.

Similarly, we have discussed at length how the UN investiga-tion concluded that no massacre ever took place at Jenin. No doubt human rights violations did occur, but five hundred people were not killed and buried in a mass grave, and Israeli troops did not rape women or kidnap women and girls to sell as sex slaves.

But once again, who cares if it really didn't happen? Who cares if in reality the bomb-making terrorists of Jenin used civilians as human shields and ambushed and killed twenty-three Israeli sol-diers who entered Jenin on foot— not from safe airplane heights and not in tanks. It's the Israeli soldiers who have been accused in the international media, found guilty, and sentenced to infamy around the world, regardless.

QUESTION 13: *So who is today's new anti-Semite?*

ANSWER: An ever-increasing crowd of naive and misinformed students who truly believe that Israel is a racist, colonialist, apartheid state; long-standing right-wing Jew haters who now have popular opinion on their side and find themselves in the surprising position of being politically correct; Islamofascists and anti-Western terrorists who see Israel as America's outpost in the Middle East and who intend to terrorize and defeat both America and Israel; some women and men, both Jewish and non-Jewish, whose hearts bleed for the Palestinians but who are embarrassed and outraged by the specter of Israelis fighting for their lives; some old-fashioned left ideologues who cannot distinguish between American imperialism and the Jewish struggles for survival; and finally, Western anticapitalist, antiglobalist, pro-environment, antiracist activists.

Criticizing the Jewish state is no proof of anti-Semitism. But there's no question that today's new anti-Semite hides behind the smoke screen of anti-Zionism. She or he knows that it's unfair and inaccurate to hate and blame the Jews for all of the conflict in the Middle East, the decline in the world economy, the price of gasoline, and so on, but because they really do hate and blame Jews, they've found that anti-Zionism is a popular and politically respectable way to do so.

Israel has always had its critics, including its Jewish and Israeli critics. Such individuals have sought to improve the state of Israel, not wipe it out because it is imperfect.

The new anti-Semitism is being waged on many fronts—military, propaganda, political, economic—throughout the world. Anyone who denies this anti-Semitism or blames the Jews for provoking it is, in my opinion, an anti-Semite. Anyone who falsely accuses Israel of genocide and racism is an anti-Semite. Anyone who cannot talk about Israel's mistakes, failures, and imperfections without demonizing Israel and the Jews is an anti-Semite. Anyone who does not distinguish between Jews and the Jewish state is an anti-Semite.

QUESTION 14: *Are Jews in more danger today than ever before? What about Jews in America? For that matter, are Americans safe?*

ANSWER: I am not a scholar of anti-Semitism. I do not know whether Jews are more endangered today than they were sixty—or two thousand—years ago. While anti-Semitism has existed for thousands of years in both Christian and Muslim lands, never before have so many unstable, fanatic leaders and individual terrorists had such easy access to weapons of mass destruction. Never before have anti-Semites had a communications system in place to indoctrinate hundreds of millions of people virtually around the clock.

The Islamic world is quite safe for Jews—because it is Judenrein (free of Jews). As a Jewish state, Israel remains a permanent bone lodged in the throat of the Islamic Middle East. This was true long before Israelis ever occupied the West Bank and Gaza. Will this ever change, will the Arab, Muslim, and Palestinian world ever really be willing to live in peace with Jewish Israelis? I certainly hope so but the facts do not encourage any optimism.

The prolonged and systematic demonizing of Israel by the United Nations, Soviet Russia, and the Islamic world on four continents, and by Western-based international human rights organizations, academics, intellectuals, and left and pro-peace movements has now entered a new phase. North African Muslim immigrants in Europe are desperately unhappy and "offended." They wish to retain an Eastern identity but on a Western dollar. Their crime rates and voting power have led their former European colonizers to allow this population to "vent" against the Jews and Israelis—which has resulted in life becoming quite dangerous and unpleasant for the scapegoated Jews of Europe.

I think that America is a safe place for Jews. Nothing is stopping us from leading our lives as individuals or collectively as Jews. Recent attitude surveys have measured some anti-Semitic beliefs but only among 3 to 37 percent of the American population. Thus, anywhere from 63 to 97 percent of Americans interviewed are *not* anti-Semitic.

Attitude surveys, however elegant, cannot totally predict what people will do given new circumstances. America may be the safest place yet for Jews and for immigrants from all other countries, including Muslims in flight from persecution in Islamic countries. However, in the past, when bad things happened to good pagans, Christians, and Muslims, they all tended to scapegoat the Jews. Will twenty-first-century Americans do this too? Who can say? I am optimistic but uneasy. Also, I do not believe that Jews anywhere (including in America) can be safe or whole without a strong and independent Israel.

What will happen to the Jews if America endures a series of 9/11 attacks? (May this never happen.) Or, if the short- and long-term consequences of invading Afghanistan and Iraq include biological and nuclear warfare against America? Will ordinary, terrified American civilians continue to support Israel after the terrorists make it clear that Israel and the Jews must be sacrificed if the attacks on America are to stop? It does not matter that such terrorists will be lying, that they will not stop their crusade with the destruction of Israel. (May this too never happen.) The point is that terrified Americans might believe them, or might be willing to sacrifice anyone and anything to get their own immediate suffering to stop.

What will Americans, including American Jews, do once their beloved children and cities are destroyed, laid waste? How much "cover" can Jews and Israelis expect from any country, including America, in the face of sustained or intermittent Islamofascist terrorism?

Jews have always survived. We have survived the destruction of Jerusalem and Israel before. We have survived both persecution and exile. Perhaps we may have to do so again.

And what of my country, America, which has had a civil war but never a foreign war on its soil? Also, like the rest of the world, Americans continue to suffer a permanent war against the poor, against the racially despised, and against women. These so-called "quiet" wars are intensified by military combat. How much suffering lies in our future? Who can say? What can stop it?

QUESTION 15: *Is there any hope for the future? Can the new anti-Semitism and anti-Western terrorism ever disappear or diminish?*

ANSWER: That is in the hands of the good people of Planet Earth. How we decide to respond to evil—not only to terrorism, but also to all kinds of prejudice, including anti-Semitism, and to all forms of injustice, such as poverty, homelessness, disease, illiteracy, and gross violations of human rights—is what will, in the long run, make the difference between human evolution and devolution.

America is the greatest power in the world. We must continually endeavor to use our power to do good on Earth: humbly, carefully, without arrogance. We must forever battle the greed and selfishness that have nearly overwhelmed our economy. While we must learn ever-greater tolerance for differences, we must also hold and attempt to enforce a single standard of human rights for both men and women, and for peoples everywhere on Earth. The era of cultural relativism must end. The era of American isolation must also end. If it is within America's power to open up torture chambers and free the prisoners, we must try and do just that. Educational outreach, economic and scientific cooperation, and military might will all play a role.

We must stand up to evil. Honesty and heroism are our only human alternatives. I only hope that the price in human lives and suffering is not too great to bear.

It would be wonderful if people were taught to identify themselves first as human beings, as all God's children. Secularists may certainly identify themselves as all Earth's children. This would be preferable to exclusively identifying oneself as a member of one tribe, one ethnicity, one religion, one nation-state, one philosophy or ideology that remains at permanent war with all others. However, based on the last four thousand years of human and Jewish history, I would like the Jews and the Israelis to be among the last of such new internationalists, not among the first.

As to anti-Semitism diminishing: I am not optimistic, but neither am I pessimistic. Things are bad, they could get worse, but they might also improve. Again, the outcome is entirely in human hands. If people will continue to expose the Big Lies against the Jews; if people of faith, people of color, Americans, Christians, Buddhists, and Muslims understand that what happens to the Jews and to the Israelis is a symbol of what has—and can—happen to all other racially or religiously marginalized people and to any other child of Earth and God; if America and the West use their military might to protect Israel and their economic might to help uplift and democratize the Arab Islamic world; if the Israeli Defense Forces remain strong; if the Jewish people remain united—then the forces of anti-Semitism *may* once again be defeated in our time.

# Notes

## Chapter One: 9/11 and the New Anti-Semitism

1. Bin Laden's speeches on video and audiotape have been excerpted by the Anti-Defamation League and may be found at [http://www.adl.org/terrorism_america/bin_l.asp]. On Sept. 23, 2001, Bin Laden referred to "martyrs in Islam's battles against the new Christian-Jewish crusade led by the big crusader Bush under the flag of the Cross"; on Dec. 26, 2001, he referred to "blessed attacks against the global infidelity, against America."

2. Seymour Martin Lipset, "The Socialism of Fools: The Left, the Jews and Israel," *Encounter*, Dec. 1969, p. 24.

3. Friday Sermon by Sheikh Ibrahim Madhi, The Sheikh Ijlin Mosque, Gaza, Aug. 3, 2001. Available in translation at the Web site of the Middle East Media Research Institute [http://www.memri.org/video/index.html]. Accessed Dec. 15, 2002.

4. On Sept. 19, 2002, former president of the Czech Republic Vaclav Havel delivered an address in New York City that was published shortly thereafter in the *New York Review of Books*: Vaclav Havel, "A Farewell to Politics" (Paul Wilson, trans.), *New York Review of Books*, Oct. 24, 2002.

5. David Warren, "Wrestling with Islam," *David Warren Online*. First posted Dec. 3, 2002. Available at [http://www.davidwarren online.com/miscell/index02.shtml]. Accessed Dec. 15, 2002.

6. Michael Wines, "Mourners at Israeli Boy's Funeral Lament a Conflict with No Bounds," *The New York Times*, Dec. 1, 2002.

7. Ari Shavit, "No Man's Land," *New Yorker*, Dec. 4, 2002.

8. Riva Rubin, "True Lies: Two Israeli Novelists on War and Oranges," *Forward*, Nov. 29, 2002.

9. Wines, "Mourners."

## Chapter Two: The Old Anti-Semitism

1. The "scapegoat" is presented in Aharei Mot (After the Death), right after the high priest Aharon's two sons, Nadav and Avihu, who are also Moses' nephews, have died because they worshiped God improperly, or with "strange fire." Perhaps they were overly enthusiastic or still overly pagan in their practice; perhaps approaching God is always dangerous. In any event, Aharon is now instructed in when and how to approach God in God's sanctuary. The high priest must choose two identical goats by lots. The priest himself does not decide; chance (or God) does that. One goat is a burnt offering. The second goat has a red thread tied around its horn and is sent to *Azazel*, which has been interpreted to mean sent to a hard and cutoff place and then thrown off a cliff. Torah scholar Rivka Haut, who has studied this, explains that the second goat was initially quite battered by the Jews, who viewed it as literally carrying the very sins they wished to be rid of, and thus the priests constructed a special ramp for the goat so it would not be abused by the populace in the Temple. The point I wish to make is that the goat is spared the battering and is also not allowed to wander; thus the Jews as a people, long abused in exile but with a remnant always remaining, are in no way a metaphoric continuation of this original second goat.

2. The idea that Christians are also wrestling with their own intractable paganism is Freud's in *Moses and Monotheism* (New York: Vintage, 1967).

3. Freud, *Moses and Monotheism*.

4. Daniel Jonah Goldhagen, *A Moral Reckoning: The Role of the Catholic Church in the Holocaust and Its Unfulfilled Duty of Repair* (New York: Knopf, 2002).

5. Jerome A. Chanes, *A Dark Side of History: Antisemitism Through the Ages* (New York: Anti-Defamation League, 2000).

6. Chanes, *A Dark Side of History.*

7. From "Dreyfus, Alfred," *Encyclopedia Judaica,* Vol. 6: Dl-Fo (Jerusalem: McMillan, 1971), pp. 224–230; Amos Elon, *Herzl* (Austin, Tex.: Holt, Rinehart and Winston, 1975); Alex Bein, *Theodore Herzl,* trans. from German by Maurice Samuel (Philadelphia: Jewish Publication Society, 1941).

8. Theodor Herzl, *The Jewish State: An Attempt at a Modern Solution of the Jewish Problem* (Mineola, N.Y.: Dover, 1988; originally published 1895).

9. Herzl, *The Jewish State.*

10. Herzl, *The Jewish State.*

11. Gil Elliot, *Twentieth Century Book of the Dead* (New York: Scribner's, 1972).

Of course, the number of Jews who have died over a two-thousand-year period in pogroms, expulsions, and autos-da-fé, (burnings at the stake), and whose lives have been cut short by poverty and exile, is almost unimaginable.

12. Dennis Prager and Joseph Telushkin, *Why the Jews? The Reasons for Antisemitism* (New York: Simon & Schuster, 1983).

13. Jean-Paul Sartre, *Anti-Semite and Jew,* trans. George J. Becker (New York: Shocken Books, 1995).

## Chapter Three: Modern Anti-Semitism Before 9/11

1. David Ben-Gurion, *Memoirs* (New York and Cleveland: World, 1970), pp. 55–58.

2. [http://www.us-israel.org/jsource/history/mandate.html]. Accessed Nov. 26, 2002.

3. [http://www.mfa.gov.il/mfa/go.asp?MFAH01dc0]. Accessed Nov. 21, 2002.

4. Ben-Gurion, *Memoirs,* pp. 190–192.

5. [http://www.eretzyisroel.og/~samuel/britainriots.html]. Accessed Nov. 22, 2002.

6. [http://www.palestinefacts.org/pf_mandate_riots_1936–39.php]. Accessed Nov. 25, 2002.

7. "Palestine and Trans-Jordan for the Year 1936." [http://domino.un.org/UNISPAL.NSF]. Accessed Nov. 25, 2002.

8. [http://www.us-israel.org/jsource/History/mandate.html]. Accessed Nov. 26, 2002.

9. [http://www.us-israel.org/jsource/History/mandate.html]. Accessed Nov. 26, 2002.

10. [http://www.realolam.com/channels/default.asp?page=1&articleid=1500&channel=38]. Accessed Nov. 21, 2002.

11. Ben-Gurion, *Memoirs*, pp. 86–87.

12. [http://www.realolam.com/channels/default.asp?page=1&articleid=1500&channel=38]. Accessed Nov. 21, 2002.

13. [http://www.us-israel.org]. Accessed Nov. 26, 2002.

14. [http://www.mfa.gov.il/mfa/go.asp?MFA01dc0]. Accessed Nov. 21, 2002.

15. [http://www.jcrc.org/main/terror.htm]. Accessed Oct. 7, 2002.

16. Alan M. Dershowitz, *Why Terrorism Works: Understanding the Threat, Responding to the Challenge* (New Haven, Conn.: Yale University Press, 2002), p. 54.

17. "La mort d'Abou Nidal" [The death of Abu Nidal], *Le Monde.fr*, Aug. 19, 2002. Available at [http://www.lemonde.fr/article/0,5987,3218—287733-00.html]. Accessed Dec. 29, 2002.

18. Letty Cottin Pogrebin, *Deborah, Golda and Me: Being Female and Jewish in America* (New York: Crown, 1991).

19. "La mort d'Abou Nidal."

20. Anti-Defamation League, "ADL Urges Buenos Aires to Bring Amia Murderers to Justice," press release, July 20, 1998. Available at [http://www.adl.org/presrele/terrorismintl_93/3202_93.asp]. Accessed Dec. 29, 2002.

21. Stephen Roth Institute for the Study of Contemporary Anti-Semitism and Racism, University of Tel Aviv, "Anti-Semitism Worldwide 1997/8: Why Argentina? Police Involvement In Argentinean Anti-Semitism." Available at [http://www.tau.ac.

il/Anti-Semitism/asw97–8/la-int.html]. Accessed Dec. 29, 2002. (The Stephen Roth Institute for the Study of Contemporary Anti-Semitism and Racism at Tel Aviv University began operating as the Project for the Study of Anti-Semitism in fall 1991. It is housed in the Wiener Library, which contains one of the largest collections of anti-Semitic, Nazi, and extremist literature in the world. The Institute monitors manifestations of anti-Semitism and racism worldwide and operates a computerized database of contemporary anti-Semitism and extremist right-wing and other hate groups.)

22. Larry Rohter, "Argentina, a Haven for Nazis, Balks at Opening Its Files." *The New York Times*, March 9, 2003.

23. Larry Rohter, "Argentine Judge Indicts 4 Iranian Officials in 1994 Bombing of Jewish Center." *The New York Times*, March 10, 2003.

24. Brigitte Sion, "Fighting Anti-Semitism in Switzerland," *Lilith*, Winter 2002.

25. Stephen Roth Institute for the Study of Contemporary Anti-Semitism and Racism.

26. Stephen Roth Institute for the Study of Contemporary Anti-Semitism and Racism.

27. Stephen Roth Institute for the Study of Contemporary Anti-Semitism and Racism.

28. Federal Bureau of Investigation, *Robert F. Kennedy Assassination: Report of Independent Special Counsel Thomas F. Kranz* (Washington: Federal Bureau of Investigation, 1977). Available at [http://foia.fbi.gov/rfkassum.htm]. Accessed Dec. 29, 2002.

29. Federal Bureau of Investigation.

30. Federal Bureau of Investigation.

31. Jeffrey Goldberg, "In the Party of God," *New Yorker*, Oct. 14 and 21, 2002, pp. 180–195.

32. Associated Press, "Attacks Against the United States," Interactive Web guide. Available at [http://wire.ap.org/APpackages/globalterror]. Accessed Dec. 29, 2002.

33. Goldberg, "In the Party of God," p. 185.

34. [http://www.cnn.com/2001/US/10/16/inv.embassy.bombings. connections.]

35. [http://www.jcrc.org/main/terror.htm]. Accessed Oct. 7, 2002.

36. Dershowitz, *Why Terrorism Works*, p. 70.

37. [http://www.jcrc.org/main/terror.htm]. Accessed Oct. 7, 2002.

38. Marilyn Safir, personal and Internet communications on the Israeli Feminist Forum, August 11–20, 2000.

39. Safir.

40. Frances Raday, personal and Internet communications on the Israeli Feminist Forum, n.d.

41. Anonymous, personal interview with the author, n.d.

42. Anonymous, personal interview with the author, n.d.

43. Safir.

44. Safir.

45. "New York Adjusts Terrorist Death Toll Downward," Cable News Network, Aug. 22, 2002. Available at [http://www.cnn. com/2002/US/08/22/911.toll/index.html]. Accessed Dec. 29, 2002.

46. [http://www.ict.org.il].

47. [http//www.cnn.com/2002/world/asiapcf/south/02/26/pearl. videotape].

48. "Pearl Murderer Defiant After Verdict," BBC News, July 15, 2002. Available at [http://japantoday.com/el?content=news& cat=8&id=386166]. Accessed Apr. 11, 2003.

49. "Karachi Bus Blast Kills Fifteen," BBC News, May 8, 2002. Available at [http://news.bbc.co.uk/2/hi/world/south_asia/ 1974377.stm]. Accessed Dec. 29, 2002.

50. James Risen with Neil MacFarquhar, "New Recording May Be Threat from bin Laden," *New York Times*, Nov. 13, 2002, p. A1.

51. Jane Perlez, "Suspect Tells Police That Target of Bali Bombing Was Americans, Not Australians," *New York Times*, Nov. 9, 2002.

52. Risen with MacFarquhar, "New Recording May Be Threat from bin Laden," p. A1.

53. Risen with MacFarquhar, "New Recording May Be Threat from bin Laden," p. A1.

54. "McDonalds to Pull Out of Middle East," *Japan Today*, Nov. 12, 2002. Available at [http://japantoday.com/el?content=news& cat=8&id=386166]. Accessed Apr. 13, 2003.

55. Reuters, "Blasts Rock U.S. Fast-Food Outlets in Lebanon," Nov. 12, 2002, 5:39 A.M. ET.

56. Reuters, "Blasts Rock U.S. Fast-Food Outlets in Lebanon."

57. I am not saying that genocide and femicide have not been active agents everywhere else in world history; sadly, they have. Europeans and Americans are not the only ones who enslaved, subordinated, and exterminated those whom they deemed enemy and other, including those upon whom they also depended. Everyone has done likewise.

   I could create a fairly long and infinitely depressing list of victims, but I will not do so at this time. I am certain that each instance of slavery (including wage and indentured servitude) and of forced starvation is evil. I am only uncertain about whether all reprehensible behavior is a form of racism or not, and whether each instance of slavery and mass murder rises to the level of genocide. We must be very careful here not to conflate one evil with another—and in so doing to lose sight of the precise nature of each offense.

58. Bernard-Henri Lévy, *Réflexions sur la guerre* [Reflections on War] (Paris: Grasser, 2001).

59. [http://www.jcrc.org/main/terror.htm]. Accessed Oct. 7, 2002.

60. [http://www.mfa.gov.il/mfa/go.asp?mfa/hojy30].

61. [http://www.adl.org/Israel/israel_attacks.asp].

62. [http://www.jcrc.org/main/terror.htm]. Accessed Oct. 7, 2002.

63. [http://www.adl.org/Israel/israel_attacks.asp].

64. [http://www.ict.org.il].

65. [http://www.haaretzdaily.com].

## Chapter Four: What's New About the New Anti-Semitism?

1. Jonathan Stevenson, "Al Qaeda's Threat Is Now Truly Global," *Wall Street Journal,* December 2, 2002.

2. David A. Harris, "Saudi Schools Keep Sowing Seeds of Hate," *The Forward,* March 7, 2003.

3. *Al-Hayat Al-Jadidah,* Jan. 4, 2000; Mar. 9, 2000; Mar. 22, 2000; June 29, 2001; Apr. 23, 2000; Apr. 17, 2000; Aug. 27, 1999; Sept. 9, 1999; Dec. 30, 1999; May 6, 2000; Feb. 26, 2000; Apr. 25, 2000; July 20, 2000; Feb. 24, 1997; Jan. 23, 2001; Feb. 4, 2001; Mar. 15, 2001; Jan. 17, 2001; Jan. 27, 2001; Jan. 22, 2001; Jan. 16, 2001; Feb. 8, 2001; Jan. 18, 2001; June 14, 1999; May 16, 1999; Aug. 29, 1999; May 22, 1999; May 20, 1997; June 24, 1997; June 22, 1997; May 6, 1997; Mar. 9, 1997.

   *Al-Hayat Al-Jadidah,* Dec. 30, 1999: Between an old man representing the twentieth century and a young one representing the twenty-first century, a dwarfed Jew is labeled "the Disease of the Century."

   Apr. 23, 2000: A Jew is depicted as a louse on an Arab's head.

   June 29, 2001: A hideous ghoul represented as a Jew is sucking on "Palestinian Blood" and "Palestinian Water" while eating a sandwich made of "Palestinian Land."

   No date: Worms in skullcaps are eating at the word *peace*.

   May 6, 1997: An Arab is tied to a gigantic candle that will obviously burn him up. The caption reads, "Memorial Day for the Holocaust Martyrs!!!?!"

   Feb. 4, 2001: Ariel Sharon and Ehud Barak's electoral competition is drawn as a footrace up a mountain of skulls.

   May 6, 2000: Former Israeli Prime Minister Ehud Barak stands in front of a chopping block in a blood-spattered apron wielding an axe. On the block is the body of an Arab in thirds that Barak has just mutilated, spilling copious amounts of blood. The caption reads, "Barak's Palestinian State."

4. Agence France-Press, "Iran Leader Hits Out at Zionist Conspiracy of Drugs, Prostitution," February 25, 2003. [http://quickstart.clari.net/qs_se/webnews/wed/aq/Qiran-prostitution-drugs.Rhjs_DFP.html]. Accessed March 11, 2003.

5. "Why Israel's Image Suffers: Interview with GPO Director Danny Seaman," *Kol Ha'Ir*, Oct. 12, 2002, trans. by Israel News Agency. Seaman named the Associated Press, Reuters, the Washington Post, the BBC, and CNN. He singled out four reporters: Suzanne Goldenberg, the *Guardian*; Lee Hockstader, the *Washington Post*; Sandro Contenta, the *Toronto Star*; and Gillian Findlay, ABC. The reporters Seaman specifically named have all been reassigned. One wonders why.

6. Peter Maass, "When Al Qaeda Calls," *New York Times Magazine*, Feb. 1, 2003.

7. Ted Harwood, "Back Home Again at the Al Rasheed." Letters to the Editor, *Wall Street Journal*, March 7, 2003.

8. Jeffrey Goldberg, "In the Party of God," *The New Yorker*, Oct. 14–21, 2002.

9. *Muslim Woman Magazine*, hosted by Doaa 'Amer, Iqraa TV, May 7, 2002. Aired from Egypt, trans. by the Middle East Media Research Institute. Available at [http://memri.org/ video/ segment1_basmallah.html]. Accessed Dec. 21, 2002.

10. The "Life Is Sweet" Show, Iqraa TV, Apr. 24, 2002. Aired from Jordan, trans. by Middle East Media Research Institute. Available at [http://memri.org/video/segment5_lifesweet.html]. Accessed Dec. 21, 2002.

11. Tamim Ansary, *West of Kabul, East of New York* (New York: Farrar, Straus & Giroux, 2002).

12. Ansary, *West of Kabul, East of New York*.

13. David Sangan, "Seven Lies About Jenin," *Ma'ariv*, Nov. 8, 2002. Trans. by Israel Government Press Office.

14. Sangan, "Seven Lies About Jenin."

15. Sangan, "Seven Lies About Jenin."

16. Sylvana Foa, "Life Under Israeli Occupation: Letter from Jenin," *Village Voice*, Nov. 6–12, 2002.

17. Foa, "Life Under Israeli Occupation."

18. Foa, "Life Under Israeli Occupation."

19. Interestingly, in 2002, one year later, Enderlin published a book titled *Le Rêve brisé* [The Broken Dream] in which he described former Israeli Prime Minister Ehud Barak as a "criminal of peace." Enderlin has been much lauded and published by the leading pro-Palestinian/anti-Israeli French intellectuals.

20. Quoted in Ellis Shuman, "German TV: Mohammed a-Dura Likely Killed by Palestinian Gunfire," *IsraelInsider*, Mar. 20, 2002. Available at [http://www.israelinsider.com/channels/ diplomacy/ articles/dip_0182.htm]. Accessed Dec. 21, 2002.

21. Herb Keinon, "(18:15) German Documentary Casts Doubt on Palestinian Icon," *Internet Jerusalem Post*, Mar. 19, 2002. [http:// www.col.fr/judeotheque/archive.web/ German%20documentary20casts%20doubt%20on%20Palestinian%20icon.htm].

22. Clement Weill Raynal, *"L'Agence France Presse: Le récit contre les faits"* [Agence France Presse: The Account Versus the Facts], *L'Observatoire du monde juif*, Mar. 2002, Bulletin no. 2, pp. 2–11.

23. "Why Israel's Image Suffers."

24. The Jewish Community Federation of Louisville, Inc. "Violence Started Before Sharon's Visit to the Temple Mount." [http:// www.jewishlouisville.org/news/sharon.shtml] Accessed Feb. 25, 2003.

25. Raynal, *"L'Agence France Presse."*

26. Raynal, *"L'Agence France Presse."*

27. Raynal, *"L'Agence France Presse."*

28. Nabil Salam, Untitled article in the official Palestinian newspaper, *Al-Hayat Al-Jadidah*, Sept. 3, 1997.

29. "The Jews and the Media Monopoly," *Al-Hayat Al-Jadidah*, July 2, 1998.

30. "Muslim Who Stabbed Jew to Be Detained in Hospital," *Guardian*, Sept. 19, 2002. Available at [http://www.guardian.co. uk/race/story/0,11374,794731,00.html]. Accessed Dec. 29, 2002.

31. Francis Marion, "Algerian Freedom Fighter Detained for Bold Counterterrorist Act," *Nationalist Free Press*, no date given. Available at [http://www.liesexposed.net/nfp/issue0102/fighter.html]. Accessed Dec. 29, 2002.

32. Avi Becker, "Under Cover of Intellectualism," *Haaretz*, Oct. 7, 2002.

33. "Alain Finkielkraut: C'est reparti comme en cinquante!" *Le Figaro*, Mar. 16, 2002; Alain Finkielkraut, "Une croix gammée à la place de l'etoile" [A Swastika in Place of the Star of David], *L'Arche*, May–June, 2002.

34. Alan M. Dershowitz, *Why Terrorism Works: Understanding the Threat, Responding to the Challenge* (New Haven, Ct.: Yale University Press, 2002).

35. Timur Moon, "Leila Khaled: Hijacked by Destiny," *Arab News*, Oct. 17, 2002.

36. "Newspaper Publishes Interview with Barayev," *The Russian Journal*, Oct. 28, 2002.

37. Alexandra Stiglmayer, *Mass Rape: The War Against Women in Bosnia-Herzegovina* (Lincoln and London: University of Nebraska Press, 1994).

38. Stiglmayer, *Mass Rape*.

39. Phyllis Chesler, "What Is Justice for a Rape Victim?" *On The Issues*, Winter 1996.

40. Chesler, "What Is Justice for a Rape Victim?"

41. Amir Taheri, "Saddam Hussein's Delusion," *New York Times*, Nov. 14, 2002, p. A-35.

42. As told to the author by Douglas Gillison, whose mother is anthropologist Gillian Gillison.

43. Don Radlauer, "An Engineered Tragedy: Statistical Analysis of Casualties in the Palestinian-Israeli Conflict, September 2000–September 2002," International Policy Institute for Counter-Terrorism at the University of Herzliya, Sept. 29, 2002. Available at [http://www.ict.org.il]. Accessed Dec. 21, 2002.

44. Radlauer, "An Engineered Tragedy."

## Chapter Five: The Betrayal of Truth, Part One

1. Quoted in Paul Berman, "Bigotry in Print. Crowds Chant Murder. Something's Changed," *Forward*. May 24, 2002.

2. Unless otherwise noted, all information on anti-Semitic events in this chapter were taken from the following annual reports by the Stephen Roth Institute for the Study of Contemporary Anti-Semitism and Racism at the University of Tel Aviv: "Antisemitism Worldwide 2000/1" and "Antisemitism Worldwide 2001/2." The Institute's eminently readable reports are available at [http://www.tau.ac.il/Anti-Semitism].

3. Lawyers Committee for Human Rights, "Fire and Broken Glass: The Rise of Anti-Semitism in Europe," Aug. 2002. Available at [http://www.lchr.org/IJP/antisemitism/antisemitism.htm]. Accessed Jan. 13, 2003.

4. European Monitoring Centre on Racism and Xenophobia, "Diversity and Equality for Europe: Annual Report," Nov. 2001, p. 45. Available at [http://eumc.eu.int/publications/ar00/AR_EN.zip]. Accessed Jan. 10, 2003.

5. *Les Antijeufs: Le Livre Blanc des Violences Antisemites en France depuis Septembre 2000* (Paris: Calmann-Levy, 2002).The book had two corporate authors: UEJF, which stands for the Union of Jewish Students of France (Union des Étudiants Juifs de France), and SOS-Racisme, an antiracist, not-for-profit organization. They both collected the information contained in the book. The title has a slang word that is hard to translate accurately but the best I can give you is this: "The Anti-Jews: The Official Report on Anti-Semitic Violence Since September 2000."

6. Anti-Defamation League, "Global Anti-Semitism: Selected Incidents Around the World in 2002." Available at [http://adl.org/Anti_semitism/anti-semitism_global_incidents.asp]. Accessed Jan. 13, 2003.

7. Stephen Roth Institute for the Study of Contemporary Anti-Semitism and Racism. [http://www.tau.ac.il/Anti-Semitism/asw2001-1/germany.htm].

8. Anti-Defamation League, "Germany: September 5, 2002." Available at [http://adl.org/Anti_semitism/ anti-semitism_ global_incidents.asp]. Accessed Jan. 13, 2003.

9. Stephen Roth Institute for the Study of Contemporary Anti-Semitism and Racism [http://www.tau.ac.il/Anti-Semitism].

10. "Les faits: une Atmosphere d'insécurité" [The Facts: An Atmosphere of Fear]. *Observatoire du Monde Juif*, Nov. 1, 2001, pp. 2–6.

11. Anti-Defamation League, "France: January 21, 2002" and "France: April 28, 2002." Available at [http://adl.org/Anti_ semitism/anti-semitism_global_incidents.asp]. Accessed Jan. 13, 2003.

12. Luc Bronner and Xavier Ternisien, "*Manifestation contre 'l'appel au boycott' des universités d'Israël*" [Demonstration Against the "Call to Boycott" Israeli Universities]. *Le Monde*. Jan. 7, 2003.

13. Sharon Sadeh, "Paris U. Boycott Raises French Furor." *Haaretz English*, Jan. 7, 2003.

14. Daniel Ben Simon, "French Establishment Supports Stabbed Rabbi," *Haaretz English*, Jan. 9, 2003.

15. "*Non aux boycotts*" [No to boycotts], *Le Monde*, Jan. 6, 2003. [http://lemonde.fr/article/0.5987.3208—304415-.00.html].

16. [http://news.bbc.co.uk/go/pr/fr/-2/hi/europe/2806627.stm]. Accessed Feb. 27, 2003.

17. Anti-Defamation League, "UK: July 11" and "UK: May 6, 2002." Available at [http://adl.org/Anti_semitism/anti-semitism_ global_incidents.asp]. Accessed Jan. 13, 2003.

18. Quoted in Omayama Abdel-Latif, "That Weasel Word," *Al-Ahram Weekly*, April 4–10, 2002. Available at [http://weekly. ahram.org.eg/2002/580/cu2.htm]. Accessed Dec. 8, 2002.

19. Rod Liddle, "Watch Who You Call Nazis," *Guardian*, July 17, 2002. Available at [http://education.guardian.co.uk/higher/ worldwide/story/0,9959,756723,00.html]. Accessed Dec. 15, 2002.

20. Stephen Roth Insitute for the Study of Contemporary Anti-Semitism and Racism [http://www.tau.ac.il/Anti-Semitism].

21. Anti-Defamation League, "Italy: July 17, 2002" and "March 31, 2002." Available at [http://adl.org/Anti_semitism/anti-semitism_global_incidents.asp]. Accessed Jan. 13, 2003.

22. Stephen Roth Institute for the Study of Contemporary Anti-Semitism and Racism [http://www.tau.ac.il/Anti-Semitism].

23. Stephen Roth Institute for the Study of Contemporary Anti-Semitism and Racism [http://www.tau.ac.il/Anti-Semitism].

24. Stephen Roth Institute for the Study of Contemporary Anti-Semitism and Racism. [http://www.tau.ac.il/Anti-Semitism/asw2001-2/sthafrica.htm]. Accessed March 9, 2003.

25. Avi Becker, "Under Cover of Intellectualism," *Haaretz*, Oct. 7, 2002.

26. Paix Juste au Proche-Orient Web site: [www.pjpo.org].

27. Private communication on Oct. 21, 2002, from Barbara Spack, national vice president of Hadassah, who showed me the actual correspondence.

28. Board of Deputies of British Jews, "Finnish Government Refusal to Supply Gas Kits to Israel," Nov. 12, 2002 (Ref. 112/02). Available at [http://www.bod.org.uk/cgi-bin/archive/archive.pl?id=458]. Accessed Jan. 20, 2003.

29. "Failure to Address the Health Toll of the Middle East Crisis," Editorial, *The Lancet*, April 13, 2002 [http://www.thelancet.com/journal/vol359/iss9314/full/llan.359.9314.editorial and review].

30. From *Haaretz* Service, by Relly Sa'ar, Oct. 25, 2002.

31. Amnon Rubinstein, "The Cheshire Smile of Anti-Semitism," *Haaretz*, March 11, 2003.

32. Board of Deputies of British Jews, "Board Dismayed at Irish Hotelier Who Refused Israeli Tourists," Apr. 10, 2002 (Ref. 94/02). Available at [http://www.bod.org.uk/cgi-bin/archive/archive.pl?id=438]. Accessed Jan. 20, 2003.

33. BBCi, "Uefa Suspends Israeli Euro Ties." Available at [http://news.bbc.co.uk/sport2/hi/football/uefa_cup/1857962.stm]. Accessed Jan. 13, 2003.

34. Board of Deputies of British Jews, "Board Joins Criticism of UEFA's Tel Aviv decision," Mar. 11, 2002 (Ref 23/02). Available at [http://www.bod.org.uk/cgi-bin/archive/archive.pl?id=370]. Accessed Nov. 22, 2002.

35. Alain Finkielkraut, "*Une croix gammée à la place de l'étoile*" [A Swastika in Place of the Star of David], *L'Arche*, May-June 2002.

36. Thomas L. Friedman, "Nine Wars Too Many," *New York Times*, May 15, 2002.

37. Edgar Morin, Sami Nair, and Nanterre Danièle Sallenave, "*Israël-Palestine: le cancer, par Edgar Morin, Sami Nair et Danièle Sallenave*" [Israel-Palestine: The cancer, by Edgar Morin, Sami Nair and Danièle Sallenave]. *Le Monde.fr*, June 3, 2002.

38. Gilles Paris, "*Les attentats-suicides, arme du désespoir des Palestiniens*" [Suicide Attacks: The Palestinians' Weapon of Despair]. *Le Monde*, June 13, 2002.

39. Ian Gilmour, "Let There Be Justice for All, Mr. Bush." *Observer*, Mar. 31, 2002.

40. "The Battle for the Truth: What Really Happened in Jenin Camp?" *Guardian*, Apr. 17, 2002. Available at [http://www.guardian.co.uk/Archive/Article/0,4273,4395504,00.html]. Accessed Jan. 13, 2002.

41. Quoted in Tom Gross, "Jeningrad: What the British Media Really Said." *National Review*, May 13, 2002. Available at [http://www.nationalreview.com/comment/comment-gross051302.asp]. Accessed Jan. 13, 2003.

42. Quoted in Tom Gross, "Jeningrad: What the British Media Really Said."

43. Tom Gross, "Jeningrad: What the British Media Really Said."

44. Middle East Media Research Institute, "The Palestinian Account of the Battle of Jenin," Apr. 23, 2002 (no. 90). Available at [http://www.memri.org/bin/articles.cgi?Page=archives&Area=ia&ID=IA9002]. Accessed Jan. 13, 2003.

45. HonestReporting.com, "Media Critiques: Dishonest Reporting 'Award' for 2002." Available at [http://www.honestreporting.

com/articles/critiques/Dishonest_Reporting_Award_for_2002. asp]. Accessed Jan. 13, 2002.

## Chapter Six: The Betrayal of Truth, Part Two

1. Stephen Roth Institute for the Study of Contemporary Anti-Semitism and Racism [http://www.tau.ac.il/Anti-Semitism].
2. "White House Condemns Lawmaker's Remarks on Jews, Iraq." Reuters. Updated 11:06 A.M. ET March 11, 2003.
3. Pat Buchanan, "Whose War? A Neoconservative Clique Seeks to Ensnare Our Country in a Series of Wars that Are Not in America's Interest." *American Conservative*, March 2003. Available at [http://www.amconmag.com/03_24_03/ cover.html]. Accessed Apr. 11, 2003.
4. Posted on CNN Web site, March 13, 2003.
5. "Study: Dems More Anti-Semitic Than GOPers: Survey Finds Bias Against Jews Greater Among Young," *WorldNetDaily*, Jan. 15, 2003. Available at [http://www.worldnetdaily.com/news/ article.asp?ARTICLE_ID=30503].
6. "Study: Dems More Anti-Semitic Than GOPers: Survey Finds Bias Against Jews Greater Among Young." Accessed Jan. 18, 2003.
7. Anti-Defamation League, "Anti-Semitism on Display: Marches and Rallys." Available at [http://www.adl.org/Anti_semitism/ arab/as_rallies.asp]. Accessed Jan. 13, 2003.
8. "Hatred in Canada," *Jerusalem Post*, Dec. 25, 2002. Available at [http://www.onejerusalem.org/ItemDetail.asp?Language= English&ItemID=1321]. Accessed Feb. 12, 2003.
9. "Toronto Jew Murdered by Skinheads," *CBC News*. Available at [http://www.cbc.ca/stories/2002/07/14/hate_murder0200714]. Accessed Jan. 13, 2003.
10. Quoted by Michigan professor Zvi Gitelman in "Divest from the Only Democracy in the Mideast?" *Michigan Daily*, Oct. 17, 2002.
11. Compare [www.israel-divest.org] and [www.divestment.org], which provide the following information:

*Original divestment campuses:* Princeton University, Harvard University, Massachusetts Institute of Technology, Cornell University, University of California system, University of Pennsylvania, University of Illinois, Barnard College of Columbia University, University of Maryland, Virginia Commonwealth University, Yale University, Tufts University, University of Michigan, and Wayne State University. Information at Campus Watch [www.campus-watch.org] indicates that similar activities are also ongoing at Georgetown University, the University of Massachusetts, and the University of Washington.

*Campuses that adopted the Feb. 17, 2002, statement:* Antioch College, Ohio; City College of San Francisco; City University of New York; Concordia University; DePaul University; McGill University; Long Island University; Merced College; Ohio State University; University of California, Davis; University of California, Los Angeles; University of California, Santa Cruz; University of Illinois, Chicago; University of Illinois at Urbana Champaign; University of Minnesota; and Vista College, Berkeley.

12. Telis Demos, "Bollinger Dismisses Faculty Petition for Israel Divestment," *Columbia Spectator,* Nov. 8, 2002.

13. Michael Rosen, Ian Saville, Irene Bruegel, Micahel Kustow, Mike Marqusee, Steven Rose, Leon Rosselson, and thirty-eight others, "We Renounce Israel Rights," *Guardian,* Aug. 8, 2002. Available at [http://www.guardian.co.uk/letters/story/0,3604, 770893,00.html]. Accessed Jan. 13, 2003.

14. Divest from Israel Campaign, "I Renounce My Right to Israeli Citizenship!" Available at [http://www.divest-from-israel-campaign.org/renounceMR.html]. Accessed Nov. 22, 2002.

15. Debra J. Saunders, "Food Fight in Tofu-Land." *San Francisco Chronicle,* Dec. 5, 2002.

16. Anti-Defamation League, "2001 Audit of Anti-Semitic Incidents," Apr. 10, 2002. Available at [http://adl.org/2001audit/adlaudit2001.pdf]. Accessed Jan. 20, 2003.

17. Quoted in Nat Hentoff, "Who's an Anti-Semite? Hating Not Just Israel but Jews," *Village Voice*, May 2, 2002. Available at [http://www.villagevoice.com/issues/0219/hentoff.php]. Accessed Nov. 25, 2002.

18. Anti-Defamation League, "2001 Audit of Anti-Semitic Incidents."

19. Alisa Solomon, "Tipping Toward Hate," *Village Voice*, May 15–21, 2002. Available at [http://www.villagevoice.com/issues/0219/hentoff.php]. Accessed Nov. 25, 2002.

20. Anti-Defamation League, "Anti-Semitism in America 2002," June 2002. Available at [http://adl.org/anti_semitism/2002/as_survey.pdf]. Accessed Jan. 13, 2003.

21. Anti-Defamation League, "2001 Audit of Anti-Semitic Incidents."

22. Anti-Defamation League, "Anti-Semitism in America 2002."

23. Laurie Zoloth, personal communication to the author, May 10, 2002.

24. "Save Canadian Magen David Adom." Available at [http://www.petitiononline.com/savemda/]. Accessed Mar. 3, 2003.

25. Margaret Wente, "Scary Times for Jews on Campus." *Globe and Mail*, Mar. 13, 2003.

26. James Kirchick, "Ranting Poet's Visit Makes for a Disturbing Week at Yale," *The Forward*, Mar 7, 2003.

27. Margaret Wente, "Scary Times for Jews on Campus."

28. Alexander Cockburn, "What Sontag Said in Jerusalem," *The Nation*, June 4, 2001.

29. A partial version of Sontag's lecture is available at [http://www.durand-gallery.com/html/sontag.html]. Accessed Jan. 20, 2003.

30. Cockburn, "What Sontag Said in Jerusalem."

31. Noam Chomsky, *Pirates and Emperors* (New York: Black Rose Books, 1991, 1995).

32. "Noam Chomsky on Israel, the U.S. and Palestine," *Socialist Worker*, Mar. 24, 2001.

33. Kyle J. Berkman, "Protests Greet Chomsky's Speech on Middle Eastern Policy," *Harvard Crimson*, Nov. 26, 2002. Available at

[http://www.thecrimson.com/article.aspx?ref=255553]. Accessed Dec. 4, 2002.

34. Noam Chomsky, "Constructive Action?" *Z* Magazine, May 11, 2002. Available at [http://www.zmag.org/content/Mideast/chomskyconstr.cfm]. Accessed Jan. 15, 2003.

35. George Jochnowitz, "Chomsky, Apologist for bin Laden," *Midstream,* Sept.-Oct. 2002.

36. Jochnowitz, "Chomsky, Apologist for bin Laden."

37. *Al-Quds Al-Arabi,* Mar. 16, 1999.

38. The Middle East Media Research Institute, "Edward Said's Lecture in Gaza," Mar. 18, 1999, Special Dispatch Series, no. 27. Available at [http://www.memri.org/bin/articles.cgi?Page=countries&Area=palestinian&ID=SP2799]. Accessed Dec. 4, 2002.

39. Edward W. Said, "What Israel Has Done," *Nation,* May 6, 2002. Available at [http://www.thenation.com/docprint.mhtml?i= 20020506&s=said]. Accessed Dec. 4, 2002.

40. The Middle East Media Research Institute, "Edward Said Compares the Holocaust and the Palestinian Disaster: 'Every Human Calamity Is Different'; 'but . . . There Is Value in Seeing Analogies and Perhaps Hidden Similarities,'" Oct. 2, 2002, Special Dispatch Series, no. 424. Available at [http://memri.org/bin/articles.cgi?Page=archives&Area=sd&ID=SP42402]. Accessed Dec. 4, 2002.

41. Christopher Hitchens, "Jewish Power, Jewish Peril," *Vanity Fair,* Sept. 2002, pp. 194–202.

42. The following thirty-two names of feminists appeared as signatories in the *New York Times* article "Not in Our Times" (there may be many more; the letter claims to have 45,000 signatures): Ros Baxandall, Judith Butler, Bell Chevigny, Angela Davis, Kimberly Crenshaw, Sheila DeBretteville, Carol Downer, Roxanne Dunbar-Ortiz, Barbara Ehrenreich, Vivian Gornick, Sandra Hale, Susannah Heschel, bell hooks, Laura Flanders, Evelyn Fox Keller, Harriet Lerner, Lucy R. Lippard, Robin Morgan, Linda Nochlin, Grace Paley, Katha Pollitt, Frances Fox Piven, Rosalind Pecheskey, Margaret Randall, Adrienne Rich,

Charlotte Sheedy, Nancy Spero, Starhawk, Gloria Steinem, Alice Walker, and Rebecca Walker.

43. Karen Laub, "Reservists Can't Refuse to Serve in Territories," Associated Press, online at the *Washington Times*.

## Chapter Seven: Is Anti-Zionism the New Anti-Semitism?

1. Charles Krauthammer, *New Republic*, Sept. 8, 1997.

2. Sabra cacti are hard on the outside but sweet on the inside. Native-born Israelis have been called sabras.

3. Phyllis Chesler and Rivka Haut, *Women of the Wall: Claiming Sacred Ground at Judaism's Holy Site* (Woodstock, Vt.: Jewish Lights, 2003).

4. Anonymous, personal communication to the author, n.d.

5. Anonymous, personal communication to the author, n.d.

6. Amos Elon, *New York Review of Books*, Dec. 19, 2002.

7. Abba Eban, *New York Times*, Nov. 3, 1975.

8. Frances Raday, personal communication to the author, n.d.

9. Raday, personal communication to the author, n.d.

10. Deborah Greniman, personal interview with the author, n.d.

11. Petronella Wyatt, "Poisonous Prejudice," *Spectator*, Nov. 30, 2002. Actually, this anti-Semite made this statement to a friend of *Spectator* journalist Petronella Wyatt. Available at [http://www.spectator.co.uk/article.php3?table=old§ion=current&issue0%20–12–08&id=1399]. Accessed Dec. 8, 2002.

12. Barbara Amiel, "Islamists Overplay Their Hand but London Salons Don't See It," *The Daily Telegraph*, Dec. 17, 2001. Available at [http://www.telegraph.co.uk/opinion/main.jhtml?xml=/opinion/2001/12/17/do1701.xml]. Accessed Dec. 8, 2002.

13. Amiel, "Islamists Overplay Their Hand but London Salons Don't See It."

14. Tom Gross, "Prejudice and Abuse," *National Review*, Jan. 10, 2002. Available at [http://www.nationalreview.com/comment/comment-gross011002.shtml]. Accessed Dec. 8, 2002.

15. Gross, "Prejudice and Abuse."

16. Richard Pipes, "Solzhenitsyn and the Jews, Revisited: Alone Together," *The New Republic*, Nov. 25, 2002.
17. Please understand that I believe in military means of self-defense when all else has failed. I certainly admire the principles of nonviolence, and ideally would always choose nonviolent over violent approaches to conflict. However, as I have previously noted, most Western "pacifists" seem personally very angry, and without the requisite Gandhian courage. For example, 100,000— even 10,000—pacifists from Europe and North America did not put their bodies where their principles were; they did not start riding the buses in Israel to prevent suicide bombings, nor did they come to stay in peaceful Palestinian villages (not the villages that are essentially bomb factories, such as Jenin) to prevent shootings by settlers or threatened transfer by the Israeli government. Their record speaks for itself.

By the way, Gandhi had something of an attitude toward Jews himself; more specifically, on the eve of World War II, and in response to the events of Kristallnacht, Gandhi advised the Jews, but not the Germans, the Jews in Palestine, but not the Arabs, to proceed only in a nonviolent way. In 1938, Gandhi wrote:

Suffering voluntarily will bring [the Jews in Germany] an inner strength and joy, which no number of resolutions of sympathy passed in the world outside Germany can. . . . The calculated violence of Hitler may even result in a general massacre of the Jews. . . . But if the Jewish mind could be prepared for voluntary suffering, even the massacre I have imagined could be turned into a day of thanksgiving and joy that Jehovah had wrought deliverance of the race even at the hands of the tyrant. For to the God fearing, death has no terror.

Let the Jews who claim to be the chosen race prove their title by choosing the way of nonviolence for vindicating their position on earth. Every country is their home, including Palestine, not by aggression but by loving service. Given the will, the Jew can refuse to be treated as the outcast of the West, to be despised or patronized. He can command the attention and respect of the world by being the chosen creation of God, instead of sinking to brute who is forsaken by God. They can add to their many contributions the surpassing contribution of non-violent action.

Harijan, Nov. 11, 1938. Excerpted from M. K. Gandhi, "The Jews in Palestine 1938." *My Non-Violence* (Ahmedabad: Navajivan, 1960).

I would like to thank Judith Antonelli for calling my attention to Gandhi's letter.

18. Jacques Givet, *The Anti-Zionist Complex* (Englewood, N.J.: SBS, 1982).

19. Yoram Hazony, *The Jewish State: The Struggle for Israel's Soul* (New York: Basic Books, 2001).

20. Traditionally, international law recognized and protected only one entity: the sovereign nation-state. (See Henkin and others, *International Law: Cases and Materials* [Belmont, Calif.: West Wadsworth, 1993].) This traditional approach brought criticism from various groups that wanted recognition and protection for minority groups, women, and other individuals, and peoples who desired self-determination.

First, let us begin with the legal definition of a state. A state should possess a permanent population, a defined territory, a government, and a capacity to enter into relations with other states. (See article 1 of the Convention on the Rights and Duties of States adopted by the seventh international conference of American States, 1934; see also section 201 of the 3rd Restatement of Foreign Relations Law.) One important duty of current states is not to unlawfully recognize a nonstate entity as a state, for this is considered interference with the internal affairs of a current state. (See article 8 of the Convention on the Rights and Duties of States, and comment to section 201 of the 3rd Restatement of Foreign Relations Law.) Thus, any country (there are so many) that recognizes Palestine as a state when it is not one is violating a key international law duty.

Articles 1(2) and 55 of the UN charter (1945) both recognize the principle of self-determination and agree to respect equal rights and self-determination because they play crucial roles in maintaining international peace. Further, Article 1 of both the International Covenant on Civil and Political Rights and the International Covenant on Economic, Social and Cultural Rights (both entered into force in 1976) states that "all peoples have the right of self-determination. By virtue of that right they freely determine their political status and freely pursue their economic, social and cultural development." Are the Jews not as worthy as others to claim such a right?

Finally, UN General Assembly resolutions 1514 (1960) and 2625 (1970) promise dedication to the principle of self-determination, especially in granting independence to colonial countries and peoples, and places a duty on states to encourage and aid this process. Resolution 2625 also recognizes different modes of self-determination, including "the establishment of a sovereign and independent State, the free association or integration with an independent State or the emergence into any other political status freely determined by a people."

Are Israel and the Jews such an instance that would merit self-determination? Yes. It can be said that the two most common claims to self-determination have been made by those with territorial claims (colonies) and by people of a shared culture, religion, and ethnicity who live contiguously with groups who control them. Yet a claim to self-determination cannot be made if it would directly conflict with a legitimate sovereign in place. (See UN General Assembly resolution 1514, which also provides that attempts to disrupt national unity are incompatible with the right of self-determination.) Thus, a claim must show that sovereignty is irrelevant either because it is not there in law or fact, or because the territory has been given some sort of international status.

Is Israel not the quintessential example of this? In the case of Israel and the Jews, it is clear that the only sovereign in place in 1917 (Balfour declaration) and 1947 (UN partition) was Britain, which willingly relinquished its claim to the land. Thus, the claim for self-determination by the Jews was completely valid because Jews constituted a legitimate group of people (that is, one that could be objectively seen as a group) and because their claim would not interfere with any existing sovereign state. Further, the UN and the international community in 1947 gave special status to the territory in question by formally and justly dividing the land between two groups of peoples (Jews and Arabs who lived there), who each had legitimate claims for self-determination. It is not acceptable that the Arabs alone thought they should obtain nationhood and yet not extend that same right to the Jews, which has led them to war against the Jews of Israel since even before it was created.

It is true that Israel is a unique situation in that the countries created from decolonization were basically countries that already existed, were then taken over, and then allowed to become sovereign nations much later (for example, Algeria).

## Chapter Eight: What We Must Do

1. Amos Elon, "How Israel Hurts Itself," *New York Review of Books*, Dec. 10, 2002. May I say that this title is offensive?
2. James Bennet, "Suicide Bombing on Bus in Israel Kills 15," the *New York Times*, Mar. 6, 2003.
3. Uri Dan, "Israel's Bus Bomber's Final Note Hailed 9/11," the *New York Post*, Mar. 6, 2003.
4. Ze'ev Schiff, "Analysis: Looking Back After Two Years," *Haaretz*, Jan. 20, 2003.
5. Thomas L. Friedman, "The New Math," *New York Times*, Jan. 15, 2003.
6. Ari Shavit, "Travels with Mohammed." *Haaretz*, Jan. 4, 2003.
7. Shavit, "Travels with Mohammed."
8. Oriana Fallaci, *The Rage and the Pride* (New York: Rizzoli, 2002). On October 22, 2002, Fallaci delivered "A Sermon for the West," based on her book, to the American Heritage Institute. Available at American Enterprise Online [http://www.theamericanenterprise.org/taejf03a.html]. Jan. 10, 2003.

9. Oriana Fallaci, "The Rage, the Pride, and the Doubt," *The Wall Street Journal*, March 13, 2003.

10. Fallaci, "The Rage, the Pride, and the Doubt."

11. United Nations Joint Programme on HIV/AIDS and World Health Organization, *AIDS Epidemic Update: December 2002*, UNAIDS/02.58E. Available at [http://www.unaids.org/worldaidsday/2002/press/Epiupdate.html]. Accessed Dec. 29, 2002.

12. Food and Agriculture Organization of the United Nations, "Food, Security, Justice and Peace," *World Food Summit: Five Years Later: Multi-Stakeholder Dialogue*, June 10–13, 2002. Available at [http://www.fao.org/worldfoodsummit/msd/Y6808e.html]. Accessed Dec. 29, 2002.

13. Food and Agriculture Organization of the United Nations, "Foetal Hunger Can Mean Adult Ill Health," *World Food Summit: Five Years Later: Focus on the Issues*, June 10–13, 2002. Available at [http://www.fao.org/worldfoodsummit/english/newsroom/focus/focus3.html]. Accessed Dec. 29, 2002.

14. "Illiteracy: World Illiteracy Rates." *Columbia Encyclopedia*, 6th ed. (New York: Columbia University Press, 2002). Available at [http://www.bartleby.com/65/il/illitera.html].

15. United Nations Environment Programme, *The State of the Environment: Past, Present, Future?* Press release, May 22, 2002. Available at [http://www.unep.org/GEO/press.htm]. Accessed Dec. 29, 2002.

16. Barbara Crossette, "Study Warns of Stagnation in Arab Societies," *New York Times*, July 2, 2002. Available at [http://www.nytimes.com/2002/07/02/international/middleeast/02ARAB.html]. Accessed Dec. 22, 2002.
United Nations Development Programme, Arab Fund for Economic and Social Development: Arab Human Development Report 2002

17. Anne Bayefsky, *The UN Human Rights Treaty System: Universality at the Crossroads* (New York: Transnational Publishers, 2001). Following this, Bayefsky published an editorial in the

May 22, 2002, *New York Times*, "Ending Bias in the Human Rights System." Available at [http://www.nytimes.com/2002/05/22/opinion/22BAYE.html].

18. Steven M. Cohen, "Jews Hardline, Yet Detached, in New Survey," *Forward*, Jan. 24, 2003.

19. Eva Fogelman, personal and Internet communication to the author, n.d.

20. International Fellowship of Christians and Jews, "Stand for Israel." Available at [http://www.ifcj.org/subpage.asp?id=252]. Accessed Jan. 29, 2003.

21. Rabbi Harold Kushner, "Fate and Destiny," Yom Kippur Sermon 5763. This was widely reprinted on the Internet. Available at [http://www.tiofnatick.org/index.html?kushneryk5763.htm].

22. Kushner, "Fate and Destiny."

23. Fouad Ajami, "Palestine's Deliverance," *Wall Street Journal*, June 27, 2002. Available at [http://opinionjournal.com/editorial/feature.html?id=110001900].

24. David Remnick, "Rage and Reason: Letter from Jerusalem," *New Yorker*, May 6, 2002. Available at [http://www.newyorker.com/fact/content/?020506fa_FACT].

25. "An Appeal," *Al-Quds Al-Arabi.*, June 21, 2002. Signatories include Professor Sari Nusseibeh, PLO commissioner of Jerusalem; Hanan Ashrawi, Palestinian Legislative Council; Saman Khoury, Palestinian National Council, Central Committee of the Palestinian Democratic Union (FIDA); Salah Zuheika, secretary general, Fatah, Jerusalem; Mamdukh Nofel, advisor to Yasser Arafat; Hana Seniora, editor, *El-Fajr* in English; Muhamed Ishtaya, general director, Palestinian Economic Council for Development and Reconstruction; Salah Raafat, secretary general, FIDA; Professor Manuel Hassassian, president, Bethlehem University; Munther Dajani, professor of political science, Al-Quds University.

26. Yossi Klein Halevi, Israel correspondent of the *New Republic*, is author of *At the Entrance to the Garden of Eden: A Jew's Search for Hope with Christians and Muslims in the Holy Land* (New York: HarperCollins, 2001).

27. "Study: Dems More Anti-Semitic Than GOPers: Survey Finds Bias Against Jews Greater Among Young," WorldNetDaily, Jan. 15, 2003. Available at [http://www.worldnetdaily.com/news/article.asp?ARTICLE_ID=30503]. Accessed Jan. 18, 2003.

28. This material has been obtained from the following five sources: Forbes.com; Jan. 7, 2002, issue of the *Nation*, article by Mark Crispin Miller; Mediachannel.org; www.hearstcorp.com; and www.lemonde.fr.

29. In the Forbes 2002 list of the world's wealthiest individuals, only 30 names out of 497 appear to be Jewish, with a combined wealth of $87.3 billion.

30. Following are the top ten media corporations, with their CEOs in parentheses: AOL/Time-Warner (Steve Case, to be replaced by Dick Parsons in May 2003), GE (Jeffery Immelt), Viacom (Summer Redstone), Walt Disney (Michael Eisner), Liberty Media Corporation (John C. Malone), AT&T (David Dorman), News Corporation (Rupert Murdoch), Bertelsmann (Reinhard Mohn family and Bertelsmann Foundation), Vivendi Universal (Jean-René Fourtou), SONY (Nobuyuki Idei).

Following are the media outlets that each of the above corporations controls:

Walt Disney: all of ABC's TV and radio networks (ABC, ESPN, Disney Channel, and so on).

AOL/Time-Warner:
TV: HBO, Cinemax, CNN (CNN International, CNNSI, CNNfn, Headline News, TBS, TNT, Cartoon Network).
Magazines: *Time, Fortune, Life, Sports Illustrated, People* (120 million readers).

GE: NBC, CNBC, MSNBC (with Microsoft).
Viacom: CBS (two hundred affiliates plus CBS radio networks), MTV, VH1, Nickelodeon, Paramount, and so on.

Liberty Media Corporation: Discovery and TLC plus minority shares in many other channels, stakes in fourteen stations, eighteen million cable viewers in Europe, and largest cable provider in Japan.

AT&T: largest cable provider in United States, owns 8 percent of News Corporation, and has a share in many channels along with AOL/Time-Warner, Liberty, and Comcast.

News Corporation: Fox, FX, Fox Sports World, National Geographic Channel, and Sky Satellite Networks. Extensive cable and satellite holdings in Europe, Asia, and Latin America. Twenty-six local stations in the United States alone. Print: *New York Post, The SUN* (UK), *News of the World* (UK), the *Times* (UK), *Daily Telegraph* (Australia), the *Weekly Standard*.

Bertelsmann: Europe's largest broadcaster, with 35 to 100 percent stakes in twenty-two European TV channels, eighteen European radio stations, and eleven daily newspapers. One of the largest publishers in the world (books, newspapers, you name it, in the United States and Europe).

Vivendi Universal: USA networks, Canal+ and Canal Satéllite. Print: *L'Express, L'Expansion*, and France's free papers. Publisher: Houghton Mifflin.

SONY: stakes in Telemundo and twenty-five international channels in India, Spain, Japan, and Latin America.

31. The *Los Angeles Times* is owned by the Tribune Company (John W. Madigan, chairman; Dennis Fitzsimmons, CEO). The *San Francisco Chronicle* is owned by the Hearst Corporation (private; George R. Hearst, chairman; Victor F. Ganzi, CEO). The *Washington Post* is owned by the Washington Post Company (Donald E. Graham, chairman and CEO). The *Philadelphia Inquirer* is owned by Knight Ridder (P. Anthony Ridder, chairman and CEO). The *Boston Globe* and the *New York Times* are

owned by the New York Times Company (private; Arthur O. Sulzberger Jr., chairman—the only Jew so far).

32. Interestingly, Prince al-Waleed bin Talal is the highest-placed Arab on the 2002 *Forbes* 500 list, at 11, with $20 billion. Saleh Kamel was the eighth Arab on the list, at 191, with $2.2 billion.

33. Rabbi Shimon ben Gamliel states, "The world endures on (or is standing upon) three things: justice, truth, and peace." The rabbis conduct a wonderful discussion of what these three things really mean and how they are to be accomplished. This seems to contradict another mishna, which states that the world exists because of Torah, avodah (service to God), and gemilut chasadim (kindness to human beings). Various sages reconcile this by suggesting that God created the world in order that Torah, service, and good deeds can come into it. If humanity does these things they will be partaking in or becoming partners with God in creation. But in order for the world itself to endure and stand, we must have law and justice, truth, and peace Pirke Avot Treasury, 1:18 (Brooklyn, New York: Artscroll Mesorah, 1995).

## Questions and Answers

1. Paul Johnson, *A History of the Jews* (New York: HarperCollins, 1988).

2. Sylvana Foa, "Letter from Israel," *Village Voice*, July 31, 2002.

3. *Jerusalem Post*, Nov. 2, 1991.

4. *Jerusalem Post*, Nov. 2, 1991.

5. Myths and Facts Online [http://www.us-israel.org/jsource/myths/mf1.html]. Accessed Mar. 1, 2003.

6. Myths and Facts Online [http://www.us-israel.org/jsource/myths/mf1.html]. Accessed Mar. 1, 2003.

7. David Rosen, personal interviews with the author, 2002–2003.

8. Yashiko Sagamori, "Who Are the Palestinians?" Available at [http:/www.think-israel.org/sagamori.html].

9. Myths and Facts Online  [http:/www.jewishvirtuallibrary.org/jsource/myths/mf22.html#v1].

10. Myths and Facts Online [http:/www.jewishvirtuallibrary.org/jsource/myths/mf22.html#v1].

11. Myths and Facts Online [http:/www.jewishvirtuallibrary.org/jsource/myths/mf22.html#v1].

12. Simon Wiesenthal Center, "How You Can Counter the Lies and Misperceptions." Available at [http://www.iacnet.org/take/lies.pdf}. Accessed Mar. 10, 2003.

13. Hertzl Fishman, *The Challenge of Jewish Survival* (West Orange, N.J.: Berman House, 1993).

14. Charles Krauthammer, *The New Republic*, Sept. 8, 1997.

15. Simon Wiesenthal Center, "Israel Is Fighting for Her LIFE!" A Simon Wiesenthal Publication, 2002.

16. Yossi Klein Halevi, "The Great Israeli Settlement Myth," *Los Angeles Times*, June 20, 2001.

17. The Mitchell Report is available at [http://www.us-israel.org/jsource/Peace/Mitchellrep.html].

18. Yossi Klein Halevi, *Jerusalem Post*, Mar. 4, 2001.

19. Clement Weill Raynal, "L'Agence France Presse: le recit contre les faits" [Agence France Presse: The Account Versus the Facts], *L'Observatoire du monde juif*, Bulletin 2, Mar. 2002, pp. 2–11.

20. Raynal, "L'Agence France Presse."

21. Ellis Shuman, "German TV: Mohammed a-Dura Likely Killed by Palestinian Gunfire," *IsraelInsider*, Mar. 20, 2002. Available at [http://www.israelinsider.com/channels/diplomacy/articles/dip_0182.htm]. Accessed Dec. 21, 2002.

# Suggested Reading

Afkhami, Mahnaz. *Faith and Freedom: Women's Human Rights in the Muslim World*. Syracuse, N.Y.: Syracuse University Press, 1995.

Ajami, Fouad. *The Arab Predicament: Arab Political Thoughts and Practice Since 1967*. New York: Cambridge University Press, 1992.

Ansary, Tamim. *West of Kabul, East of New York*. New York: Farrar, Straus, and Giroux, 2002.

Badran, Margot, and Miriam Cookie. *Opening the Gates: A Century of Arab Feminist Writing*. Bloomington: Indiana University Press, 1990.

Bard, Mitchell G. *Myths and Facts: A Guide to the Arab-Israeli Conflict*. Chevy Chase, Md.: American-Israeli Cooperative Enterprise, 2001.

Bein, Alex. *Theodore Herzl*. (trans. from German by Maurice Samuel). Philadelphia: Jewish Publication Society of America, 1943.

Bellow, Saul. *To Jerusalem and Back: A Personal Account*. New York: Penguin Books, 1976.

Ben-Gurion, David. *Memoirs*. New York and Cleveland: World, 1970.

Ben-Zvi, Rachel Yanait. *Before Golda: Manya Schochat—A Biography*. New York: Biblio Press, 1989.

Biale, David. *Culture of the Jews: A New History*. New York: Schocken Books, 2002.

Blanch, Lesley. *The Wilder Shores of Love*. London: Readers Union, 1956.

Bodansky, Yossef. *Islamic Anti-Semitism as a Political Instrument*. Houston: Freeman Center for Strategic Studies, and Israel: Shaarei Tikva: Ariel Center for Policy Research, 1999.

Brooks, Geraldine. *Nine Parts of Desire: The Hidden World of Islamic Women*. New York: Anchor Books, 1996.

Bruce, Tammy. *The New Thought Police: Inside the Left's Assault on Free Speech and Free Minds*. New York: Random House, 2001.

Buckley, William F., Jr. *In Search of Anti-Semitism*. New York: Continuum, 1992.

Cantor, Aviva. *Jewish Women, Jewish Men: The Legacy of Patriarchy in Jewish Life*. San Francisco: HarperSanFrancisco, 1995.

Chanes, Jerome A. *Antisemitism in America Today: Outspoken Experts Explore the Myths*. New York: Carol Publishing, 1995.

Chanes, Jerome A. *A Dark Side of History: Antisemitism Through the Ages*. New York: Anti-Defamation League, 2000.

Chesler, Phyllis. *About Men*. New York: Simon and Schuster, 1978.

Chesler, Phyllis. "And the Walls Came Tumbling Down," *On The Issues*, Spring 1989.

Chesler, Phyllis. "Women at the Wall in Jerusalem: A Lawsuit on Behalf of Women's Right to Pray," *On The Issues*, Summer 1990.

Chesler, Phyllis. "Foreword." In Kayla Weiner and Arinna Moon, eds., *Jewish Women Speak Out: Expanding the Boundaries of Psychology*. Seattle, Wash.: Canopy Press, 1995.

Chesler, Phyllis. "Claiming Sacred Ground." *On The Issues*, Spring 1996.

Chesler, Phyllis. *Women and Madness*. New York: Four Walls Eight Windows, 1997.

Chesler, Phyllis. "Wailing at the Wall." *On The Issues*, Fall 1997.

Chesler, Phyllis. "Give Harmony a Chance." *Hadassah*, Mar. 1998.

Chesler, Phyllis. "Jewish Women in America." *Tikkun*, May/June 1998.

Chesler, Phyllis. *With Child: A Diary of Motherhood*. New Edition with preface by Ariel Chesler. New York: Four Walls Eight Windows, 1998.

Chesler, Phyllis. "The Rape of Dina in Vayishlach: A D'var Torah." *Nashim: A Journal of Jewish Women's Studies and Gender Issues*, 1999-2000, 3.

Chesler, Phyllis. "Jewish Mother and Son: The Feminist Version." In Rachel Josefowitz Siegel, Ellen Cole, and Susan Steinberg-Oren, eds., *Jewish Mothers Tell Their Stories: Acts of Love and Courage*. Binghamton, N.Y.: Haworth Press, 2000.

Chesler, Phyllis. "When the Afghans Are Free of War." *New York Times*, Nov. 2001.

Chesler, Phyllis. "Women of the Wall." *New York Times*, Editorials/letters, June 2002.

Chesler, Phyllis. *Woman's Inhumanity to Woman*. New York: Plume Books, 2003.

Chesler, Phyllis, Esther D. Rothblum, and Ellen Cole. *Feminist Foremothers in Women's Studies, Psychology, and Mental Health*. Binghamton, N.Y.: Haworth Press, 1996.

Chesler, Phyllis, and Rivka Haut. *Women of the Wall: Claiming Sacred Ground at Judaism's Holy Site*. Woodstock, Vt.: Jewish Lights Publishing, 2003.

Dawidowicz, Lucy S. *A Holocaust Reader*. West Orange, N.J.: Behrman House, 1976.

Dawidowicz, Lucy S. *What Is the Use of Jewish History?* (Neal Kozody, ed.). New York: Schocken Books, 1992.

Dershowitz, Alan M. *Why Terrorism Works: Understanding the Threat, Responding to the Challenge*. New Haven: Yale University Press, 2002.

Des Pres, Terrance. *The Survivor: An Anatomy of Life in the Death Camps*. New York: Oxford University Press, 1976.

Elliot, Gil. *The Twentieth Century Book of the Dead*. New York: Scribner's, 1972.

Elon, Amos. *Herzl*. New York: Holt, Reinhardt and Winston, 1975.

Fallaci, Oriana. *The Rage and the Pride*. New York: Rizzoli, 2002.

Fanon, Frantz. *Black Skin, White Masks*. (Charles Markham, trans.). New York: Grove Press, 1967.

Fanon, Frantz. *The Wretched of the Earth*. New York: Grove Press, 1968.

Fernea, Elizabeth Warnock. *In Search of Islamic Feminism: One Woman's Global Journey*. New York: Anchor Books, 1998.

Fishman, Hertzl. *The Challenge of Jewish Survival*. West Orange, N.J.: Behrman House, 1993.

Fogelman, Eva. *Conscience and Courage: Rescuers of Jews During the Holocaust*. New York: Anchor Books, 1994.

Freedman, Samuel G. *Jew vs. Jew: The Struggle for the Soul of American Jewry*. New York: Simon and Schuster, 2000.

Freud, Sigmund. *Moses and Monotheism*. New York: Vintage, 1967.

Frymer-Kensky, Tikva. *Reading the Women of the Bible*. New York: Schocken Books, 2000.

Givet, Jacques. *The Anti-Zionist Complex*. Englewood Cliffs, N.J.: SBS, 1982.

Goldberg, Jeffrey. "In the Party of God." *New Yorker*, Oct. 14–21, 2002.

Gordon, Lucie Duff. *Letters from Egypt*. London: Virago Press, 1983. (Originally published 1865.)

Grayzel, Solomon. *A History of the Jews*. Philadelphia: Jewish Publication Society of America, 1965.

Gruber, Ruth. *Exodus 1947: The Ship That Launched a Nation*. New York: Museum of Jewish Heritage, 1998 [Originally published in 1947].

Gruber, Ruth. *Haven: The Dramatic Story of 1,000 World War II Refugees and How They Came to America*. New York: Three Rivers Press, 2000. [Originally published 1983.]

Hazony, Yoram. *The Jewish State: The Struggle for Israel's Soul*. New York: Basic Books, 2000.

Herzl, Theodor. *The Jewish State*. Mineola, N.Y.: Dover, 1988. (Originally published 1895.)

Hunter, Edward. *The Past Present: A Year in Afghanistan*. London: Hodder and Stoughton, 1959.

Jenkins, Robin. *Dust on the Paw*. New York: Putnam, 1961.

Johnson, Paul. *A History of the Jews*. New York: HarperCollins, 1988.

Keddie, Nikki R., and Beth Baron. *Women in Middle Eastern History: Shifting Boundaries in Sex and Gender*. New Haven, Conn.: Yale University Press, 1991.

Langbein, Hermann. *Against All Hope*. New York: Paragon House, 1994.

Leitner, Isabella. *Fragments of Isabella: A Memoir of Auschwitz*. New York: Crowell, 1978.

Lerner, Michael. *Healing Israel/Palestine: A Path to Peace and Reconciliation*. San Francisco: Tikkun Books, 2003.

Lerner, Michael, and Cornel West. *Jews and Blacks: Let the Healing Begin.* New York: Putnam, 1995.

Levi, Primo. *The Reawakening.* New York: Collier Books, 1965.

Levi, Primo. *The Periodic Table.* (Raymond Rosenthal, trans.). New York: Schocken Books, 1984.

Levi, Primo. *The Drowned and the Saved.* (Raymond Rosenthal, trans.). New York: Summit Books, 1988.

Lewis, Bernard. *The Jews of Islam.* Princeton: Princeton University Press, 1987.

Lewis, Bernard. *The Middle East: A Brief History of the Last 2,000 Years.* New York: Simon and Schuster, 1997.

Lewis, Bernard. *The Crisis of Islam: Holy War and Unholy Terror.* New York: Modern Library/Random House, 2003.

Londres, Albert. *The Jew Has Come Home.* New York: Richard R. Smith, 1931.

Mackworth, Cecily. *The Destiny of Isabelle Eberhardt.* New York: Ecco Press, 1975.

Mahdi, Muhsin. *The Arabian Nights.* New York: Norton, 1990.

Memmi, Albert. *Portrait of a Jew.* New York: Viking Press, 1976.

Memmi, Albert. *The Liberation of the Jew.* New York: Viking Press, 1966.

Mernissi, Fatima. *Beyond the Veil: Male-Female Dynamics in a Modern Muslim Society.* New York: Schenkman, 1975.

Millett, Kate. *Going to Iran.* New York: Coward McCann, & Geoghegan, 1981.

Morton, Leah. *I Am a Woman—and a Jew.* New York: J. H. Sears, 1926.

Oren, Michael B. *Six Days of War: June 1967 and the Making of the Modern Middle East.* New York: Oxford University Press, 2002.

Ostow, Mortimer. *Myth and Madness: The Psychodynamics of Antisemitism.* New Brunswick: Transaction, 1996.

Pardes, Illana. *Countertraditions in the Bible: A Feminist Approach.* Cambridge, Mass.: Harvard University Press, 1993.

Perlmutter, Nathan, and Ruth Ann Perlmuttter. *The Real Anti-Semitism in America.* New York: Arbor House, 1982.

Peters, Joan. *From Time Immemorial: The Origins of the Arab-Jewish Conflict over Palestine.* New York: J. Kap, 1985.

Pogrebin, Letty Cottin. *Deborah, Golda and Me: Being Female and Jewish in America.* New York: Crown, 1991.

Prager, Dennis, and Joseph Telushkin. *Why the Jews? The Reasons for Antisemitism* (New York: Simon & Schuster, 1983).

Quinley, Harold E., and Charles Y. Glock. *Anti-Semitism in America.* New York: Macmillan, 1979.

Rashid, Ahmed. *Taliban: Militant Islam, Oil and Fundamentalism in Central Asia.* New Haven, Conn.: Yale Nota Bene, 2001.

Rashke, Richard. *Escape from Sobibor: The Heroic Story of the Jews Who Escaped from a Nazi Death Camp.* Boston: Houghton Mifflin, 1982.

Rubin, Theodore Issac. *Anti-Semitism: A Disease of the Mind: A Psychiatrist Explores the Psychodynamics of a Symbol Sickness.* New York: Continuum, 1990.

Rushdie, Salman. *The Satanic Verses*. New York: Viking Press, 1989.

Sartre, Jean-Paul. *Anti-Semite and Jew* [Réflexions sur la question juive, 1948] (George J. Becker, trans.). New York: Shocken Books, 1995.

Segev, Tom. *Elvis in Jerusalem: Post-Zionism and the Americanization of Israel*. New York: Metropolitan Books, 2001.

Sevela, Ephraim. *Farewell Israel!* South Bend, Ind.: Gateway Editions, 1977.

Shaaban, Bouthaina. *Both Right and Left Handed: Arab Women Talk About Their Lives*. Bloomington: Indiana University Press, 1991. (Originally published 1988.)

Shapira, Anita. "Did the Zionist Leadership Foresee the Holocaust?" In Yehuda Reinharz (ed.), *Living with Antisemitism: Modern Jewish Responses*. Hanover, N.H.: University Press of New England, 1987.

Spencer, Robert. *Islam Unveiled: Disturbing Questions About the World's Fastest-Growing Faith*. San Francisco: Encounter Books, 2002.

Stiglmayer, Alexandra. *Mass Rape: The War Against Women in Bosnia-Herzegovina*. Lincoln and London: University of Nebraska Press, 1994.

Stillman, Norman A. "The Response of the Jews of the Arab World to Anti-semitism in the Modern Era." In Yehuda Reinharz (ed.), *Living with Antisemitism: Modern Jewish Responses*. Hanover, N.H.: University Press of New England, 1987.

*Tanakh: The Holy Scriptures-The New JPS Translation According to the Traditional Hebrew Text: Torah, Nevi'im, Kethuvim*. Philadelphia and Jerusalem: Jewish Publication Society of America, 1985.

Wallach, Janet. *Desert Queen: The Extraordinary Life of Gertrude Bell-Adventurer, Adviser to Kings, Ally of Lawrence of Arabia*. New York: Anchor Books, 1999.

Waskow, Arthur. *Godwrestling, Round 2: Ancient Wisdom, Future Paths*. Woodstock, Vt.: Jewish Lights, 1995.

Wharton, Edith. *In Morocco*. New York: Hippocrene Books, 1920.

Wittig, Monique. *Across the Acheron*. Chester Springs, Penn.: Dufour Editions, 1988.

Yahil, Leni. *The Holocaust: The Fate of European Jewry*. New York: Oxford University Press, 1987.

Ye'or, Bat. *The Decline of Eastern Christianity Under Islam—From Jihad to Dhimmitude: Seventh–Twentieth Century*. Madison, N.J.: Fairleigh Dickinson University Press, 1996.

Ye'or, Bat. *Islam and Dhimmitude: Where Civilizations Collide*. Madison, N.J.: Fairleigh Dickinson University Press, 2001.

## Selected Internet Resources

Anti-Defamation League: http://www.adl.org

*B'Tselem:* http://www.btselem.org

*Haaretz* English: http://www.haaretzdaily.com

Human Rights Watch: http://www.humanrightswatch.org

International Policy Institute for Counter Terrorism at the University of Herzliya: http://www.ict.org.il/home.cfm

Israeli Ministry of Foreign Affairs: http://www.mfa.gov.il/mfa/home.asp

Israel/Palestine Center for Public Research and Information: http://www.ipcri.org/index1.html

Jerusalem Post: http://www.jpost.com

Jewish Virtual Library: http://www.jewishvirtuallibrary.org

Middle East Media Research Institute: http://www.memri.org

Lawyers Committee for Human Rights: http://www.lchr.org. See especially, "Fire and Broken Glass" [http://www.lchr.org/IJP/antisemitism/antisemitism.htm].

Middle East Intelligence Bulletin: http://www.meib.org

*New York Times* Middle East Coverage: http://www.nytimes.com/pages/world/middleeast

Stephen Roth Institute for the Study of Contemporary Anti-Semitism and Racism at the University of Tel Aviv: http://www.tau.ac.il/Anti-Semitism

# The Author

PHYLLIS CHESLER is the author of the landmark feminist classic *Women and Madness*, as well as many other notable books including *Women, Money, and Power*; *About Men*; *With Child*; *Mothers on Trial: The Battle for Children and Custody*; *Letters to a Young Feminist*; *Woman's Inhumanity to Woman*; and *Women of the Wall: Claiming Sacred Ground at Judaism's Holy Site*. Dr. Chesler is an Emerita Professor of Psychology and Women's Studies at CUNY, a psychotherapist, and an expert courtroom witness. She has lectured and organized political, legal, religious, and human rights campaigns in the United States, Canada, Europe, the Middle East, and the Far East.

Dr. Chesler is a cofounder of the Association for Women in Psychology and The National Women's Health Network. She has lived in Kabul, Afghanistan, and in Jerusalem and Tel Aviv.

She invites readers to contact her at the website www. phyllis-chesler.com.

# Index